SCORING

Also by Reg McKay

SCORING

AN EXPERT'S GUIDE

FRANK McAVENNIE
WITH REG McKAY

CANONGATE

Thanks to . . .
Every footballer supporter who has paid to watch me play –
whoever you support.
My Mum and family who have stood by me when others
would have walked away.
Nicky – a better man than me.
Mark for sticking by me through thick and thin.
Ray Winstone for being more polite than he could have been
at the beginning of this book.
My son Jake for giving me the strength to go on.
Last and never least, to my wife Karen for giving me
my life back.

First published in the UK in 2003 by
Canongate Books, 14 High Street, Edinburgh, EH1 1TE

10 9 8 7 6 5 4 3 2 1

British Library Cataloguing-in-Publication Data
A catalogue record for this book is available
on request from the British Library

ISBN 1 84195 428 4

Typeset by Palimpsest Book Production Limited,
Polmont, Stirlingshire

Printed and bound by
Creative Print and Design, Ebbw Vale, Wales

www.canongate.net

DEDICATION

This book is dedicated to my father, Bernard McAvennie.
My biggest fan, my biggest critic, always there for me.

You done that deal yet, Dad?

CONTENTS

FOREWORD

Frank? Frank the fuck who?

It was my first thought about the bold boy as it was for other West Ham supporters the summer of 1985. We'd had a dodgy season the year before and needed to strengthen the pool. Who did we get? Some unknown git called Frank McAvennie from a Scottish team that wasn't Rangers or Celtic. It wasn't a good time to be a Hammers supporter.

Upton Park, first game of the season, I'm standing there with those jittery butterflies you get before kick-off. On come our lot, the old familiar faces in the old familiar colours. There's a flash of peroxide and I wonder if we'd signed a girl. When the sod smiled I reached into my breast pocket for my sunglasses. Frank McAvennie wasn't going to go unnoticed and it's been that way ever since – on and off the field.

When their team is playing well the lives of football supporters soar. It's the perfect happy pill and no harmful side effects. Well, not many. Sad bastards? Maybe but I like it. Within weeks Frank and Tony Cottee were scoring the goals and thousands of people in London's east end were hovering three feet off the ground. Frank always did it with that smile. God knows how it made the opposition feel but that wide grin did it for me.

So I was shooting a film called *Tank Mallon*. Me and the other crew had established our headquarters in the Burford Arms, a little pub at the back of Stratford Fruit Market. One day, Frank comes strolling in looking for a drink, naturally. I eyed him and said,

'I'm not fucking buying you one. You're playing tomorrow.'

He just grinned. So he got one and the rest. One drink's no damn good for anyone. Is it? Certainly not for Frank who stayed a while and we've been stuck with each other ever since.

I never did all that poncing about with Frank in the glitzy clubs, not my scene. But I've always loved him for having no airs and graces. One night he'd be rubbing shoulders with the lah-di-dah, ordering chilled champagne, an arm wrapped round some page three dolly and getting his pic in the papers. The next night he'd be holding up the bar in an east end boozer, wedged between a greyhound and some old guy with no teeth and be as happy as Larry.

The east end folk sensed that Frank was one of their own. Okay, in the beginning no one could understand what he said but that was short-lived. Besides, attitude overcomes language difficulties every time and Frank loves people. Especially the down-to-earth, working class mob. That's the stock he's from back in Glasgow. One time he offered to buy his old dear and dad a nice house in an upmarket area but they refused to budge from the house they'd had since he was a kid. There's a lot of that in Frank. The boy knows where he's from and will never forget.

I've plenty of special memories of Frank on and off the field. To me there's not two sides to Frank, just the one guy who happens to love chasing a ball. But sometimes parts of his life overlap into another. One time against Leicester City I think it was, Frank just wasn't on form. By then his reputation for a good time was well known and I reckoned the bugger had been on the sauce the night before. The ball came sailing over into the opposition box with Frank just standing there looking the other way. The ball only thumps him on the top of the head, sails up over the keeper and into the net. Even with a hangover he did the business. Lucky sod. He celebrated with glee, pretending he'd planned it all of course. We all knew better but we didn't bloody care.

Most of Frank's goals were deliberate and skilful as hell. It was one of the great pities that there was a TV dispute on that season and the rest of the country's football supporters were denied a glimpse of his magic that year. Hell mend them, I say, they should have come to Upton Park.

Why people love Frank can be explained by a football story when he wasn't there. He had just left West Ham for Glasgow Celtic, the team he had supported since he was in nappies. West Ham were playing at home and were down 3–0 which doesn't happen to them often to be honest. As you can imagine, Hammers' supporters weren't best pleased. Bloody depressed more like. There were radios scattered throughout the crowd giving half-time results from the rest of the country. Celtic were winning 3–0 and Frank had scored the lot. It was as if he was smiling back at us with that cheeky grin. First there was shaking of heads then an enormous cheer filled the stadium. The players on the pitch stopped and looked at the crowd, puzzled what the fuss was about. Frank, that's what. He was one of us. Still is.

These days I meet up with Frank most often when we play for the same charity football team. Twin strikers – Winstone and McAvennie – how does that sound? But I'll tell you he's a selfish bugger. Every time I think of having a crack at goal he's right there in front of me, getting in the way. I swear. Couple of weeks ago he couldn't make it and I was on my own. What a bloody goal I scored. Ace. So I 'phone him to tell him that I'm right and he's been getting under my feet all along. Bugger just laughed at me. What do you think of that? And he's supposed to be a friend.

The boy's got plenty of front, that's for sure. He enjoys life in every way every chance every day and has some stories to tell, most of them from off the park. This book won't be long enough and it better be fireproof. If all this sin and damnation stuff is right it's odds on that Frankie will end up in Hell but he won't be lonely – most of his friends will be there and it will be the best party in town – it always is. I'll make the Margueritas as usual, Frank. Deal?

If you walk on the edge you expect to teeter now and

then and from time to time Frank's hit problems. Been there myself once or twice. I always say to him that it doesn't matter how you fall into the shit it's how you climb out of it. As ever, he comes strolling through smelling of roses, with that wide, friendly grin, a story to tell and moving right on to the next adventure.

That's my mate Frank for you.

Ray Winstone
London, April 2003.

WHO ME? (LONDON, 1985)

I was standing on this table, a bottle in one hand, a half-full glass in the other. Saturday night in London and I was letting loose as usual. Music was swimming round the room, bouncing off the walls. Beautiful, long-legged women wearing pelmet-length skirts were jigging to the beat. Life was good.

Somewhere below me a hand reached out and tugged at my sleeve. They would have to do better than that. I ignored it. Another tug, more insistent this time. Peering down at Margot Mitchell whose lovely face looked uncharacteristically serious, troubled.

'There's a stack of photographers outside, Frank,' she said, as if that were adequate explanation. Obviously it had nothing to do with me. We were in Stringfellows in London for God's sake. Earlier that night I'd spotted Jack Nicholson sitting at a nearby table. The place was mobbed with faces from TV, the movies and the music world and that didn't include the really big names who had slipped upstairs to stay out of the public eye. Me, I was just a young guy from Glasgow out to have a good time.

'What's that got to do with me?' I asked.

'You play football,' she replied.

'So?'

'And something to do with you being on a TV show last night,' Margot smiled a little ironic grin.

'Shit!' the penny clanged to the floor as did I.

Okay I was scoring loads of goals for West Ham United then riding high at the top flight of English football. But I was only months into my first season and there was a television blackout due to some dispute. Nobody knew what I looked like, who I was or what I did with my spare time. The night before I'd appeared on the Terry Wogan TV show

1

along with Dennis Law. Wogan was a British institution at that time and went out three times a week to many millions of viewers a go. But to me it was just a good chat with some friendly people. I was born to drink and talk – I'm a natural, still am. Never did I think that a pleasant half hour would have any repercussions like the tabloid paparazzi hovering by the door. I should have but it just didn't occur to me. Here I was about to make my first splash in print that wasn't lodged at the back of the newspapers and here I was half drunk as usual. Then there was Anita Blue, my partner of the time. It had been a big enough decision for her to up sticks from Glasgow and move with me here to London, now without warning she was about to be spread across the headlines – if we let them.

'We need to get out of here, Margot.' I made an instant decision, another habit of mine – sometimes good, sometimes bad. This time it was the right decision.

'No problem,' she smiled again. To me Stringfellows was just a good pub. Half the time I'd be gabbing to some guy at the bar not realising who he was till he'd left and Anita would whisper in my ear he was a rock star or whatever. In truth I didn't care who they were, just what their patter was like. But Stringfellows cared in more ways than one.

Before I knew it, John and Dennis, a couple of male members of staff, slung a coat over my head and headed me to the main, front door closely followed by Anita. I felt a right phoney. Like these things happened to Elvis not to Frank McAvennie from Milton, Glasgow. All the way, bent under that coat, I couldn't stop laughing, staring down at the moving pavement and the shuffling feet of men demanding to know who was under the wraps. They were told sod all, of course.

John and Dennis huckled us into the back of a large stretch limousine with blacked out windows, one of many waiting for the patrons at Stringfellows. I wish I could say it was mine but it belonged to some sheikh or what not. Anita and I had arrived by mini-cab. The bored chauffeur had agreed to give us a lift home and away from the pursuing photographers and reporters. He must have assumed that we were staying at some of the nearby luxury hotels in the West End of London because when I explained we lived in Essex – a good forty-minute drive away – I could hear him cursing under his breath, softly and politely but still not pleased at all. I didn't care. I just poured us a drink from the well-stocked booze cabinet, stretched back into the luxurious leather seats and listened to the purr of the engine as early morning London floated past the window.

Not long ago I had been a road digger. A few years previously I didn't even play football. Three months before I still lived in Glasgow. I lit a fag, leaned back and, not for the last time, wondered just how the hell I got here.

NICE TO BE NICE (1979)

My hangover had almost lifted, I was heading to the bookies and all I had in my pocket was a five-pound note. Just another Saturday.

Except this one was worse than most. It wasn't so much the dank air and cold chill on the feet that was a typical Glasgow winter, but the Celtic weren't playing. Every second Saturday I'd take in their home games come hell or high water and most of their away games in between. Always had since I was a nipper and planned to continue forever. But ground frost and lack of under-soil heating all contributed to a cancellation. I was not a happy man.

My usual routine was to call at Smith's the bookmakers in Glasgow city's centre and bet a few quid on the horse racing before each match. Just because the Celtic game was off I didn't see why I should break that habit. Besides I was unemployed at the time and permanently skint. With only five pounds in my pocket I needed to win a few quid to save me from having to borrow to get out that night, never mind the long wait till my next giro.

Smith's lay behind the Apollo, then one of the largest, most successful music venues in the UK. Glasgow was high on the itineraries of every major group and singer in the world and the Apollo was inevitably where they performed. Early on Saturday afternoons the street outside was also the meeting place for all the minor league football teams to congregate for their buses to take them to their games. Most Saturdays as I strolled on my way to Smith's I'd pass the guys standing there and think,

'It takes all kinds. Imagine choosing ninety minutes of playing third rate football rather than watching a decent game.' That Saturday was different.

'Ho, Frank,' a voice shouted from across the street.

'How you doing?' I waved back at the familiar face.

'You up to much?'

'No, just heading to the bookies.' I strolled across the street towards the congregated footballers.

'Shame about the Celtic game eh?'

'Aye.'

'You at a loose end?'

'Well, I'm just going to the . . .'

'Fancy playing for us then?'

'Eh, well I've not got any kit.'

'Who's this?' An older man had joined the group, the team coach I surmised.

'This is Frank.'

'Is he any good?' Fair question from a football team coach but I could feel the hackles on the back of my neck bristling a wee bit at being talked about, questioned when I was standing right there in front of him.

'Aye, he's good.' Heads nodded around the group from guys who had played in kick-abouts with me in the local Deaf School playground on Sundays (first team to score 21 goals won) or in similar 20-a-side games in the street when we were younger.

'Look,' I interrupted, 'thanks for the offer but even if I was Pele I've got a slight problem – no boots.' I started to head slowly off towards the bookies.

'What size you take, son?' the coach asked.

'Eights.'

'So happens I have a spare pair of eights.' The coach raised his eyebrows waiting for an answer, the final obstacle removed. Those guys must have been a man short and really desperate. Nice to be nice I reckoned so I agreed to play. Besides, I enjoyed football and had only a fiver to last me the week. If I'd gone to the bookies I probably would have lost the lot. A good, cheap afternoon and I would have some fun too.

Now, aged twenty, I was going to play a rare competitive match. A few months earlier I had turned out for a junior team called Kilsyth St Pat's but they had shown me the door saying I wasn't good enough. So I set off that afternoon with no other thoughts than to have a good time. Not like me really.

The 200 Club was a good team but placed somewhere between pub league and junior football. It was obvious even travelling on the bus to that game that the other guys loved the sport for its own sake and I could identify with that. I had been a football fanatic from an early age, every boy in Milton was. Well, every boy I knew and I was on first name terms with most.

Milton was a typical peripheral council housing scheme in north-west Glasgow near Maryhill. A nice place in my memory. The kind of area where you knew all your neighbours, felt safe and kids could grow up unharmed. Later it would be seen as a bit dodgy as hard drugs ravaged nearby Ruchill, Possil and Maryhill. But I liked the scheme, still do, as my Mum lives there.

One of my pals when I was younger was Jackie Norval. We ended up doing a milk round together early in the morning. After we had finished work we would stop at Jackie's place for a fry-up breakfast made by his father. Milton was that type of place. But a wee while later, Jackie's father was arrested. He was Walter Norval, the godfather of crime in charge of a massive gang who were ruthless armed bank robbers.

During the trial the High Court in Glasgow was bombed, the judge and jury provided with armed protection; all hell broke loose. The police were really pissed off when Walter Norval only got 14 years and said as much. But I never asked Jackie about his father or questioned what was going on. We just got on with being friends and still are. That's what Milton was about.

Milton had its own claim to football fame being where Kenny Dalglish grew up. The Milton guys who used to play impromptu football with Kenny would say that he was so rubbish he was always last to be picked and shoved in goal, between the jumper goalposts. Maybe aye maybe no but I reckon not. Every boy I knew wanted to be Dalglish except me. He was my hero. A genius. A one-off. No one else could be Kenny. I just wanted to watch him. Poetry in motion. When he left Celtic for Liverpool it broke my heart.

I seemed destined to be a football spectator rather than a player from boyhood. At school, St Augustine's, I was banned from playing for the school teams because I was too small and frail. The school worked two teams and I was always put in the second. The teacher in charge of organising the football was Mary Clark, a family friend to this day. One day both teams were playing on nearby pitches. Another teacher went to fetch Mary, telling her she had better come and see something happening in the second team's game. She stood and watched as I ran rings round the opposition. But still she reckoned I was too small for the first team. Of course, I frequently remind her of this to this very day.

At one point I managed to get into an organised boy's game but ended up having a punch-up with an opposing player – another wee weakness – and that's when my father, Bernard, imposed another lifetime ban. Sine Die as the Scottish Football Association used to say when kicking the bad boys out forever, as if using Latin made it more polite. And you didn't argue with my old man.

I didn't even argue with him when I was young. I was the kind of kid who always wanted to be just so in the latest fashion. My old dear, Jean, bought all my clothes, of course, and it seemed to me she deliberately conspired never to get the gear quite right. So if I wanted eight-inch turn-ups on my trouser legs that had to be four inches short of my Doc Martens (I know, I know, but it was fashionable then, honest) she'd bring home trousers that had two-inch turn-ups and lay on top of my boots.

I made the mistake of lusting after a leather bomber jacket at one point. It really knocked me out when one night I came home from school and my mother presented me with the said bomber. Brown leather, baggy, just long enough to lie on the high waistband of my trousers – it looked the part all right. When I tried it on it felt – well, kind of stiff – but I just wrote that off to it being new and assumed it would loosen up over time. A couple of my mates were in our house at that time and I noticed them smirking.

'Nuh,' one declared, 'cannae see where that jacket was cut out at all. Must be underneath.' Then two of them were levering the couch back and peering at the underside looking for the cut-out shape of my jacket. My father was an upholsterer by trade and had just re-covered our three-piece suite in brown leather. The same brown leather as my jacket, not being a man to waste anything. I matched the bloody sofa.

My pals gave me pelters – that's Glaswegian for a relentless flow of sarcastic ribbing – and continued giving me pelters at every opportunity. Not to put too fine a point on it, I was mortified – well, I was a young teenager – and let my folks know about it sharpish. All to no avail, of course. I would wear it leaving the house in the morning, dump it at a mate's house, shiver all day in the Glasgow winter and put the bloody thing back on before I went home at night. Like I said, you didn't argue with my old man. But be fair, would you have worn a jacket made out of your Mum's suite when you were that age? At any age?

A couple of years later I exacted some form of revenge for the walking three-piece suite. Typically, some mates and myself decided that we wanted to form a rock group. My old dear splashed out and bought me an electric guitar and a small amplifier – a big investment in a family that never had a lot of spare cash. Not that I could strike a chord, I just intended to be a superstar. A few months later, when I was 16-years old, some friends were heading to the Isle of Man on holiday and I was desperate to go with them. With a bit of persuasion my parents said I could go but just one problem – no dough. Determined not to miss out on a lads' fortnight away, I secretly flogged the guitar and amp without telling my Mum. We lost out on the deal but it was enough to give me a great time – beach football in the mornings, boozing in the afternoon, dancing at the discos and women. Boatloads of good-looking girls from all over. In case you think it was all a blast, we did organise a game of football, Scotland versus England, my first international. Scotland won, of course. In many ways that holiday was to set the pattern of my adult life, which was just fine by me.

I had left school at 15-years old – the earliest opportunity . Not that I disliked school but I just couldn't see the usefulness of algebraic formulae and all that palaver. I wanted to get out there and start real life, so I did pronto, right into glamorous jobs like working in a clothing factory. In fact that turned out to be a good number with a little unofficial distribution on the side. We specialised in housecoats and when the queue formed at the ice cream van in Milton, it was a fashion parade of all our multi-coloured blagged goods. At one time I got a job as an apprentice motor mechanic – with the help of Kenny Dalglish's father. I loved working on the big flash cars and used to take them for a wee spin. One day the gaffer saw me waltzing past in a high-spec Citroën worth a load of money. Trouble is I didn't have a driving licence. Instant dismissal. Later I found work as a waiter in a restaurant owned by Billy McPhail, a former Celtic player. To me, having a Celtic man as my boss was as close to the ideal employer as I reckoned I was going to achieve. It almost compensated for the long hours and the low wages. But I was good at the work and enjoyed it eventually. Then there was van boy delivering bread before dawn, a year on the dole, and labouring jobs after labouring jobs including bin man and road sweep. Road sweep – nothing wrong with that. But as an 18-year old you are so aware of your public image. I mean the job was fine, useful even but what if my pals saw me? It would be a sherricking for life. I was out there pushing my cart for a full twenty minutes before I decided to chuck it in. Back to the base with the tools, resigned and headed to the dole office on the bus. Trouble was they found out I had voluntarily packed it in and promptly stopped my dole money for six weeks. Looking for work again and on to whisky bonds, shifting furniture in a charity shop and a stack of other jobs. All by the age of twenty.

The jobs were mostly grimy, gruelling grinds but I didn't care – much. Little more than some muscle was demanded of me and I was paid just enough wages to pay digs to my Mum and concentrate on having a good time. If I got fed up with one, or argued with the gaffer, I'd just resign and move on to another. I'm never confident I quite remember them all but I reckon I had more than fourteen jobs in four years. Who can be bothered to count that type of nonsense?

My ambition was to be a lorry driver. Sitting on my ass, travelling the country and being paid enough to support my pleasures. Seemed like a great deal to me. But football? No way was football ever an option. You watched that and only the select few ever got paid to play.

But here I was, hungover and broke on a cold Glasgow Saturday, heading for a game of competitive football aged 20-years old. It wasn't going to be the last time I would decide to do something on the spur of the moment. At the time I didn't analyse it at all. It's not what all young people do is it? Something happens, they make a decision and the next you know . . . except I never did quite grow out of that spontaneous approach to life. Later on I would find myself in the hot seat being demanded to explain my actions by some lawyer claiming I had planned them all out carefully with illegal intent. In truth, then as now, most of the time there was no agenda in my life, no plot. Yet some people find it hard to accept the answer, 'It seemed a good idea at the time.'

But that's for later. On that cold Saturday in Kirkintilloch a couple of miles from Glasgow I was getting kitted out for a game of football for precisely that reason.

Even if I say so myself I played a blinder. As all around

me twenty-one other players and two hoarse-voiced coaches took every pass and kick with life or death seriousness, I relaxed and played them off the park. I was a skinny young guy – as thin and white as a lollipop stick – but I liked the ball at my feet. My opposite number was given a right hard time as I beat him to every ball, won every tackle and nutmegged him at will. Poor guy. What I didn't know was that among the hundred or so spectators half a dozen scouts were there specifically to watch him. If someone had just told me I would have made sure the guy looked good. I mean I was only passing a couple of hours, just there for the kick about. No skin off my nose. Besides, I knew well enough that even the best players can go to pieces when they are being watched. But no one whispered in my ear did they? So the guy looked like an arsehole that day when he was probably an ace player most Saturdays.

We won and, celebrating after the game in a pub, the 200 Club coach, Tam McAulay, the man who had produced the size eight boots, was all for me being a regular. I looked about me and felt the pent-up enthusiasm of my new found team-mates and enjoyed the buzz. Anything can be forgiven if there's a good dose of enthusiasm. But I wasn't so sure I had that in me. If I agreed to play for the 200 Club I would feel obliged to turn up for all future games and wondered how long it would take for a big Celtic match or a heavy night on the town to turn my head. Saying yes then letting people down is something I was brought up to avoid at all costs. But, on the whim of the moment, I said yes and meant yes. Tam McAulay smiled and said something wry about bringing my own boots along next time. Later I found out I'd worn his boots that day and wonder what would have happened if he took size nines or tens.

Drinking my beer slowly to make it last, laughing at the antics of the other players getting quickly pissed in the post-adrenalin rush of the match, I was told that someone wanted to see me. Now the game had been played just a hundred yards from where some relatives of mine lived but because I didn't know I'd be playing I hadn't even had the chance to tell them to come along to spectate. At the time I thought it was to be a one-off, my last competitive game of football. But who else would want to talk to me there?

It was a scout from Johnstone Burgh, one of the best junior sides in Scotland. The guy had come along to watch my opposite number and decided to sign me instead. Now playing for Johnstone Burgh would be a different matter entirely. There's nothing childlike or amateurish about junior football. The leagues are full of guys who almost made it professional and former pros on the way down. It's hard, vicious and very, very serious. You even had to go to regular training for God's sake. Didn't like the sound of that at all.

But I liked the idea of Johnstone Burgh. They were based just outside Glasgow and the inevitable sectarian tensions that hung around the city, permeating the football. Likewise, none of my mates supported them so I wasn't going to get catcalled from the terracing every week. Apart from that Johnstone Burgh were up against mobs like Kilsyth Rangers. Now giving any team with Rangers in their name a beating was worth some effort. As far as I was concerned it had nothing to with religion. I'm a Celtic supporter. It was football and much more important than religion. That sealed it, I signed within the week, getting a one-off fee of £500 and a job set up for me in the Roads Department of Strathclyde Regional Council.

From a chance meeting on a freezing Saturday, I'd gone from hangover king with a fiver in my pocket to a fully-fledged and paid footballer. I was sure of only one thing – I may not be any good at the game but I was going to have a ball. Guaranteed.

NO CHANCE, SON (1980)

S kin as white as bleached bone, carrot red hair and skinny as a twig – I must have looked like the ideal midfield dynamo – not. But that's where Johnstone Burgh played me and it clicked. From day one I was rated, playing regular first team games and making a bit of an impact on the field as a newcomer with no past – well, no football past. There was a fair bit of transfer activity between junior clubs and their scouts were pretty comprehensive in taking in the games of all the other teams they scoured for talent. Me, I just popped out of nowhere, came in off the street – literally. So I took the opposition by surprise.

Within a couple of months Partick Thistle came for me. In a sense Partick was my home team being based just down the road in Maryhill. But there's only one home team when you're a Celtic or Rangers supporter regardless of where you live. Just go to the supporters' clubs in the USA, Ireland, Australia, the Middle East and everywhere else and you'll see what I mean. So to me Partick Thistle were, at that time, a top Scottish club and that was the end of the significance.

Partick Thistle, known as the Jags, were the unpredictable pixie team of Scottish football – just as likely to thrash the top team in the world, as they had the all-conquering Celtic in 1971, as to be relegated. They had a proud tradition as the wee Glasgow team who sometimes played sparkling football and became giant killers. In their day they have produced top-class players just seldom at the same time. Alan Hansen played for the Jags before going on to play most of his career with Liverpool then becoming a leading pundit on the box. Alan Rough, one of the longest serving Scottish international keepers was also a Jags player but more of him later. And more, much more, of Mo Johnston who was playing for Partick Thistle at that time before moving on to Watford.

The Jags were managed by Bertie Auld, one of Celtic's Lisbon Lions, the first British team to win the European Cup in May 1967. A Celtic legend you might say and a kind of hero of mine – they all were. So, when I went along to play my trial I was on tenterhooks just because Bertie Auld was watching me, never mind the chance to go from being an unemployed labourer to part of a senior football team's pool in a matter of weeks. My first trial went okay but then they asked me to come back. The second trial went all right I thought until I was told that there would be a third game. It was a bit much to be honest. At that time the teams would watch you, maybe ask you along for one trial and a bit of training and then make up their minds. With Partick it felt like an endurance test and I'm not too fond of those.

At the third trial I ran my legs off. Once again I thought I'd done well enough to be signed. After I'd showered and changed, I was ordered to report to the manager's office. There he was, old jaw-face himself, Bertie Auld. He had this public demeanour where he would always appear dressed in a suit and woollen coat, looking dapper and wearing a tight-lipped grin as he brandished a big cigar. That day the grin was rather thin and not a Panatella in sight.

'You'll never make it. No chance, son.' He came to the point sharp and sweet and that was me shown the door. I expected the theme tune from the Hamlet cigar adverts to come on but no, it was just the rumble of the traffic outside Firhill. As I made my way home, I lit a fag and muttered under my breath, 'No chance eh? No fucking chance? Well, I'll show you.'

I was already playing and training with Johnstone Burgh and, unknown to them, turning out for the 200 Club on the side some weeks. This was decidedly against the rules even then while these days the pen-pushing bureaucrats

14

who run football would have you hung, drawn and quartered for the misdemeanour of playing for two clubs. They even take kids' football far too deadly serious these days, trying to organise everything out of sight. All young people want to do is have fun and that's what they should be left to do. It's the suits who run football and have never kicked a ball I blame for the falling standards of the Scottish game. They should just leave well alone. But back then it was at least a little more relaxed and I took full advantage.

So I was getting fitter and stronger without giving up my quest for a good time. Still dating several women at a time, hanging around with the same half dozen guys, moving from pointless job to another, hitting the pubs when we had dough. Not so much troubled or tearaways just lost, looking for something and whatever that was we hadn't a scooby-doo between us. Now and then we would get into a bit of trouble. Thankfully, as in my boyhood, I never got caught, being too fast on my feet.

But the football gave me a regular purpose. Not that I had become an athlete or anything so daft. But I enjoyed the playing for its own sake. When I walked on to a football pitch I thought that nothing and no one could touch me. I was safe from whatever other issues were about. For ninety minutes, I was at home – a fish in the water, a bird on the wing. So I turned up for every game, even training, and was getting stronger and fitter without even trying.

Ten months into my time with Johnstone Burgh, St Mirren came for me. They were in what was then known as the Scottish First Division (now the Premier). A great club from Scotland's largest town, Paisley, lying on the periphery of Glasgow. The famous players who have been through St Mirren's books are too endless to mention. Of note at that time, a certain Alex Ferguson had been their manager before moving on after a major fall out (sacked in other words) in 1978. Ferguson had made Aberdeen into the Scottish team of the decade, winning the European Cup

Winners Cup in 1983 and a score of domestic trophies. Of course, he would take over Manchester United and our paths would cross at a later stage when he was Scotland boss. Just as Paisley prided itself on being different and every bit as good as big neighbour Glasgow, so St Mirren had the audacity and the courage to try for the top. Folk from Paisley are called Buddies and you either are or you aren't one of them. I liked that self-confident swagger and what is more I liked the idea of playing for St Mirren.

Just before my 21st birthday I played my trial game against Morton. Everything was going well till I got into a fight with an opponent and ended up being given my marching orders by the referee – again. I headed for the dressing room with my head down, despondent. Blown it for sure. All right, I had only been playing football for ten months but I was impatient to succeed. It's not in my make-up to accept failure at anything. Sitting there in the dressing room, a towel wrapped over my head waiting to be told I had failed, Jim Clunie, St Mirren's Manager, came in. I held my breath and waited.

'Well, son, I knew you could play a bit but . . .' Just get it over with quickly eh. '. . . I never knew you had the bottle. Now I do.' I was used to getting bawled at by coaches for losing the place on the park. Never dreamed that one day it would get me signed for a top club. But sign for St Mirren I did and in November 1980, just before my 21st birthday.

The night of my signing I went out to celebrate with my sister, Marie, and a few friends. Though Marie was a few years older than me we got on well together. I didn't know it but her habit of nagging me like hell was going to serve as perfect preparation for coping with football managers. There's really not that much difference except that maybe I paid more attention to my sister. We wanted to make the celebration a big night out but it was mid-week and it was gay night at the only club that was open late. Didn't bother us one bit. Mind you it was interesting the number of guys

I knew who I met in there who were somewhat abashed to see me.

Back to day-to-day reality, the only way that smaller clubs like St Mirren could survive in the top flight was to have a handful of full-time players and most, like me, on part-time contracts. With that came part-time wages of £50 per week and not enough to live on. So the jobs would have to continue. But I didn't care. Rangers, Celtic, Aberdeen, Hibernian – come ahead. We could show them a thing or two if I had anything to do with it.

Jim Clunie, who had just signed me was fired two weeks later. Don't know if at the time he thought I was a Jonah or what but since then I've teased him that it was the best signing he had ever made as well as his last.

The new manager, Ricky MacFarlane, the club's former physio, announced I wasn't ready for first team football and I played in the reserves. Still as thin as a rake with a mop of unruly red hair, Ricky used to call me Swan Vesta, as in the brand of matches. I didn't care, I had arrived at a top football club.

There were some real hardened pros around St Mirren, like team captain Tony Fitzpatrick – a man of incredible stature who had played in England with Bristol City. In spite of being a full-time professional with one of Scotland's senior clubs, Tony still lived in Possilpark, perhaps one of the shittiest schemes in Glasgow. Tony took me under his wing professionally and personally. He knew the part-time wages were crap so every day he would drive the mile or so to my folks' place in Milton and give me a lift to the club. He is the type of pro I still hold with utmost regard. Never forgot his roots, never will.

Training was a different matter. Jimmy Bone was the team captain. A real tough professional who had taken no prisoners at every level of football, having played previously with Celtic, Norwich City and Partick Thistle among others. Looking at Jimmy was enough to scare most grown men and on the training park he howled at me constantly.

If I had been two foot taller and broader, as well as being backed up by a mob of my pals I might, just might, have considered giving him a square go. As it was I just had to get on with it.

One day at training the football caught me full belt on the goolies. For those of you who haven't had this dubious pleasure it's sheer, seething agony joined swiftly by a deep sense of dread that your equipment is never going to work again. Not good. It made more than my eyes water.

'Here, son,' said Jimmy, coming over all concerned, 'better rub some of this on them.' He squeezed some magic ointment out on the palm of my hand and I immediately did as he instructed. Well, my balls were aching fit to burst and I reckoned that the top football teams had to have some fancy potion to deal with what is a regular professional risk. The heat built up slowly to start with then took off like a bloody steam train. But I'm the new guy, the young bloke and I'm from Milton so I'm saying nothing to nobody – just kept on training, pretending I didn't care. 'Wee bit hot, Frank?' Jimmy eventually enquired, his face deadpan.

'Aye, a wee bit,' I conceded.

'Better go have a shower eh,' he helpfully suggested and I didn't need to hear it twice, sprinting to the changing rooms at full speed, behind me the whole St Mirren squad cackling with laughter. Ralgex. Deep Heat. Choose a brand name, I don't care. My balls were on fire and not in a way I ever wanted to experience again. I had been caught out by football's version of sending the apprentice welder for a bucket of blue steam or telling the new telephonist that there's a Mr G. Raff on the phone for her. It was a nippy-sweetie all right but, thank God, no permanent damage was done. If there had been, the rest of my story would be a wee bit different that's for sure. But then I was never that good at thinking with my brain and it would land me in great times and terrible times, as you'll see.

GOING DUTCH (1981/85)

I trained regularly and worked hard to build myself up, all to no avail. Seems like so many men from the Glasgow schemes I was destined to stay a runt of the human race. Reserve football was okay – certainly a step up from the junior leagues even though the atmosphere tended to be non-existent. Against Rangers and Celtic it was a different matter, with more supporters turning out for their reserve matches than for most of the top Scottish games. The boss kept saying I wasn't ready for the first team pool even though I knew my form was excellent and I could handle the knocks – you learned that fast in the junior game which is not for the fainthearted. But he was the boss so I played out the remainder of the 1980/81 season in the reserves.

My first breakthrough came right at the start of season 1981/82 with my League debut against Airdrie when I played midfield as usual and scored two goals in a 4–3 victory. It was the best of starts and not bad for a wee guy who had only started playing football eighteen months before. Well, it was all a case of I didn't take it that seriously. I just enjoyed playing – much better than working for a living. Besides I was used to scoring and it turned heads in the squad.

Heads turned in the boardroom as well for a different reason. The younger of my two older brothers, Jim, had managed to buy himself a black blazer, grey slacks, pristine white shirt and a St Mirren tie. Togged out like that he looked every part the club director. After my first game he waltzed right into the Board's lounge and chatted away like he had just bought major shares in St Mirren. Me? As a new face I had to convince the commissionaire that I was actually in the squad in spite of having just ran my ass off

19

on the field for ninety minutes. Jim's a chancer, of that there is no doubt.

My first season as a professional footballer was going well. While I wasn't scoring two goals every game, of course, I was well on my way to becoming St Mirren's top goal scorer from the midfield, my regular position. Not bad for a new kid on the block.

St Mirren still couldn't afford to pay me full-time so I was missing out on some training and chances to learn, sharpen my game. I realised that big Jimmy Bone wasn't taking just the piss when he was roaring at me on the field, always criticising every mistake. In his own way he was as helpful as the calm, considered Tony Fitzpatrick, getting me wiser about the game. But, not being a guy for half measures, I wanted more.

A family conference with my parents resulted in them offering to support me to go full-time while still on the part-time wages of £50 per week. They saw their boy had a chance to make something of himself and like all decent parents were willing to make sacrifices, to take the risk. All they asked in return was that I had the chance. They weren't looking for big-time success or a rich son, knowing well enough that only a smattering of people ever make it in football. While I was the youngest of their four children and the others had left home, there still wasn't a great deal of money around. Ours was the kind of working class family where poverty would never visit us but we were always just two steps up a very long ladder towards financial security. It was a gift of love from my Mum and Dad and one I'll never forget.

So I went full-time on part-time wages. Upped the training and felt the benefits. That first season, 1981–82, St Mirren reached the semi-finals of both the League Cup and the Scottish Cup. I was selected for Scotland's under-21 team and was awarded the Young Player of the Year award. Life was looking up, that's for sure.

My football went from strength to strength over the next

few years as did St Mirren's fortunes. They never quite won the league or a cup but were there or there about. It got to the stage where even every team feared coming to Love Street, St Mirren's ground. It was a time of dominance by the so-called New Firm of Aberdeen and Dundee United. Maybe their success had lifted the ambition of Scottish clubs, no longer scared of the football monoliths of Celtic and Rangers. For me running out at Parkhead as a player after a lifetime as a supporter was weird, uplifting and heady at the same time. Not least of my worries was that out there in the packed terraces were all my friends and most of my family. If I made an arse of a move I reckon I'd pick their voices out in the massed howls. But as soon as the game was kicked off I adapted, always feeling safe on a football park.

Rangers and Ibrox was another matter. I hated playing there even though I loved the idea of beating them. It was all to do with a group of headbanger supporters who, at every home game, made a point of taking up positions above the tunnel and spitting down on the opposing team as we ran out. When I say spit I mean it rained green lumps of gob. Standing ready for the kick-off you'd be smeared over your hair and shirt with their filth. I can take as much heat from the opposing supporters or my own (and have) but that was disgusting.

Eventually, my folks' support and my consistent good form paid off and I was given a full-time contract. The club were getting close to winning major competitions but always being knocked out at the semi-final stage and it felt like we were falling foul of Celtic and Rangers all the time. I recall in one semi – the Scottish Cup, I think – we were leading Rangers 1–0 and there were minutes left. Davie Cooper of Rangers, one of the best ball artists I have ever seen and now sadly dead, ran past me on the pitch and said, 'We'll score before the whistle.' Davie said it with such conviction, like he knew it to be true. Maybe it had something to do with the grin spread across my face at the

21

prospect of my first cup final at Hampden, Scottish football's spiritual home. At the time I just reckoned he was trying to put me off my concentration. Fat chance. We had run them ragged the whole game, besides he'd left it too late. Sure enough, injury time seemed to drag on forever and I couldn't remember there being that many casualties. Then Rangers scored, just as Davie Cooper predicted. Rangers scored the winner in extra time, of course, and I had learned a valuable lesson.

As a supporter I was acutely aware of the friction between the Rangers' and Celtic's supporters – you had to be to survive. But as a St Mirren player I became aware of the dominance of the two teams that seemed to permeate everything and everyone – especially referees' judgements. A few minutes added on for injuries that didn't happen, a fair but hard tackle rewarded by a penalty, a handball ignored – all the stuff that the pundits and punters argue about endlessly after the match. But, as a player, take it from me that many Scottish referees favour Rangers and Celtic. It could be religious bias or plain fear at the enormity of their support. Don't ask me why – it is just so. For all the other teams it's like starting one goal behind.

On the personal front I was having a whale of a time, ably supported by a half decent full-time wage. The club scene in Glasgow was exploding during that period and I was sponsoring them all – Bar Luxembourg, Henry Afrika's, Pump House, the Warehouse. Favourites were the Toledo Junction on Mondays and Paris in Paisley especially on Wednesday nights when the regular DJ was Richard Park, who moved on to Radio Clyde then Capital Radio. Glasgow's a small village of a city and for a footballer who liked to party everybody knew me and a hell of a lot about me. Like I played for St Mirren, was a Celtic supporter, was with a different woman every night and came from Milton. Now any single one of those attributes is a recipe for bloody disaster in Glasgow's clubs and pubs –

apparently. But I never had one whiff of trouble. It wasn't till later I found out that the people who ran the clubs were taking care of me, making sure nobody tried to step in. For that I'm truly grateful. It gave me a sense of freedom, joy in life, a continuing love affair with the city of Glasgow that's with me still.

On the football park, St Mirren manager, Ricky MacFarlane, had been appointed as the boss of Scotland's Under-21 team. Teams were allowed two over-age players then and Ricky promptly picked me when I was 22-years old. I was in good company, playing alongside people like Steve Nicol of Liverpool, Ray Stewart of West Ham, Gary Gillespie of Coventry City and Jim Bett of Rangers. The team was doing well in what was then called the UEFA Under-21 Championship. We were drawn against Italy away from home in the quarter-finals. No Scotland team at any level had ever beaten Italy let alone Italy in Italy. Everyone, even the most partisan of Scots, wrote off our chances. But we didn't know any better. In the north of Italy, slap bang in a territory where they take their politics and football very seriously, we won 1-0 to a McAvennie goal knocking them out of the tournament. Chuffed as hell with ourselves we celebrated and headed for the tunnel only to be met by a mob of Italian fans charging us and bottles falling like arrows from the sky. Didn't bother me one whit. It was just like an average Saturday night out in Glasgow. Besides I had scored.

In the semi-finals of the competition, England knocked us out over two legs. Like every Scot playing for Scotland I was desperate to beat our neighbours. But there's nothing racist in the sentiment. It's more to do with sibling rivalry. Love your brother but beat him to the goal. Just that old rivalry runs fierce at times – well, ninety minutes a go for me. But that's old hat. What the game gave me was a taste for the wider world of football. Here I was playing against the Italians and the English. I could use that and maybe play alongside them. The seed of ambition was planted – I could go anywhere, play with anyone.

I didn't have long to wait for another taste of the European scene when St Mirren won through to the UEFA Cup and were drawn against Feyenoord, the masters of total football, led by the chain-smoking maestro himself, Johan Cruyff. Over the two legs we were beaten but in the Netherlands I won Man of the Match award. In Amsterdam the play was going well. We were holding our own and I was learning a hell of a lot from the other team. Then St Mirren's Frank McDougall got sent off and headed for the tunnel with the usual mixture of anger, disappointment and a big, petted lip. When unfortunate enough to be red-carded it's important that the victim carries it off with a certain panache. Walk away like you don't care. The Glasgow way. Trouble is Frank McDougall disappeared down the wrong tunnel heading towards Feyenoord's dressing room. I spotted his error as the game went on around me and stood there in hysterics knowing he had to come back out. Some of the Dutch players were throwing me strange looks and making screwball signs at me. Five minutes or so passed and no sign of him. Knowing Frank a wee bit, I knew he had to be standing in there, totally embarrassed, waiting till he thought no one would see him slip out and head towards the right tunnel and our changing room. Sure enough, he emerged, almost tiptoeing into the stadium, and was met with a huge roar of laughter from the 40,000 or so spectators. They were waiting for him too. Poor Frank McDougall was blushing for a week.

Nothing much had changed in my personal life – I just got better at it. Looking back I laugh at the fuss the media made about my so-called champagne lifestyle when I made it to London. I was behaving like that and worse long before then and nobody gave a hoot.

Just before my twenty-third birthday, I bought my first flat and I was going to employ my new freedom to party, as you do. It was the usual boozy affair with loud music and very little food. But it was my birthday and I expected presents. I mean it was traditional, right? Everybody obliged apart from these two sisters, gorgeous blonde twins who were part of our group. A little bit miffed, at first I didn't say anything, tried to be cool and act the gentleman. As ever, that disappeared as the booze kicked in late into the evening. So I cornered the two blondes and challenged them.

'We have brought you a present,' they insisted almost in unison, a habit of theirs they didn't notice.

'Well?' I asked not unreasonably.

'It's just . . . we can't give it to you till later.' Giggles this time. My head was too befuddled with the bevy to comprehend. So they drew me aside and privately opened a holdall I'd noticed them bring into the house earlier on. In the bag were pairs of stockings, suspenders, basques – two of each. Now I clicked.

Try as I might I couldn't get my friends to leave the house even though it was my house. The girls were insistent that the present wouldn't get delivered till we were on our own. The other partygoers knew the sisters well and the girls had to retain some dignity. So I told my mates to fuck off. They smiled and told me to fuck off back. It was the kind of relationship we had and for a while that night I regretted it.

Eventually in the early hours of the morning we three were on our own. As I lay on my back, their naked flesh wrapped round me from either side, I just knew that was the best birthday present ever. What a life! Making it as a professional footballer and now a three-in-a-bed romp with blonde twins.

'This will do me nicely for the rest of my life,' I thought. If only I knew what was round the corner.

I met and got engaged to a beautiful woman called Vivian (we'll spare her surname to save her blushes). But me, I was getting engaged all the time. So much so that a few years later, a good-looking young woman was trying to get to speak to me at a football club. First she had to get past the staff.

'But I'm a friend, honest,' she pled. The grim-faced guy at the door eyed her up and down. Long blonde hair, leggy, big breasts – she looked the part all right. 'Look, we're getting engaged,' she argued.

'Aye right, join the fucking queue, hen,' he replied, pointing to a group of young women waiting on the pavement and slamming the door in her face.

This time with Vivian must have been serious since we made a date for the wedding and she moved into my flat. As the day of the nuptials drew closer I started to sweat till finally I called it off. The worst part was telling her father. I thought he would go mental. But no, he said he was relieved that I'd not gone through with it if that was how I felt. A real gentleman.

Vivian and I decided there was no point in wasting the honeymoon so went off together to Calla d'Or. It was a bit embarrassing when the hotel started plying us with champagne and roses as newlyweds but not so much as we didn't drink the fizz. The holiday was the customary superb mixture of booze, dancing and recovering in the sun on the beach. In a local bar one night I met Tony Hadley, lead singer with Spandau Ballet, then competing with Duran Duran for dominance of the popular music world. He didn't know it but he was my best friend. Well, he was for the duration of the holiday. I never had much time for the airs and graces of celebrities – it's not the Glasgow way. And to be fair, it wasn't Tony's way either.

Even after the honeymoon that wasn't, Vivian and I still weren't getting on any better. So, I resorted to type and hit the pubs and clubs. It was getting so I was some kind of minor celebrity, a name and face most people knew who could always be relied on to be in the bar. One night in some pub, I was asked to be a judge in a wet T-shirt competition or some such crowd puller – well, it would get me through the door. Trouble was, some of the contestants had taken cold feet or cold something and chickened out. So, the manager persuaded one of his staff, Rita Stewart, to take part. I had been chatting up Rita for ages with no luck. She had a regular boyfriend and was acting all faithful. Needless to say she won the competition but fair dos, she did look bloody great in a wet T-shirt.

Rita and I became an item for a while. Leastwise, we spent a lot of time together while I was still going out with Vivian and Rita with her regular boyfriend. Seems like her relationship wasn't working out too well either. One night in a club she asked me to dance. Now that is something I do not do and she knew that fine well. I must have been half cut or something because the next I know I'm on the dance floor. As soon as I started jigging, the floor cleared of all other couples. It was a bloody set-up as was the music – something from *Grease*. Rita's Olivia Newton John was impeccable but my John Travolta was – well, less said the better. Sarcastic bastards that run the club then presented us with a prize. The whole night summed up an aspect of Glaswegian culture – don't get too big for your boots. In Scotland I was a name, in the sports pages of the newspapers regularly, interviewed on TV. But as a dancer I made a great footballer. That was me put in my place and I love Glaswegians for that wee habit.

By 1983 I was well established as a regular player in the top flight of Scottish football. Luton Town began to show interest in signing me. Luton were at that time doing well under the management of David Pleat. I was tempted that was for sure but the deal didn't come off, with St Mirren getting a good deal from Aberdeen on Frank McDougall. David Pleat didn't give in. He was phoning my folks' house so often they were all on first name terms and chatted about this and that, just like old friends.

At that time I didn't have an agent. Well, they weren't as universal then as now and I hadn't needed one to get my position with St Mirren. Then I got a phone call from an agent called Bill McMurdo. McMurdo was full of contradictions. With long hair and a full dark beard he looked like a hippy in a three-piece business suit – not an uncommon style on the streets of Glasgow at that time. A Rangers-crazy Orangemen he draped himself in appropriate regalia. But McMurdo was totally upfront with me. Knowing my roots he invited me for a chat at his house that was like a little Ibrox. He declared that as a person he supported one team, one religion. But as a businessman he was entirely objective with only his clients' interests at heart. I liked his style, his bluntness and took to him right away. We shook hands on working together. That was it – no lawyers, no negotiations, no signed agreement in triplicate. McMurdo said that if I was ever unhappy about how he represented me I should always feel free to walk away. In all the time I worked with Bill McMurdo I never had any formal contract. Yet he was the new kid on the block as far as football agents were concerned and the hungriest, sharpest and most successful of the lot. It was one of the best business moves I was ever to make.

One day in 1985 Bill phoned to say that Luton were showing interest in signing me. Was I interested? Luton were doing well at the time, a rising team performing against the best English clubs. David Pleat's persistence had also impressed me so I agreed to signing talks. St Mirren under their new manager Alex Millar were willing to sell me for what would've been an entirely profitable transaction for them. They confessed they knew I would go sooner or later. Better I go for good money and move out of Scottish football than better money and start playing against them. So the meeting was set up and we headed south. As we flew off I knew they all reckoned that it was a done deal. Me, I had reservations. More of a dull feeling in the pit of my stomach I found hard to explain. But soon the answer would become clear in something like a scene out of a James Bond movie.

SECRET MEETINGS
AND CREAM TEAS (1985)

It felt a little awkward at first being the centre of such attention. I was used to scoring goals, getting cheered or jeered by thousands of supporters but in the peace and quiet of the meeting room, surrounded by the suits from St Mirren and Luton it felt, well, ineffectual or false. They were mincing about too much for me. Too indirect and too bloody polite. The questions were quite simple. Who do I play for? How much do I get paid? When do I start? I'd do the rest on the pitch.

St Mirren were easily satisfied with the transfer fee offered since it was going to be their biggest to date. Bill McMurdo hedged around and had extra terms built into the contract, taking care of my interests. All eyes eventually settled on me. I had to agree for the deal to be on.

'Any questions, Frank?' David Pleat asked. I liked his style and his perseverance. A good man I thought and obviously a great manager given Luton's success.

'Yeah, just one. How much do I get paid?' Some guy from the Luton mob, probably an accountant, wittered on about bonuses for this and extras for that . . . again.

'No,' I interrupted. 'How much will be in my pay packet at the end of every week?' It was a simple enough question, too simple for them it seemed as the same answers came rolling off their tongues. I was on the point of repeating the question for the umpteenth time when the Luton chairman waltzed into the room. David Evans was a Tory MP, close confidant of Margaret Thatcher and in charge of a club peaking in the top ten of English football, some of the best in the world. He had every right to be pleased with himself.

'Macca, old boy,' he said in a plummy, toffee-nosed

accent, slapping me on the back. 'Welcome aboard.' What I wanted to reply was, 'Who the fuck are you calling Macca?'

Football supporters, copied by the press, had given me that name a couple of years before. It was my nickname, a familiarity that supporters had every right to use but this guy? Who the hell was he? Screwing the nut, instead I just asked,

'I've been trying to find something out.'

He raised his eyebrows and smiled with dead eyes. Patronising prejudice was wiped across his expression. This geezer thought he was better than me, probably better than everyone else, certainly all footballers. 'What's my wage? How much will I get paid each week?' I asked again. Blow me but he just repeated the same spiel his people had been throwing at me, except in his case Evans kept chucking in that name, Macca. 'Look,' I interrupted, 'all I want to know is what will be the bottom line in my pay packet every week.' I was a simple man with a simple request, that's how it seemed to me. What could I spend? Was that too much to ask? I would have had the same question whatever the job, wouldn't you? Instead he started on the same palaver over again.

'Fine,' interrupted someone from the St Mirren group, 'we'll think about it overnight and let you know in the morning.' Whoever it was knew me very well. I was on the point of giving David Evans a verbal slap, telling him to stick his team where the sun don't shine. Bad enough that he seemed to be deliberately avoiding my question but his patronising assumption that I would join his team and his repeated slaps on my back accompanied by another over pronounced MACCA really pissed me off.

As we headed to the door somebody from the St Mirren group, thinking I wouldn't hear, mumbled, 'He's not going to sign.'

How well these guys knew me. My mind was made up. Literally within yards of the Luton group, Alex Miller turned to me and Bill McMurdo and murmured,

'West Ham are interested in you.' It took all my self-control not to explode right there and then. Instead through gritted teeth I asked,

'Why the hell wasn't I told this before?' Alex just looked back stony-faced and kept walking out of the building as if he had said nothing at all.

West Ham, you beauty. It was the Academy of Football. Bobby Moore, Geoff Hurst, Martin Peters, Trevor Brooking, Billy Bonds and the whole heap of bloody wonderful talent. It was the tops. The place to be. I wouldn't give a monkey's what the pay was. It didn't matter to me that the Hammers had narrowly escaped relegation the season before while Luton were on the up and up. I'd play for West Ham for free.

'Make a call, Alex,' whispered Bill McMurdo through his beard.

'Aye, as soon as we're out of here.'

We kept walking, straight-faced, sombre, careful Scots, as if we were still considering the Luton deal. Me, I was already dreaming of Upton Park.

Back at our hotel a phone call was put into John Lyall. The conversation went something like this,

'You're interested in signing Frank McAvennie, John?'

'Yes. Absolutely.'

'Good. There's one catch.'

'Go on . . .'

'The signing talks have to be tonight.'

'What? You're kidding right?'

'No, we're in London and available now but leave in the morning.'

'Who are you down to see?'

'It wouldn't be right to . . .'

'Okay. I understand.'

'So it's tonight or . . .'

'Gotcha! Right meet me, at . . .'

The next I knew we were driving through one of those

huge parks that grace London. In the pitch dark, deer flitted across the headlights of the taxi, disappearing again just as quickly. It felt more like a night trip in the Highlands of Scotland than a journey in one of the world's largest cities. This was getting to be bizarre.

We had to be careful. Luton had paid the St Mirren delegation's travel and hotel expenses. They would be far from chuffed to know we had gone to signing talks with another team and they had picked up the tab. John Lyall had given us directions to meet him at Toddington service station. By the time we got there it was the early hours of the morning and the cafeteria was almost deserted, aside from a scattering of long distance lorry drivers and some sad, lost-looking folks. Mind you, the bunch of grown men in expensive suits, huddled round one small table in straight-faced, earnest discussion must have looked pretty bloody suspicious.

John Lyall was ace. I took to him in five minutes. Open, honest, straight-forward and gave me my place. He knew that this was one of my biggest decisions in my life and it was more important to him that I wanted to play for West Ham than the issues concerning the money people on either side of the negotiations. But he did all that as a normal, everyday human being with a matter of fact approach. Now that was a seller to me. I'd never understood why some people get all po-faced, solemn and fierce just because they are dealing with something important. I liked John Lyall.

By the time we parted, the transfer fee of £340,000 and most aspects of the contract were agreed. Next morning phone lines between Upton Park and our hotel were red-hot smoothing out some wrinkles. Sitting on the plane flying back to Glasgow only one matter had to be resolved – my personal signing-on fee, though I actually forget the precise figures. Money has never been that important to me in spite of enjoying its fruits more than most. In fact it's likely that I would have earned a damned sight more if I had signed for Luton, even though they had been somewhat obscure on the matter. West Ham had offered me a signing-on fee of something like £10,000, a lot of dough in those days. Just to be awkward I was holding out for £15,000. Don't ask me why. There was no significance to the figure and I certainly didn't feel undervalued by the one tabled. With that issue still to be settled I just got on with my life like nothing had happened.

By then I'd managed to pass my driving test and get my first car – a racing green Capri 2.9. I thought it was the bee's knees. Probably on the back of St Mirren's regular good form, some company decided to give the players sponsored cars. While that was a regular feature for players at the top clubs, it was a definite boon for us at St Mirren. One Friday the company took my car off me and gave me a brand new Metro for the weekend. The following day we were play-ing Celtic and got thrashed 7 – 1. No way was I leaving the house after that. In the village that is Glasgow I would have been slagged off by every guy I met and a whole host of women, too. Besides, I hated getting beaten. So that Saturday night, I invited some friends round to my flat for a few drinks – well, a good few drinks as usual. Near the witching hour we all caught the booze munchies and I decided to get us a carry out curry. In spite of having been drinking I drove down to the restaurant to collect the meals, reasoning that it was close by and I was far from drunk. The curries safely lodged on the back seat I headed for home. Before I had travelled far a taxi suddenly pulled out of the dark in front of me and I ran right into it.

No matter how cool a customer you are, an unexpected car crash is always a disorientating fright, stunning you for a second. In the unreality of the post-crash adrenalin rush, I sat there trying to figure out what the hell had happened. Suddenly I was aware that my head and body were burning hot and there was a terrible stink. My guts had been ripped open, my skull crushed for sure, I reck-oned, and I responded in that manly way by passing out.

The next I knew I came to, lying on a bed in a hospital

Accident and Emergency ward. The burning sensation had abated and the smell reduced though still there.

'Is it bad?' I croaked to the nurse fussing over me.

'Not too bad,' she soothed.

'Tell me the worst.' The panic over, I wanted to know the score.

'Well, there's good news and bad,' she responded, a grave expression on her face.

'Just tell me the worst,' I insisted, thinking this was no time for joking.

'The bad news is you're going to go hungry,' she replied. Ignoring my perplexed look she continued, 'But the good news is you'll be able to play football again.'

'Whaaat?' I had decided that the crash had scrambled my brains and this crazy conversation was some fevered, coma-tose nightmare. The nurse smiled, wide and welcoming,

'Apart from getting covered in hot curry, you've no injuries at all.'

Did I feel embarrassed. If it wasn't for the Tikka sauce staining my face, the nurse would have witnessed a rare event – a Frank McAvennie blush. But the blush soon turned to worry when the police turned up. They were happy that the evidence at the scene indicated that the crash was the taxi driver's fault but would I mind blow-ing into this bag? Just routine. Well, I did mind but had little choice. I failed the breathalyser as I knew I would. What the hell was I going to do? Family clubs like West Ham were known to dump players guilty of any offence and drunk driving is one of those socially irresponsible acts. Easy, I pled not guilty even though I knew I was guilty as sin. That plea would mean that the court case wouldn't be for many months – long after the deal with West Ham was well struck. And if they found out about it in the mean-time – well, I was innocent till proven guilty, wasn't I? Nothing was going to stand in the way of me playing for West Ham. Nothing.

Not even the outstanding dispute over the signing-on fee.

But when John Lyall phoned me to say that the club had agreed my demands I accepted the extra dosh, naturally. Having disposed of that point, John asked me to fly down to London immediately and carry out the formal signing of contracts. A few days after that I was to go down again for my medical. Now you have to remember that I had hardly been out of Glasgow in my life. My first trip to London was for the signing talks with Luton. The short flight to the capital to me was a pain in the ass. I hummed and hawed. But John wanted the deal signed pronto. So, next morning very early I met him at the hotel at Glasgow airport. A cup of coffee, the contracts signed and he stepped on to the next plane back to London. Toddington service station, now Glasgow airport – we really had to stop meeting like that. Thankfully we did.

Training at West Ham started on something like 18 July, a Thursday. John Lyall wanted me down for the day before to settle into the hotel the club had arranged for me. But I insisted it was to be the Friday before that or not at all. He must have thought me off my nut. It was the close season, I was doing nothing else other than waiting for the biggest move of my life. Nevertheless I insisted and he agreed.

What he didn't know was that I was coming down for Live Aid which was to be held on Saturday 13 July, 1985. The biggest rock and pop bonanza in history, organised by Bob Geldof and Midge Ure to raise money for the starving of Mozambique, Ethopia and a stack of other countries – and to be held at Wembley Stadium. Us Glaswegians like our music, prefer it live and I'm no exception. No way was I going to miss out on a chance to see U2, Sting, Elvis Costello, Style Council, Paul Young, David Bowie, Elton John, Freddie Mercury, The Who and cross-Atlantic links with the likes of Bob Dylan and Simple Minds, as well as all the other wonderful talent. So, West Ham sponsored my trip and Graham Mills, a mate of mine, came along just for the gig.

We arrived the day before Live Aid. John Lyall and

Eddie Bailey, West Ham's chief scout, met us and took us to the hotel. They hung around chatting for bloody ages and we were champing at the bit for them to leave so we could hit the town. Eventually they split and we immediately got dressed up in our best glad rags and went looking for a good time. Like any tourists Graham and I wanted to go for the best sites but forget your Tower of London and Buckingham Palace – we headed directly to Stringfellows where we were promptly, though politely, refused entrance. As you'd imagine, I have reminded Peter Stringfellow of this numerous times since and he's countered by replying that maybe his staff got it right the first night. Undeterred we ended up in the Hippodrome which was great and became one of my regular haunts for years. Next day we ignored our hangovers and headed for the concert.

From afar that is Glasgow, Wembley was as familiar to a football supporter as his own street. Whatever the competition between Scotland and England, Wembley was the place of World Cup victories, the twin spires of top international matches. It was an icon. Trouble is, we expected it to be right there close at hand and, of course, it wasn't. Nothing in London is just around the corner. We wandered about the streets asking folks the way to Wembley. Some just ignored us, others spoke in dialects we couldn't understand. Others rattled off the directions by underground which was very helpful except they didn't tell us that was what they were doing. The North Circular and all that guff might as well have been double Dutch to us. Here I was signing for a top English club and couldn't find my way to the national stadium. Eventually, one expensive taxi ride later, we found the bloody place.

The effort was worth it. In spite of being late, I was determined to get as close to the stage as I could. Using the usual McAvennie method of just going for it with a grin, we weaved our way down on to the cram-packed pitch. Before long, I'm right in front, in the middle of a bunch of guys jumping to the music. In a break, Graham turned to me and said,

'Think this is the last time you'll do this without being recognised, Frank.' I looked around me and we're slap-bang in the centre of a group of heavy blokes wearing West Ham team colours of claret and blue and Bubble tattoos, as in their anthem, 'I'm Forever Blowing Bubbles'. I reckoned that he might be right. That day the Hammers supporters treated us well, offering us drinks from their carry out, a toke of a joint. I took to them right away. They reminded me of Glasgow guys – working class, down to earth, full of humour – just with different accents. It might have been the last time the West Ham supporters didn't recognise me but it was only the start of us partying together. In fact, I still party with them from time to time. They are my kind of people.

Half deaf and our heads still ringing with the music, we crawled back to our hotel after dawn exhausted but happy. When we eventually stirred the next day, I decided I couldn't be bothered hanging on in London for the few days before training started. Somehow I had got it into my head that training started on Tuesday instead of the Thursday. Those two days made the world of a difference to my boredom tolerance limit. Hanging around a hotel on my own in a city I didn't know was going to be too dull for words. So, off to the airport and on the next flight back to Glasgow with Graham.

It was an afternoon shuttle and, as is customary, the stewardesses came round with tea, coffee and scones. We thought we had arrived. There we were, two boys from the housing scheme of Milton, catching a flight from London to Glasgow just because we could. With the trays of food and do-dahs in front of us we just helped ourselves as cool as you like. Then I looked around and saw that we had mucked up. We had stuck those little pots of clotted cream into our coffee rather than on to our scones. I'm sure nobody noticed and if they did they couldn't have cared less. Somehow that little faux pas summed up for me my naïvety and inexperience. I could walk the most dangerous street in Glasgow. Handle any pub trouble going. On a pitch with a ball at my feet I didn't care who was watching. My approach to women was brazen and successful. Yet I didn't know where you put the clotted cream.

You can take the boy out of Milton but you can't take Milton out of the boy. Well, I like it that way now. But then, I was going to London and a world I knew nothing of. Bring it on, I thought. Do your worst. I can handle your best shot. Well, I would soon find out if I could.

TOO LONG IN THE BOGS (1985)

John Lyall picked me up at the airport in his flashy Jaguar. Looking back I realise this was typical of John – a personal touch that other top tier managers would delegate to some member of their backroom staff. But then this was the same guy who managed a late night, no-notice meeting with me at a motorway service station and then flew a round trip from London to Glasgow for the five minutes it took me to sign a contract. John Lyall was spoiling me for future managerial experiences. But then I reckon his approach was the right approach. It certainly got the best out of me.

Driving into London I asked him if we could go down Kings Road. I hadn't changed much from my teenaged years, always being a fussy dresser. With good money coming in and living in a city with some of the best clothes shops in the world, I knew I was going to be like a kid let loose in a sweetie shop. John obliged and headed off to King's Road so that I could fix my bearings. On the way, the traffic got stopped by a contingent of police. As we waited this cavalcade of police outriders and big black limousines cruised past. I noticed the Royal standard on the bonnets of the cars. Turning to John I said,

'You shouldn't have gone to all this bother for me.' He smiled and replied something like,

'Cheeky git. Maybe someday, eh?'

Later I was told it was Princess Diana travelling in the procession though I had no idea who it had been at the time. I was more interested in Kings Road, the clubs and pubs and, of course, playing for the Hammers.

That night, West Ham put me into a hotel in Epping. Let's say it wasn't the most salubrious of places – a little run down, tatty at the edges and as exciting as a church service at night. Obviously it had been chosen for that last aspect. If I wanted a wild time I certainly wasn't going to find it on my own doorstep. Lately I've just learned that it has been revamped into one of the hottest venues in the area. Just my bad timing eh?

At training that first day, I was introduced to the squad with guys like Alvin Martin, silky Alan Devonshire, Tony Cottee their top scorer and Ray Stewart, the only one I knew from playing together for the Scotland Under-21 team. First impression was that they were a good bunch. But football teams have a strange culture. It's a mixture of welcoming you into their group edged with having a go. I suppose it's to do with keeping the competitive edge well honed.

John Lyall and his coaching team of Ronnie Boyce and Mick McGiven were ace. That very first morning they handed me a ball. I thought they were taking the piss. The routine up at St Mirren and most other Scottish clubs was that for the first few weeks of pre-season training you did nothing but running to rinse the filth collected on your holidays out of your system and toughen you up. But I looked around me, anxious that they were taking the Mickey, and noticed that everyone had a ball even Phil Parkes the goalkeeper. I was ready for whatever they threw at me but this time no Ralgex on the testicles. Maybe they accepted that I was no longer an apprentice. John Lyall explained that the ball was our trade and we had to keep on learning how to use it. Suited me down to the ground. Football to me was about having the ball at my feet. Throw a ball on the ground and I'd chase it forever. But running for running's sake? I only ever did that to appease the coaches.

As the pre-season weeks passed I began to realise that this wonderful step up for me maybe wasn't greeted in the same way by my fellow players and West Ham supporters. During the summer the Hammers had lost their young midfield maestro Paul Allen to city rivals, Tottenham Hotspur. Worse than that, John Lyall had failed to bring in some new names he had chased hard. Spaniard Manuel Sanchez Torres couldn't move from Dutch side FC Twente because he wouldn't be allowed a UK work permit. West Ham's offer of £400,000 for Rob de Wit, brilliant star player of Ajax and a full Dutch internationalist, was turned down. Eventually they went for the lesser known Dutchman Danny Hoekman who was all set to move. Trouble was he was under twenty-one and his parents had to sign their legal approval of the transfer. Bizarrely they refused. Imagine, West Ham couldn't make a signing because his mammy wouldn't let him come out to play.

To cap that, they had just signed me for £340,000, the most expensive import from Scotland to England that summer but hardly a household name south of the border. I was well known in Scotland, sure, but unlike Celtic and Rangers, teams like St Mirren don't get covered by the London-based media. The poor supporters must have been tearing their hair out wondering Frankie Who? Did it bother me? No, I didn't even notice. Besides, put me on a football pitch and I would do the talking. I knew who I was and the Hammers crew would learn soon enough.

I decided to help them along a wee bit. I had already had my carrot-red locks dyed blonde back in Glasgow when I had received my first decent wage from St Mirren. On a trip home just before my first game, I went along to my hairdresser, Michael, for a haircut, as you do. This time I told him leave out the toner. The result was blinding, bleached blonde hair. The colour associated with brassy dames, loose women, ladies of the night. Bottle blondes. You catch the drift. The point was that when I walked on to that pitch the Hammers supporters wouldn't miss me or confuse me with someone else. No matter how I played, they wouldn't forget Frank McAvennie.

During those early weeks in London I was taking my life as seriously as I have ever done, concentrating on the football. The pre-season preparation wasn't going so well for West Ham. It reached rock bottom when we took on nearby neighbours Leyton Orient.

In spite of my knack of scoring and having been moved

41

upfront on many occasions at St Mirren, John Lyall played me in midfield, saying it was my natural position. I was happy enough there and opened the scoring for us against Leyton Orient. Then they scored three. The West Ham support went mental and who could blame them. One guy even burst into the dressing room and gave John Lyall a right bollocking that consisted mainly of four-letter words. Initially, I thought the guy was a director or something, so sure was he of his right to be there expressing his views. As a lifelong supporter of the game I knew how the guy felt. Lyall, who could come across as unapproachable, a stiff upper lip headmaster sort of a guy, just stood there and took it. Almost as if he was admitting that we deserved a rollicking. The season before, a Tony Cottee goal in the very last match had saved West Ham from relegation. The home crowds were down to much less than 20,000, even when the top teams visited. Now, here they were getting ready for the new challenge having lost their best young player and signed, well, me. West Ham were giving their supporters the jitters since, to all appearances, we were in disarray.

A couple of days before the season kicked off, John Lyall made a signing that sounded on paper like an act of desperation. Mark Ward was a twenty-two year old from Oldham Athletic. Now, the lower divisions in England, as graced by Oldham Athletic at that time, were held in equal ignorance by the top team supporters as the game in Scotland. Nobody knew who Mark Ward was or why Lyall should fork out £250,000 for him.

Mark was put up in the same hotel as me. As soon as I saw him I liked him. Given that I was banned from the game as a child since I was too small and weak, the fact that I was taller than Mark Ward gave me no end of consolation. But he was strong. He reminded me in appearances of the great Scottish wingers of my childhood like Celtic's Jimmy Johnstone or Rangers' Willie Henderson. Short, yes, but with broad shoulders and thick thighs. You wouldn't be knocking over Mark Ward easily.

Mark and I had a good few things in common. He had worked for a living after leaving school, never thinking about being a professional footballer. He was from Liverpool, a Scouser, a working class city with a population that has so much in common with Glasgow. His move from Oldham to West Ham was seen by him and his family like a dream come true. So we got on fine, at least I thought we had. A short while later we were moved out to separate hotels. Mark's wife and baby were coming down and my girlfriend Anita Blue had joined me. That seemed to be the reasoning at the time. Later, it transpired that Mark couldn't understand my Glasgow accent and I obviously wasn't coping too well with his Liverpudlian warble, even though I thought I had been. But I must have been answering all the wrong questions. Or at least he thought I was – if only he could have made out what I was saying. But communication is a damn sight more than words and he and I got on very well.

The start of the season was a bummer with us getting beaten 1–0 away to Birmingham City. I was being played in midfield just behind our strikers Tony Cottee and Paul Goddard. Goddard got badly injured in that first game and his bad luck turned out to be my good fortune. I was moved up front. Three days later we whipped Queens Park Rangers 3–1 and I scored my first goal in a competitive match for West Ham. At one point in the match, a Queens Park defender kept niggling and niggling at me and seemed to be getting off with it. I had had enough. Next time I caught him with the ball I tackled him so hard he ended up in the West Ham crowd. Poor guy had a bit of trouble getting off the terracing and back on to the pitch. It was now Frank McAvennie the striker – the guy with yellow hair who booted players off the park, when they needed it.

The next game we were beaten at home by Luton Town, the team that had tried so hard to sign me. Ironic or what? I didn't care. I knew I had made the right move. Then we went to Old Trafford and got dumped by Manchester

United 2–0. It was beginning to look like we were heading for relegation territory again. The next three games we drew, including a 2–2 result against Liverpool, now run by my childhood hero, Kenny Dalglish, as player/manager. Going to these places, taking on the big name players I idolised as a supporter might have unnerved me, except I never thought about it. Every Saturday was a kid's trip out to wonderland for me. Where are we going, who am I going to see? If I had sat down and mulled over it for days – going to Anfield to take on Hansen, Rush, Molby, Whelan, Grobbelaar, Nicol – I might have wet the bed or at least lost my nerve. But instead I just took life as it came and enjoyed myself.

A couple of months into my time at West Ham I was beginning to feel a little detached from the other players. Good guys and all that but we just didn't seem to have anything in common apart from football. One day I did an uncharacteristic thing and shared my worries with Ray Stewart.

'The other guys don't seem to like me much, Ray,' I offered.

'What makes you think that?'

'Well, they don't speak to me. Even at training.' Ray hooted with laughter,

'You silly bugger.'

'What?'

'It's your accent. Every time you shout for the ball they think you want to fight them.'

Fair comment. I wouldn't hang around with someone who was always wanting to give me a battle. From then on I started to adjust the way I spoke. Just a little, mind. I'll always be Scottish to any listener. But at least I can now ask for the ball without a team mate taking fright.

Round about the same time, I was feeling a bit homesick. This came as a big shock to me since I usually take seconds to make myself at home anywhere, anytime. And even though Anita had joined me I just felt cut off from

the world that I knew. It's a funny thing homesickness –
a low level ache that just never goes away. It saps your
spirit, deadens your humour and I don't like that one whit.

I went along to John Lyall and told him that I wanted
a move back to Scotland. Worried that it wouldn't work
out, I suppose, he asked me,

'You wanting to transfer back, Frank?'

'No, I'm not asking for a move, it's just I can't settle in
London,' I replied.

'If you did have to move, who would you go to?'

'There's only one team I'd leave West Ham for,' I reassured John Lyall, 'Celtic.' Lyall nodded as if he understood exactly what I was telling him. Now I had played
for West Ham I couldn't play for a smaller team, even if
it was successful. And there was only one team for me, the
team I had supported from childhood. Now that would
always be a step up, regardless of who I was playing for.
John Lyall put on his head master's cap and advised me
to give it a few months first, a sensible suggestion considering all the trouble he had gone through to sign me and
I was happy to oblige him.

Lyall must have had a word with the players or maybe
Ray Stewart did, because the next I know they've organised a squad night out. We hit The Ship in Gidea Park,
then the Slater's Arms in Romford, before ending up in
Stringfellows. I'd been in Stringfellows before but that
night was my proper introduction. Because there was some
dispute resulting in no football being covered by TV, no
one knew who I was. That night, Stringfellows staff were
introduced to me as Frank McAvennie of West Ham. Now
that carried clout. I was never refused admission again and
I was hardly out of the place.

The night out was great. The blokes were doing things
like standing with their arms draped round each other's
necks and then getting up to dance together. For a while
I wondered if half of them were gay. Well, swinging
enlightened London and all that jazz. Turns out they

weren't just pissed but were also taking the piss. Now both of those I appreciate.

But that's where their bad habits seemed to end. Most of the team were married and well settled down with kids and mortgages – the type of commitments that couldn't support my kind of lifestyle. Apart from the booze, none of them were up to badness that night – none of them even smoked or so it appeared. I had smoked since my teenage years but was careful with it in a particular way. When out in public, especially with other players, I always thought it best not to advertise my nicotine habit. Bad publicity, bad image, bad message for kids. So I would occasionally slip off to the toilets for a quick drag. When some of the squad cottoned on to what I was up to they would follow me out and cadge a ciggie. Part-time smokers with a special brand – OPFs. Other People's Fags.

In years to come, people would sell stories to the newspapers saying they had been in such and such a club when they noticed me slipping away to the toilets frequently. Now sometimes the more sinister headline spin of taking a line of coke might have been right – that's for later – but sometimes I was just going for a fag. Serves me right for worrying about the public image of a football club – that type of responsibility has never sat easily on my shoulders. People should just be themselves in my view. Maybe that's a weakness, maybe it's a strength. Whatever you think, it's just me.

That night in Stringfellows something magical was happening. That dull ache lifted from my guts. I was partying, relaxed, in good company and I felt I belonged, was now part of the team. The homesickness had vanished. This was my home. West Ham was my team. Bring on your football prima donnas and your West End girls. I wanted as much of both as I could manage. Little did I know that night exactly how much of both would come my way.

THERE'S SCORING AND . . . (1985)

Turning points, like big mistakes, are best recognised after the event. In football terms, the game against Leicester City was probably the turning point for me in England. At the time, it was good enough that I scored the first goal in a 3–0 win for us but looking back at the results that season it seems to stand out as the start of a good run of victories. A beginning of a time when every other team wouldn't fancy playing the Hammers – home or away. But that's for the pundits to mull over. Analysis and history are not for me. I was always too busy living life.

That game against Leicester did spell out something for me – the beauty of Upton Park. I don't care if you're a football supporter or not, the atmosphere of Upton Park is special, moving, terrifying and would reach you too. A small, compact ground, the supporters are right on, almost over the pitch. With tired legs in the 89th minute, a football park can seem too long, too wide and with too far to go to goal. At Upton Park it seemed like a tiny goldfish bowl with no hiding place from the crowd. Wrath or celebration – whatever they felt you caught the gale of their emotions. If a supporter wanted to tell you you were playing crap you smelled the stale lager on his breath as well as catching every syllable. Intimidating? For opposing teams it must have been. Especially since that year the top clubs had agreed to curtail sales of tickets for away matches in a response to growing concerns about violence surrounding football. One of the side effects was that when you played at Upton Park you were being watched almost entirely by West Ham supporters.

I could never understand the Eric Cantona Karate Kick school of thought. So what if supporters gave you a bad time? They were the geezers who paid entrance money, bought team strips, wore scarves, came back week after week however you were playing. The supporter is the boss and too many players forget that these days. But me, I loved the closeness of the crowd. I realised it that day against Leicester City – Upton Park was my kind of place, filled with my kind of folks.

I didn't realise it at the time but there was another reason I would look back on that game. In the closed season Leicester City had transferred a certain striker by the name of Gary Lineker to Everton for £800,000. It made my transfer fee look like chocolate-coated sweeties. That's never bothered me. If someone gets on and screws a few quid – good luck to them. Lineker was the blue-eyed boy of English football and a great scorer of goals. Leicester was now stuck with playing without him and it showed. I didn't give Gary Lineker a second thought – well, he wasn't on the pitch was he? But by the end of the season people would be putting our names in the same sentence. If someone had predicted that to me, early in the season of 1985/86, I would have told them to keep taking the medication. And I guess most football supporters would have agreed with me. Like I said, turning points are best recognised after the event.

That night out with the West Ham team did more for me than get rid of my homesickness. Now I spread my wings in London and I could afford a different lifestyle. The bold Bill McMurdo had all sorts of clauses stuck into my contract. My starting wage at West Ham had been £350 per week compared to the £250 per week I had been getting from St Mirren by the time I left. While a 40% increase wasn't to be sneezed at and £350 a week was a damn sight more than your average road digger earned, it wasn't the glamour salary that the public expected top flight footballers to be on. In fact, in spite of my reputation as a good time guy, I never did earn the kind of dough everybody assumed I earned. Thing is, because of McMurdo's canniness I seemed to be getting a wage rise every few weeks.

I refused nothing but blows, of course. Thank you very much, Bill McMurdo. Very grateful, West Ham. Now where can I spend the loot?

First I had to look the part. Always a fussy dresser, I went to town on suits at prices that were obscene. The height of fashion at the time, all I can say now is that they were LOUD. It wasn't deliberate on my part. Some folk might look at photographs of that time and accuse me of attention seeking, showing off. No doubt a designer label suit costing the equivalent of a few months' wages for most people did attract attention. But I didn't think that way. I had the money and the money would be spent. That had always been my way and always will be. The suits represented more a coming of an age of confidence. By then I knew I was going to do the business on the football field and anywhere else. I had yet to deliver but knew I would. Cocky? Probably. Confident? Certainly. I just did my thing and enjoyed every second of it.

Brown's, the Hippodrome and, of course, Stringfellows received a fair slice of my wages, especially Stringfellows. It was then I was told I had been approaching Stringfellows the wrong way. The celebrities only went there mid-week to avoid the rush of the great unwashed wage earners out for a special night at the weekends. Names were also meant to slip upstairs to smaller, private rooms. Sod that, I went wherever and whenever I wanted, preferring to hang around downstairs especially for a good blast out on a Saturday night when the company was good. Not famous, maybe, but great revellers nevertheless.

It is myth dispelling time. I've been given a reputation as someone who hated training, drank every night and still did the business on the field. Almost accurate. I drank most days, despised training, but always took care the night before match nights. Okay so I maybe arrived at training straight from a party with a wee hangover now and then. But never on a match day. How I hate being in the company of drinkers when I'm stone cold sober. It's like they are all talking a different, happier language from you. So I'd avoid going out at all on the nights before a game. This meant that most weeks I'd have two nights off the falling down liquid in preparation for the Saturday and mid-week fixtures. Only two nights mind. A man has to reward himself for discipline eh? Otherwise why bother? There would be no point if you couldn't go out and celebrate and I always did when I could.

Anita Blue had moved down from Glasgow and we moved into a flat together in Brentwood. Anita had been a little reluctant to move away from her Glasgow ties and who could blame her? Who was to know if it would work out for me in London? On my trip back north after Live Aid and before the season started I had persuaded her to move south sooner rather than later. After sorting out her domestic and work affairs she joined me pronto. We spent most of our social time together during those early months. It was a bit like an extended holiday in London with always another place to go to. Anita was good for me

But soon we weren't short of familiar Glasgow company. Charlie Nicholas had signed from Celtic for Arsenal a couple of years before. Charlie's lifestyle had earned him the nickname Champagne Charlie and that suited me just fine. Charlie made us very welcome and showed us around his domain of the pubs and clubs, of course. I even let him off with his nickname for me – Esther. There was also Mo Johnston. Now playing for Celtic and scoring frequently, Mo had played for a year at Watford under the management of Graham Taylor. Most Saturday nights or when there was a mid-week break in training, Mo would jump a plane to London and end up out on the town with us. His time in Watford had given him a taste for the city of London's play area and he kept on coming back. While Charlie had the reputation as the good time guy, Mo managed to keep up and more. Somehow he didn't feature in the press gossip columns as Charlie had. Maybe I should have paid a bit more attention to that and figured out how

Mo had achieved the lack of scandal. But in truth I didn't care that much about reputations, especially my own.

As regulars at Stringfellows Anita and I had met the stunning Margot Mitchell who was the club's official photographer. Margot originated from Coatbridge, a few miles out of Glasgow. Maybe it had something to do with the proximity of our origins or, then again, maybe Margot was just caring for a couple of outsiders but she certainly kept us right, showed us the ropes. Margot's job was to approach Stringfellows' customers and ask to take pictures. Unlike those who worked for the press she was polite, always asking permission and would never take a photograph when refused. This was well appreciated by the more famous customers and, as such, many of them became friends with Margot. Friends of Margot's were friends of ours and soon we were on first name terms with sheikhs, oil magnates, film producers, rock stars. My trouble is that none of that brouhaha ever impressed me and I got to know a stack of people as Ed, Paul or Joe and promptly forgot their last names, never mind what they did. Yet most others would know of them for what they did and from their pictures in the colour supplements or the TV. If I'd realised that one day I might write a book I should have kept a diary logged with Margot's ace pictures. As it was I enjoyed and trusted her company and was too bloody busy having a great time.

Out on the football field life was going as well as I had felt it would. West Ham had put together a string of results that was impressing everyone – beating Nottingham Forrest, Newcastle away, thrashing Aston Villa and dumping Everton away among others. By November we were coming across as the team to worry about and yours truly was sitting comfortably as top goal scorer in the league

Trouble was, the dispute with TV had festered on and no one aside from West Ham supporters and avid readers of our match reports had any clue what I looked like or anything else about me. One newspaper ran a competition inviting readers to describe me. Standard guesses figured I was a six foot tall, burly built, red-headed, take-no-prisoners type of bloke. I suppose when in doubt fall back on stereotype and, let's face it, the English football scene has had enough big Scots that approximated that description. Even the small maestros like Billy Bremner somehow seemed larger than life and punched more than their weight.

Then I got a call that was to change all of that. I was being invited on to the Terry Wogan show as a guest. Wogan's chat shows ran three times a week on television back then, drawing audiences of many millions at every turn. It is not an overestimate to say that he was a national institution. But it didn't occur to me as anything special to be invited to appear. It should have but it didn't. Something to do with all the Boys' Own Adventure events that had happened to me in the previous few years. From unemployed Glaswegian to striker for one of England's top football teams. I was used to anything and everything happening. Nothing was surprising me anymore. So I said yes and went along for the chat. Drinking and talking – I was born to it. Half an hour with Wogan – no problem.

The show was on a Friday night as I recall. Of one thing I'm certain, the other guests were comedian Ade Edmondson, the woman who played Dot Cotton on the TV soap *Eastenders*, the pop group Shakatak and the most important to me, Dennis Law. Now in Dennis Law I was really meeting a childhood hero. I can just picture him in a Manchester United or Scotland strip, the sleeves pulled over his hands, looking almost frail yet turning brutal defenders, adding the killer touch to the ball, riding a double-footed target and still heading towards goal. It was too much for me that some journalists were comparing my style with that of Dennis Law. Guys like Law are simply a different class, up there along with Pele, Best, Eusebio – except better – well he is a Scot after all; allow me some bias.

Law was an old hand at the chat show routine and saw fit to put me at ease while we waited in the Green Room which, of course, wasn't green at all. He had flown in from somewhere and gone directly to the studio. Unfortunately, while he had taken a fresh suit and shirt to change into, he had forgotten his shoes. Not only was he forced to wear sneakers, he also discovered to his obvious horror that the sole of one had worn in a hole. Dennis is a very dapper, smart dresser and that hole in the shoe offended him. As a past master of the ogle box, he knew a bit about camera angles and made me promise to sit at one side of him to conceal his embarrassment.

As the cameras swung on to me, Law, who knew it was my first time on TV, muttered out of the side of his mouth,

'Don't worry, Frank, there's only 14 million people watching.' A dab hand at speaking in private and not wanting to be heard, I muttered back,

'Worry? Me? I'm not the one with a hole in his shoe.'

Any possibility of nerves had now disappeared. I might be on live TV in front of millions but I was sitting with a hero, Dennis Law, with a hole in his sneaker. I suppose it was my equivalent of the advice given to folk going for an interview – imagine the interviewers to be naked. Thank God I didn't have to go that far. Wogan and Law in the scuddy! No thank you very much.

The details of the show are vague. There was a lot about me as the unknown star of English football. A bit about my suits and the loud fashion. All in all a pleasant half hour. My first TV appearance and one that set me at ease. In fact I have never been nervous in any media situation since. So thank you, Wogan and Law.

The BBC car took me home after the show and I settled down to a quiet night before the next day's game. It had been a laugh, a diversion, no more than that and by bedtime I had forgotten all about it. Little did I know the trouble it was about to bring to my life.

. . . THERE'S SCORING
(STRINGFELLOWS, LONDON 1985)

I was standing on this table, a bottle in one hand, a half-full glass in the other. Saturday night in London and I was letting loose as usual. Music was swimming round the room, bouncing off the walls. Beautiful, long-legged women barely wearing pelmet-length skirts were jigging to the beat. Life was good.

Somewhere below me a hand reached out and tugged at my sleeve. They would have to do better than that. I ignored it. Another tug, more insistent this time. Peering down at Margot Mitchell whose lovely face looked uncharacteristically serious, troubled.

'There's a stack of photographers outside, Frank,' she said, as if that were adequate explanation. Obviously it had nothing to do with me. We were in Stringfellows in London for God's sake. Earlier that night I'd spotted Jack Nicholson sitting at a nearby table. The place was mobbed with faces from TV, the movies and the music world and that didn't include the really big names who had slipped upstairs to stay out of the public eye. Me, I was just a young guy from Glasgow out to have a good time.

'What's it got to do with me?' I asked.

'You play football,' she replied.

'So?'

'And something to do with you being on a TV show last night.' Margot smiled a little ironic grin.

'Shit!' The penny clanged to the floor, as did I.

The Terry Wogan show had blown my cover. Trouble is I didn't know I needed a cover till the reporters turned up that night. Margot and two of the guys from Stringfellows smuggled Anita and me out of the front door, under a coat. The whole scene felt ridiculous, bizarre. If the guys in Milton had seen me they would've been telling me to act real. Mind you the same blokes would've told the photographers to fuck off and followed that up with a wallop and that wasn't my modus operandi. The photographers may have been stepping into our personal space but they were only doing a job, trying to earn a buck. Good luck to them.

Margot and the boys persuaded the driver of one of the long, black limousines to give Anita and me a lift home. The guy was obviously bored, hanging around outside Stringfellows waiting for his boss. There were stacks of big flash cars there in the street with fed-up drivers catching a quick smoke or polishing their wing mirrors for the umpteenth time. This guy just drew the short straw when he heard that he was to take us all the way out to Essex rather than a swanky hotel in nearby Mayfair. I didn't care. I just poured Anita and I good hefty measures from the well-stacked drinks cabinet, lit a fag and leaned back, enjoying the smooth ride through London.

It was one of those times in my life when I struggled with events. Not unpleasantly. But it was hard to avoid trying to grasp that it was the same boy from Milton being smuggled out of Stringfellows and escaping from the press in a chauffeur-driven car. Put simply, I couldn't believe my good luck. What had I done? Played a bit of football. That's all. But the experience was good for me, taught me another few tricks. As of then I was forever coming out of high class clubs and cadging lifts in black limousines, sometimes enormous stretch jobs. For years to come there would be people who assumed that I travelled everywhere in my personal chauffeur-driven wagon. Sorry, folks, it was just the Glasgow boy chancing his arm. I owned a few flash motors in my time but not as grand as the ones I hitched lifts in.

By the time we hit home, I was still laughing. A few drinks later and I was heading to bed. What a blast of a weekend was my last thought before I reassured myself it was all over. Aye, like hell. It was just starting.

The next I knew I had been picked for the Scotland squad. When Jock Stein had died of a heart attack as the game against Wales had spun out all around him I had mourned like every other football supporter. Big Jock was a hero, a legend. The boy from the pit face of the white trash scrubland of a barren country who taught the rest of the world how football should be played. If I thought my transformation from road digger to footballer was all a bit crazy, I was put in my place by two seconds of contemplation of Jock Stein's life. By birthright he was meant to have slaved down the pit from an early age in perpetual poverty till his lungs gave in to a too swift demise. Instead he crawled out to kick a ball around a park and got paid for it. When his playing days were over he applied himself to management instead of choosing the normal route of pub ownership and alcoholic oblivion. He transformed Dunfermline Athletic into a classy side and then took Celtic to the top. From a bunch of boys most of whom were born within spitting distance of Celtic Park, Parkhead, Paradise – call it what you want – he won the European Cup at Lisbon. The first British side to do it and do it in such style. The Lisbon Lions had no big names, no obscene wage earners, no big money spinners. Stein made them immortal from nothing but his wits. When The Boss collapsed and died before he saw his international team score the goal they needed to secure a World Cup play-off place I couldn't help but mourn. Any real football supporter in the world would mourn, whatever football club they were pledged to.

If Stein's heart had held out, maybe I would have had the honour of being picked by him. Now that would have been something else. But, for the play-offs for the World Cup in Mexico, Alex Ferguson, then manager of Aberdeen, was given the honour of being manager, assisted by Walter Smith. At the time, those two names didn't impress me at all.

Scotland were drawn against Australia. It was to be a home and away tie with the first leg at Hampden. Playing for your country was something else again and I can't deny it gave me one huge buzz. There was some fuss about the top English clubs not being too happy to allow their Scottish players away for the international. It was aggravated by the same clubs having an agreement with the English FA that players would be freed for their games. I didn't have such troubles. It was written into my contract that I would be freed if picked for international duty. Aside from that I reckon John Lyall wanted his players to show up on the international arena. In the tradition of West Ham, John was about producing great footballers and, if successful, that meant their national side would pick them. We need more of his approach in the sport today and get away from these naff managers who pretend their players are injured when the international matches come up. If I had been playing today and my manager was refusing to let me play for Scotland I'd tell them to stick it and go anyway. Mind you, modern day footballers tend to do what they are told.

On the night it was fantastic. My old man was in the crowd, proud as punch but saying nothing. That was his style. The careful, no showing off approach to life that so many decent working class blokes of his generation subscribed to. He didn't have to say anything. I knew how he felt. Well, when you love someone you do know, right?

Being in the squad was one thing but being picked was something else. Scotland had a lot of talent to choose from then. As Johnny Come Lately, I would not have been surprised if Ferguson overlooked me and preferred one of the tried and tested strikers. There's a load of guff written about the international platform being different from top-class league football, that some players can score for their clubs and not for their national side. Thankfully that viewpoint wasn't as prevalent then as it is now. Football is just football. I was in.

The game was played at Hampden on the evening of 20 November 1985. A cold, sharp, dark night but it might as well have been the middle of the day as far as I'm concerned. For what it was worth the team that night was: Jim Leighton, William Miller, Alexander McLeish, Maurice Malpas, Steve Nicol, Gordon Strachan (sub Jim Bett 83 mins), Graeme Souness, Roy Aitken, me, Kenny Dalglish (sub Graeme Sharpe 71 mins), David Cooper. Now you might have noticed something in that line up. I was playing alongside my all-time hero, Kenny Dalglish. While it broke my heart when Dalglish moved from Celtic to Liverpool in 1977, the thing about being a Celtic player is you never stop being identified with the club. How can you hold a grudge against your hero anyway? It's a contradiction in terms.

On paper we should have thumped the Australians off the park. They were a nation of part-time players without any big clubs. But it was around that time that the traditional football powers were just becoming aware that there was no such thing as an easy pushover on the international scene. God knows Scotland had learned that to their cost against the so-called minnows of the game, usually during world cup finals. The public mood was optimistic but tinged with a wee bit of dread that the Scottish tendency to play crap when we're favourites would rear itself again. We would have stood a better psychological chance against the Brazilians and likely to have thrashed the English against the odds. But the Aussies, they were a different kettle of fish. We were expected to beat them.

In the changing room before kick-off, we were treated to a dour, monosyllabic talking to from Alex Ferguson. I was sitting on a bench, looking at the ground, as if I was concentrating hard on every word he uttered. But I was grinning like a Cheshire cat, just delighted to be there. I kept my head down though, thinking that maybe Fergie wouldn't appreciate that I didn't appear to be taking his words of wisdom too seriously. Christ's sake, all he was telling us was that our defenders should stop them from scoring and guys like me should score goals. Like that's what I did and I hadn't come along for the ride. That night, I reckoned Fergie took himself far too seriously. So far, I haven't been proven wrong.

Out we ran into the glare of the floodlights, 60,000 mainly Scottish supporters roaring us on. Tell you, that kind of buzz was worth all of the tedious training. The first half was a nervous stalemate. We had the better of the play but every now and then they would get into a dangerous position. It would be right on script for Scotland to lose the game to one breakaway goal. That's the kind of self-destruct behaviour we were renowned for and with justification. Back in at half-time for more of a dirge from Ferguson and out again. This time it was a question of some of us getting a wee bit fed-up with the situation. We were going to sort it out our way. Less than ten minutes from the kick-off Davie Cooper scored a cracker. That was better. Me, I was running my legs off playing my usual game. Always dipping back to help the midfield, running through waiting for a chance. Then it came, as sweet a ball as you like from none other than Kenny Dalglish. Kenny had seen me in action earlier in the season, scoring both West Ham's goals in a draw with his Liverpool. The maestro had worked out my play and laid it right on me. It wouldn't have mattered if he had sliced it with his knee accidentally. It was a pass from Kenny and I lobbed in my first international goal. A perfect ending to a perfect night. God knows what happened during the rest of the match and, personally, I don't care. We had done the business winning 2 – 0 and I had scored from a Dalglish pass. What more could I want?

That night I met some new friends. Like Roy Aitken of Celtic. A total teetotaller who always seemed to be totally pissed. The big man had a bizarre sense of humour like he was on some happy drug all the time though he is the most sober person I've ever known and that includes most priests. And I made some new friends like Graeme Souness, arrogant as they come but never posted missing when the going got tough. Souness had earned the right to strut his stuff. Good luck to him.

The newspapers in Scotland were full of the victory. As a goal scorer my name figured large but I was a wee bit disappointed that when I returned to London it had hardly been noticed. West Ham had become my family and my team. I wanted them to notice. But as far as the media was concerned it was more a question of, 'Where have you been, Frank?'

Of course, the West Ham guys had looked out for the score and weren't slow to slag me off about Scotland having to fight a play-off game and only scraping two goals against a side like Australia. They could tease me all they wanted. It was just like the Glasgow scene, another way of saying well done we were thinking of you.

Three days later it was back to business as usual. Away to Coventry City I scored the winner. By the following week, I had to miss West Ham's game against West Bromwich Albion to fly out with the Scotland squad for the second leg against Australia. The Hammers did all right without me, managing to score a 4–0 victory. After feeling really good about the result, I made a mental note not to be away too often. I didn't want George Parris, Neil Orr and Alan Devonshire getting too used to getting their names on the score sheet.

It is amazing how air travel has improved over the last couple of decades. Even now, a journey to the other side of the world is exhausting but back then it was totally knackering. With the hullabaloo about English clubs freeing their players, the cheapskate Scottish Football Association had decided to cover the trip and match in as few days as possible. When we touched down in Melbourne the squad felt like the walking dead and most looked like it. To make things worse, I had bloody toothache. A couple of calls by the backroom staff and an appointment was arranged with a local private dentist. I went straight to it, simply relieved that the pain was going to get fixed. What I hadn't reckoned on was that the first game against Australia had been covered by their TV channels and newspapers. As a goal scorer my picture had been flooded all over the place. Compared with the impact of the still raging TV blackout in England, in Australia I was a celebrity. A celebrity who didn't know it.

I walked into the private dentist and was greeted by a beautiful receptionist, dressed in a white gown. Because of the emergency appointment arrangements, I would have to wait while the dentist dealt with another patient. No problem. The receptionist showed me into the waiting room and stood chatting, just being polite or so I thought. The more she talked, the more I realised she knew exactly who I was, a most unusual experience for me anywhere except in my own patches in London or Glasgow. But the language of a come-on is universal and I was hearing her loud and clear. Before I knew it, she was giving me an expert blow job right there in the waiting room. Now that's what I call a warm welcome and me in Australia for only a matter of hours. It set me wondering if all the Aussie women were so friendly. Let me tell you as an alternative to anaesthetic, a blow job does the trick.

Shortly thereafter the dentist took care of my rogue tooth, oblivious to the nookie scene that had just taken place in his very own surgery minutes before. Before I left, the receptionist cornered me and asked what I was doing that night. It was to be a night off for the squad and she was keen to meet them all. Who was I to deny the lady? Since it was before the important international, our movements were limited, under strict orders from Alex Ferguson and Walter Smith. The idea was we could have a few beers, chill out, visit some quiet local places but no more than that and under a strict bedtime curfew. When she arrived at the hotel after her work, the dentist's dolly was obviously pleased with herself. All the players were well known in

Australia. What we hadn't realised was that the chance of qualifying for the World Cup Finals for only the second time in their history was a big deal in Australia. As the players standing between them and that place, we had all been well covered in the press. As far as the woman was concerned, she was in the company of celebrities and wanted as much as she could get. When she made it clear she would do anything – and I mean anything – with anybody, I decided that I shouldn't be greedy and decided to leave her to the other boys. Besides, when it comes to the pleasures of the flesh an audience isn't really my scene. The last I saw of her she was in a hotel room in the company of a few of my colleagues. To avoid a few divorces here and there I'm going to have to leave you to decide the likely identity of the culprits. Me? For a change, I behaved myself, going out with some colleagues for a bit of sight-seeing and a couple of beers. Well, I wanted to play in the World Cup Finals too.

Apparently the Australian press and their manager, Frank Arok, were in favour of playing the match in the afternoon, under the blistering heat of their summer sun. As our squad were all based in Britain, it was winter back home and we'd had no time at all to acclimatise, it would've been a sound tactic, sure to knacker us in minutes. After some arguments between the football associations, the game was eventually played at night in Melbourne on 4 December, thank God. It was a hard fought match that ended in a dull 0–0 result. Enough to take us into the finals but not an impressive performance at all. Whenever asked about that game since, I've always played up on the lack of energy of all the Scots being exhausted after their long haul flight. That's true, of course, but you'll appreciate that somehow some of us still found the energy to play in a different game of life. Isn't that always the way of it?

After the Australian match we were allowed a night off and we headed to the clubs. Most of us ended up in what I can only describe as a disco. Loud music, flashing lights and the dance floor seething with drunken bodies. Yet again, our fellow revellers seemed to know who we were and treated us kindly, well most of them did. In the early hours of the morning, most of us well merry, I spotted Mo Johnstone across the floor in the company of a good looking woman. Right there in view of everyone else, he had slipped her top up and was stroking her naked breasts, with that wicked, self-satisfied grin all over his face. Not being one to miss an opportunity – or spoil his fun – I immediately joined them and started feeling up her free breast. Mo just kept grinning and saying, 'She's lovely, isn't she?' And I had to agree. The woman just stood there, smiling and kissing both of us in turn. Next I know, a hand grabs me roughly by the shoulder and yanks me around.

'That's my fiancée,' growled this bloke who loomed over me blocking out the flashing lights. What with the drink and the noise and my foolish expectation that Mo was making a public spectacle of a young woman he had got off with rather than borrowed – the geezer caught me by surprise. Trouble is, whatever the woman's boyfriend had actually witnessed he had assumed it was me and not Mo who had stolen his woman and Mo was not for telling him otherwise. The whole place erupted into a barney, with bodies and fists flying everywhere. I can still remember struggling with some oversized guy and catching a look of Mo Johnstone's mug, still smiling as if butter wouldn't melt.

The Melbourne papers picked up the fracas as indeed did Alex Ferguson. The boss grilled us on the basis of what he had already been told, that I started the whole thing by getting it on in public with some other guy's girlfriend. Mo – the rat – was quite happy to let this story lie. He was planning to get married and didn't want the scandal to interfere with his nuptial plans. So, I just shrugged my shoulders and took the blame. He was a good friend and besides what's in a reputation.

Three days after that night in Melbourne, I was back

playing for West Ham. The round-the-world travel hadn't bothered me that much since I scored the only goal to beat Queens Park Rangers. Nothing much had changed on the social front either. The furore caused by my appearance on Wogan was just waiting to burst through. I quickly learned that the media don't give up and started getting snapped as I headed to and from the pubs. Then there were the invitations. One of the most enjoyable was an appearance on the set of the TV soap series, *Eastenders*, which had over-taken *Coronation Street* in the ratings war. As a striker for West Ham, it was entirely appropriate that I identify with that programme based in the east end of London. It was a set up for newspapers to take photographs, carry out interviews and basically promote the programme against the backdrop of the Queen Vic, the fictitious pub. I played headers with Leslie Grantham, then acting the villain of the show, Dirty Den. Leslie and I hit it off almost imme-diately and he wasn't too bad at heading the ball either. Through that connection I made lasting friendships with him and other actors like Michelle Collins and Nick Berry. Our paths were going to cross again and again.

One night I was invited to a dinner, in honour of some guy I hadn't heard of. To be polite I went along, well that and never being slow to turn down a boozing session. It was one of the most welcoming crowds I've been in. Everyone seemed to know who I was and came up for a chat introducing themselves as Tony, Joe, Dave, Kate and Frankie. Big West Ham fans I reckoned. Well we were in the right part of London and feelings for the club ran deep. It wasn't till near the end of what was a great night that someone asked me if I knew who I had been jollying with. Yeah, of course I did. It was Tony, Joe, Dave . . . The bloke shook his head, smiling and gave me their full names. Tony Lambrianou, Joe Pyle, Dave Courtney and Frankie Fraser – just some of the leading gangster faces in London. For good measure I had also been supping with Buster Edwards and Bruce Reynolds, two of the Great Train

Robbers. Didn't make any difference to me. These people were courteous, welcoming and warm. They reminded me so much of the hardmen back in Glasgow, just with cockney accents. Without knowing who they were, I'd spent a good time in their company, judging them on their own merits and judging them well. They would do me just fine. They were great company and their morals were spot on – unlike some women I was about to meet.

SPOILED FOR CHOICE (1986)

O ver December and January West Ham's perform-
ances lost a little of its sparkle. We despatched
Birmingham City easily enough and Leicester again but
went down to Tottenham Hotspur with Clemence, Hoddle,
Waddle and a late appearance by former Hammer, Paul
Allen. A drubbing by Liverpool at Anfield later in January
set things back a bit. Even though we were up against the
likes of Ian Rush, Steve Gillespie and Alan Hansen, my
view, and increasingly that of the rest of the team was that
we were capable of taking on the best in their own back-
yard. Next game though we gave Manchester United a 2–1
doing at Upton Park – just the tonic we needed. The game
was good and life was fast becoming better.

All sorts of crazy events were now becoming normal.
An example that sticks in my mind was on a boys' night
out to Southend for a club opening. As ever the place
seemed packed out with stunning women, dressed in the
height of fashion. No sooner was I in the bar than a little
cutie approached me and asked for my autograph. This
still embarrassed me a little but I knew that it was just a
very small thing you could do in return for people's
support. So, I never refused autographs. The wee cutie
hung around without saying much, just throwing me
these big eyes.

'Is there something else you wanted?' I asked. She
nodded and smiled. 'What is it?' I asked. She just smiled
wider then led me away from the bar by the hand. A few
minutes later we were making love in the club's office.
Don't get me wrong, I'm not complaining, but I hadn't
even had a drink yet. Once we had finished and headed
back to the bar, she kissed me on the cheek and never
spoke to me again all night. In fact I've never seen or heard

from her since. And they say that it's women who feel used after sex.

Charlie Nicholas and I were hitting all the West End clubs together. They say that we've been in more clubs together than any other footballers but have still to kick a ball in the same team. Good old Charlie knew all the best places to go having carved out the alternative pisshead's map of London in his years at Arsenal. One night in Brown's I was again approached by a good-looking woman who asked me outright for sex. Being a gentleman I obliged, again in a backroom of the place. When we returned I discovered that Charlie had been sitting chatting with the woman's husband while I was fucking with his wife through the back. Now whether or not the guy knew what we were up to I'm not certain but this scenario repeated itself so often with different people I began to wonder if you had couples out trophy-hunting footballers. Not that I minded, you understand, but I did wonder what kind of relationships these people had.

Back on the football front, West Ham had started going on a spree. A 4–0 gubbing of Chelsea, dumping Spurs in spite of Ossie Ardilles's best efforts and almost everyone else in the league. It got to the stage that in nearly every game Tony Cottee and I were on the score sheet though often joined by team mates. Years later I learned that Tony had been worried about his place in the team when John Lyall had signed me. It's a lesson to me about how the unknown shouldn't be taken as a threat but an opportunity. We had become the most feared striking partnership in England and some would say that meant the world.

Tony Cottee and I wouldn't worry about whether West Ham were going to score but would actually bet on who between the two of us would score the best goal. This ran for weeks with many good-humoured rows over the fine detail. I can recall against Queens Park Rangers scoring a goal from some distance with an overhead kick when the ball had come at me from an awkward angle yet he still

67

argued. Mind you so would I if the tables had been turned. When the boss, John Lyall, discovered what we were up to he immediately fined us a hefty whack. I know the rationale behind his actions was to emphasise the need to work as a team and not care who scored. But we were what we were. I was a hard-working, run my legs off bloke who unselfishly worked for others while Tony was a poacher. And he was a bloody good poacher who also began to work harder as our partnership evolved. In truth we didn't care who scored for West Ham, we were just so confident we would score. After Lyall fined us we just kept our little wagers to ourselves . . . and kept on scoring.

Apart from regular team nights out, the other players were mainly serious, stay-at-home married types. When I arrived for training of a morning, they would claim I was wearing the gear I had on the town the night before. Usually this wasn't true no matter how late I'd been. It was simply the case that I took my clothes seriously – though some of my fashion foibles might argue against that. They just thought that the rigouts I was wearing during the day had to be night-time gear. Like I was all dressed up or something. It got to the stage that the boys would rib me regularly as if they were living through me. It was assumed that I had come straight from some club to training. I usually just let them think what they wanted and took the teasing. But that view, added to my natural disinclination for training, added up to the creation of a few myths about running around Upton Park drunk. Now, I'll confess to turning up with the occasional hangover and only a few hours sleep but that's it. I've even heard some folk who I've never played with claiming that I would turn up at games straight from a club and still go out and score a hat trick. If I ever suspected that was possible then I might just have slipped into those ways. But I didn't. All I did was party every night I could but never the nights before games. They were strictly stay-at-home times with me on the tea and no additives. I was not and still am not the kind of guy who takes a beer. One beer is not enough. I've never understood that phrase about going for a beer. A bucket load yes, but one or two beers? Don't see the point. So I'm on the booze or off and there's no middle ground. The nights before matches I was off the bevy and into bed at a decent time. I wanted to win too much to squander the chance for the sake of a night out. I could party any other night and did.

As for this palaver about some managers banning their players from having sex the night before a match – what drivel. I had nookie the night before every game. Often on the mornings of matches too. Sex was my pre-match training and I thoroughly recommend it to every player.

The media attention was building up. They had me on the Saint and Greavsie show. For those too young to remember this pair, you missed yourselves. A double act of ex-footballers. Ian St John, a Scot who played for his international team, scored the quickest hat trick in history (150 seconds for Motherwell against Hibernian) and played some of the best football of his career with Liverpool. Jimmy Greaves, one of England's all-time top scorers who had starred for West Ham, Tottenham, Chelsea, AC Milan. Greaves was the guy that many still argue should have played in England's World Cup victory in 1966. Ian St John, quiet, intelligent, the straight man. Jimmy Greaves, wisecracking cockney, chainsmoking, recovering alcoholic. They were a good pairing and made great TV. They had me on as guess who's scoring all the goals in the English First Division as a counter to the TV blackout to games. They put the question to sports writer Hugh McIlvanney and comedian Billy Connelly. I had a laugh.

I was also on Question of Sport. I was the mystery guest where they had to work out who I was – again playing up on the lack of TV coverage. I was getting to be an old hand at this media lark. Early on I sussed that all you had to do was dress presentably, turn up, relax and be yourself. That last bit is no problem to a Glasgow scheme boy. Just like the London eastenders – talking comes naturally and wisecracking is a way of life.

On the social life front, my local was Brown's but I was still a regular at Stringfellows. Through our friendship with Margot Mitchell, Anita and I were introduced to a whole range of people. Margot would befriend many of the club's clientele, sometimes babysitting for their kids. Friends of Margot's were friends of ours. Through her we met Rod Stewart, Elton John, George Michael. I was particularly impressed with Telly Savalas, the shaven-headed star of the detective series *Kojak*. He was so bloody tall. Somehow I had expected a short-legged, broad-chested sort of a guy but he towered over me. He was also such a welcoming bloke. Made us feel like his guests and old buddies at the same time. Telly liked to live life to the full and, boy, could he hold his drink. Just my type of company.

As the only West Ham player that was out and about most nights, I also had a great deal of contact with supporters. My blond hair followed up by my accent did the trick. I wasn't about to be confused with Alan Devonshire or Mark Ward. These folks were great, always courteous, full of jokes and patter. I reckon if I had accepted every drink offered to me by a West Ham supporter during those months, I would have had to move permanently into a detox clinic at the end of the season. You found West Ham supporters everywhere and in every walk of life. It's the type of club that holds allegiance through thick and thin, a lifetime commitment. A support that comes from the heart – the right type of support. And they were buzzing.

My life might have been taking off big style but the most important, positive experience of 1985/86 was the great sense of optimism in supporters who so often had a load of skill to watch but were never given a consistent run of results. These people were beginning to believe they could win the league for the first time ever. You can buy in bigtime names, use tactics that are boring but efficient, hire the most famous manager in the world and you can win titles. Stuff that. I'd rather have the heart of a West Ham supporter any day.

Since the start of the season my wages had been creeping up. This was partly through conditions of my contract negotiated by the bold Bill McMurdo – increases when I played for the Scotland team, scored so many goals, so many appearances – and partly due to the regular win bonuses. Almost without noticing, my wages amounted to a very tidy salary indeed. It was time to settle down into a house that was really ours.

I'd had a wee problem with my flat back in Glasgow. When I had left for West Ham, Vivian and I had officially split up. But I was quite happy for her to stay on in my flat – furniture, fridge, sound system, the works. It was to be the first but not the last house I walked away from leaving some woman to live there.

Around that first New Year after I had moved to London, I had heard that Vivian was planning a big party and I was not invited. I was cool about the whole break-up and all Vivian needed to do was invite Anita and me, or at least phone and tell me about the party. She chose not to so I suspected a bitter twist. I reckoned it was a last blast out. Fine by me but not for my flat to get wrecked, which I was certain was on the agenda. So, I slipped on a flight to Glasgow, hired a big van, checked Vivian was out at work and piled into the flat with some of my mates. Within a few hours the place was empty and I mean stripped bare. We took the phone out of the socket, the toilet paper from the holder, the fitted carpets from the floors, the very light bulbs out of the sockets. I'm an easy-going guy – always have been. Quite happy to let people use my stuff, spend my money, take advantage . . . till they take one step too far. If I decide that someone is taking the piss then I take no prisoners and never forgive. Vivian should have known that. Well, I guess she learned that day when she came home to a desert within four walls.

The Glasgow flat sold, Anita and I were looking for our own home, though quite happy with the West Ham-owned flat in Brentwood. A nice place, handy for travel to training, surrounded by West Ham supporters. These days, you would expect a top flight football player to buy some luxurious pad in a millionaires' retreat the moment he signed for a new club. But then, and it's only just over 15 years ago, it was a big step for most players to buy a house at all, especially in London with the high prices.

Things have moved on so much in terms of the scale of footballers' wages and I suppose I should regret that it wasn't quite as lucrative in my days. Of course I do, who wouldn't want extra dosh? But I don't think it has helped the game at all – quite the reverse. Now clubs seem to buy players because they are priced high rather than because they are in love with the game. Too much emphasis on expensive being best and it does nothing but create moaning prima donnas and smother the young, talented players before they are given half a chance.

Give me a team of players who are there for the joy of the game any day of the week. Think of the great teams, the legends and they were full of men who would be playing for their pub team if they hadn't made it professional. Those are the kind of players who produce magic rather than just mere technical proficiency that seems to be the trend today. As this book is being written there's word that most big clubs are going to have to reduce their bills and freeze wages. No bad thing in my view. No bad thing at all.

With all my extracurricular activities it might be asked how Anita and I were getting on. Very well is the answer. I was very fond of her and took good care that she didn't get hurt. All right, I was taking up offers of a quickie now and then but, in truth, I was far from ready to settle down. I suppose I should have seen the writing on the wall but I was too busy enjoying life and that included a great deal of time spent with Anita Blue. She deserved better but I just wasn't ready to give her what she wanted. With moving into the flat in Brentwood, it was a move towards settling down together. Long-term living with Anita would have been no bad thing. Trouble is, I also wanted to play the game of life and I did. It was the way I was.

On the pitch, West Ham had picked up a head of steam, dumping the likes of Arsenal, Sheffield Wednesday, Chelsea and Spurs. I was particularly enjoying victories over London rivals since that was something that gave the fans an extra buzz. A close second was whipping the northern teams like Liverpool and Manchester United who had tended to monopolise trophies for too long. There's nothing that gets the fans going quite as much as the family team of West Ham handing out a right doing to the so-called big clubs. Players are out there to win games but should never forget that the boss is the person who paid an entry fee. Besides, as well as a player, I was now a West Ham supporter.

There were now eleven games to go the end of the season 1985/86. Not only diehard Hammers supporters but even the football pundits were beginning to fancy us for the league for the first time in West Ham's history. Eleven games and no team ahead of us to fear. I had heard that Kenny Dalglish as player/manager of Liverpool had started issuing team sheets on match days with my name inserted instead of Ian Rush. All as a joke you understand but the message was clear. If the one and only Dalglish rated me and rated us we couldn't possibly lose. Could we?

PRETTY BUBBLES IN THE AIR (1986)

Brian Clough obviously hadn't been reading the sports pages of the newspapers. Nottingham Forrest, then a good team regularly fighting in Europe under Clough's management, gave us a reminder that life wasn't going to be that straightforward. A 2–1 beating away was a sobering wake-up call. The trouble was that in England the standard of the top ten teams was excellent. Even the bottom ten teams were capable of giving you a game, unlike in Scotland where the teams fighting to avoid relegation tended to be pushovers.

There were a whole heap of differences between the Scottish and English games. In England, players were more athletic, moved the ball around more on the ground. You were allowed a slow build-up but you had to know what you were doing or the next you know the opposition would have the ball down at your goal. But as a striker, the main difference to me was the approach of the defenders.

Big centre-halfs in Scotland had only one thing in mind when they got near you with the ball – hurting you. They would come rattling in on you, two-footed, studs hurtling towards your ankles. Or smash their weight against you, wrapping long legs around yours and almost scooping the ball through you and away. All they were concerned about was bulk and power. The English defenders were huge, probably bigger, but most wanted the ball at their feet. They would allow you to come on to them face-to-face with every confidence that they could take the ball off you, out-dribble you and move on.

The best defender I played against in England was Alan Hansen of Liverpool. He had a real sense of class and arrogance that he was more skilful than any striker. Many people complain that Hansen didn't get picked often enough for Scotland and I sympathise with them. Maybe his sophisticated style didn't suit Scottish managers. Then there was Terry Butcher, Gary Marbutt and the boy Pallister. Mind you, close on the heels of Hansen were our own Alvin Martin and Tony Gale, backed up by Ray Stewart. That lot made a great contribution to the team's performance that year and I certainly wouldn't like to go up against them.

Then there were the hardmen. There has to be Brian Kilcline who played with Coventry City. God how Coventry supporters loved him. He had a nickname that suited him to a tee and one he used himself. Against Coventry I'd dread long balls when I'd hear him shout, 'Killer's ball.' You just knew he was about to run right through and sometimes he even managed to take the ball as well. Killer Kilcline did not take prisoners.

But the man who was reputed to be the most fearsome in the English first division at that time was Mick McCarthy, then of Manchester City. I'd heard all about his reputation before the first meeting between West Ham and Manchester City. Not being one to change my ways, I decided I'd give him a little rattle early in the game. As the two of us went for a ball I climbed up and elbowed him in the face. Just a wee jab you understand. McCarthy hit the deck only to rise again instantly. As the play went on he ran up and stood in front of me, blood streaming from his nose.

'Listen,' he growled in that broad Midlands brogue, 'you might be a skilful wee fucker but I'm the hardest bastard on this park.' Mick McCarthy wasn't wrong. For the rest of the game he kicked seven shades of shit out of me. By the final whistle I got the impression that he wasn't quite satisfied with the damage he had wreaked. Hobbling to the dressing room, I made a mental note to look out for Mick McCarthy in the future.

One of the worries of John Lyall and his backroom boys was that I would get injured. My style of play was hard-working, putting in as many tackles as any player. I would go back and help out the midfield, then dribble forward passing the ball and getting into a scoring position if I could. As a result I was more often than not in the thick of action and picking up niggling knocks. A serious injury is always a possibility but not worth worrying about. If you do fret you start avoiding tackles, holding back at the last minute, arriving half a yard short. In my opinion that's the way to get crocked as well as being crap football. So I didn't worry, just relaxed and played my game.

When I did get injured it was usually minor and I had to report into Rob Jenkins, the physio, on a Sunday – not my best day for being capable of doing much. Rob was a right character and used to demand a tip of four cans of lager for working on you on a Sunday and he got off with it. It must have been some sort of club tradition since Rob had succeeded his father Bill as physio at West Ham. Now, some Sundays I simply wasn't fit to go anywhere through self-inflicted damage in some watering hole the night before. Reporting for training on Monday, the ever efficient John Lyall would check if all those injured on the Saturday had turned up for treatment on Sunday. Rob always covered for me and said I had but there was a price – six cans of lager. Mind you it was always worth a good night out.

Another habit of Rob's was to give one or two players a sip of brandy before a game. Now drinking before a match in Scotland would have had you out the door but one or two West Ham guys just took a little sip to settle their nerves or some strange phenomenon. Of course, I was on to them and asked for a taster. Rob handed me the bottle and I emptied it much to his red-faced fury. I couldn't see what the fuss was about. It was only a wee bottle like a miniature or maybe a quarter-gill. Apparently the other players just took a tiny drop and the bottle would last Rob weeks. Bugger that, it wasn't even a proper drink. Besides, one drink is never enough for me so I chucked the habit after that one go – to the relief of the other guys and Rob.

Early in April we beat Southampton and then Oxford United only to go down in the next game 2–1 away to Chelsea. We had only beaten the Blues 4–0 away from home the previous month but that's football for you, every ninety minutes is different. Like making love except, if you do it right, sex lasts longer.

Now we really were down to the run-in. Liverpool were the most likely to win though Everton were up there too and Manchester United were still in the hunt. Our last game of the season was going to be against Everton away from home. If it was down to the last match we believed we would whip them and take the title.

In spite of setbacks like the defeat by Chelsea, John Lyall insisted we played our usual game. Some called it skilful, others described it as swashbuckling. I thought it was the latter with a good sprinkling of the former. The West Ham team really was a mixture of individuals.

Phil Parkes in goal was a great lump of a bloke who must have been 106 years old that season. His approach to the game was so laid back he was easily mistaken for a supporter who had come along for the ride. On the way back after matches you'd catch him puffing away at a cigar and scooping back full-sized therapeutic brandies. But he was brilliant, probably the best goalie in the UK that year.

Alan Devonshire was simply one of the best players I have ever played with. Though a totally different kind of player I put him in the same category as Dalglish. Now that's the highest accolade I can pay.

Mark Ward was a right buzz wire who made the move up to the first division with talent to spare. Alvin Martin was a rock. Tony Cottee – one of the best six yard box artistes around. Neil Orr did the simple things effectively and repeatedly. I'd bet on Ray Stewart to win any tackle. Tony Gale was as much of a piss-taker on the park as off. And the others, all individuals with idiosyncrasies to spare. If before the start of the season you had listed these blokes by position, track record, weaknesses and strengths on paper – no one in their right mind would have put us together as a team. But John Lyall was just crazy enough and the magic worked. We were like the teams from the old school, a mixture of some guys who could make it anywhere and others who would always struggle. But playing together – watch out. John Lyall said keep playing our way and we did, right to the end.

Next game we saw off Elton John's Watford and then it was a visit from the Geordies. Newcastle was another place where they took their football seriously. I've always liked the city and the people from there even though the supporters gave me a hellish time – something to do with my habit of scoring goals against their team. Newcastle were going through a rebuilding phase and were heading for the middle of the table. But they had a young striker they were hopeful of, a guy by the name of Peter Beardsley who hardly got a kick that day and I remember being far from impressed – shows you what I know. We ran out 8–1 winners though I only scored one goal. Alvin Martin had the audacity to score a hat trick. Felt like tapping him on the shoulder and demanding to know what the fuck he was playing at. There was some consolation though, Tony Cottee didn't score at all.

Next we scraped a 1–0 home victory over Coventry and two days later had the same result against Manchester City. Only two days after that a late Ray Stewart penalty saw off Ipswich Town 2–1. And then it was down to the last two games.

The buzz was great. We had played and won five games in only eleven days. My training consisted of sleeping at every opportunity and, it has to be admitted, I wasn't in the mood for partying – well, just the minimum. I had a greater high in front of me – winning the league with West Ham.

The end of the season was going to be dramatic. Liverpool were to play Chelsea and would have to lose if West Ham and Everton were to stand a chance of winning the title. Liverpool's form had been slipping and Chelsea was a handy team playing at their best form. Any sensible man would have bet on Chelsea to win especially since all the Londoners wanted West Ham to win the League.

We were away to West Bromwich Albion for the second last game. West Brom were already doomed to relegation and I had no doubts we could get a result. Our last game of the season was against Everton. So, if Chelsea did the business for us against Liverpool the title would be decided by that very last game. You couldn't have scripted it any better.

People were worried that the West Ham players were exhausted. I can't talk for anyone else but I certainly wasn't worn out. Booting up for the West Bromwich game, I felt as fresh and keen as I had at the start of the season. Can you imagine modern day players fitting in five games in eleven days and not grumbling about exhaustion? The wee souls. We stood a chance of winning the League – that was our energy source. Running on to the park against West Brom, I knew I could burn myself out in the next 90 minutes and still go up against Everton buzzing, chasing every ball, determined to win the title. It all depended on the Liverpool versus Chelsea result that day playing at exactly the same time as us.

Our game started well with me scoring in six minutes. Then Tony slotted in a second and we looked as if we were cruising. West Brom obviously weren't just along for the ride and pulled one back before half-time. We had decided as a team to ignore the Liverpool game. All we could do was play to win ours and make sure we didn't shoot ourselves in the foot by losing. Our supporters gave an almighty cheer which was clearly unrelated to anything on the field. They had heard on the radio that Chelsea were beating Liverpool and we understood totally what they had heard. The rest of the game was fought out desperate and hard, made worse when West Brom drew level. Maybe our nerves and sapped legs had got the better of us but I don't think so. It was just another example of a team at the bottom of the English first division being able to give a team at the top a hard run for their money. And did they.

We were out there believing that Chelsea were beating Liverpool and all we needed to do was score a winner. A draw wouldn't have been good enough. It was like the whole year's work hung in the balance and the seconds were ticking by. Then in the 82nd minute we got a penalty. Ray Stewart stepped up and without a flicker thumped the ball into the back of the net. That's it, we had won! And Liverpool beaten. All we had to do now was win against Everton and even as we ran off that park I could feel the energy surge through us. Bring them on now if you like. We were going to thrash them and lift the title. Then we got into the changing room.

John Lyall, never one to show obvious delight even when things went entirely his way, had a face like fizz – anger, disappointment and pain written all across it. Liverpool had beaten Chelsea by a Kenny Dalglish goal. We crashed from victorious delirium down to bleak depression in a second.

God knows what happened in that crowd. Either the radio announcer got it wrong or someone heard it wrong. To this day I haven't asked about that. Understanding such human error is nothing compared to how the team and the supporters felt that day. It was a Saturday for black armbands and we were all wearing them. You could have heard a pin drop in that West Ham dressing room. Some of the guys sat with tears mixing with the sweat of their brows. I was deep in my private thoughts. If the games had gone differently I would have achieved what I can only conceive of as a boy's own dream. Instead the hero of my youth, the all-time football hero of my adulthood, had proven my worship right and robbed me of that dream. That day, and for a while after, I wished I had been wrong about Kenny Dalglish. If he could only have let me down, just for one Saturday afternoon.

I didn't dwell on my loss. I couldn't get over feeling for the supporters. As we battled to a victory over West Brom, they sang our anthem, 'Pretty Bubbles in the Air'. When I first heard that refrain it seemed a silly song for football. Then I grew to understand it. Beauty and grace. Eccentricity. Always looking for skill and who cares what others think about us. Whae's like us? Damn few and they're a' deid.

Only too well I knew how one game, one season, one campaign, could affect every aspect of football supporters' lives. There are those who would sneer at such a state of mind, seeing it as childish. I think they are jealous of the passion. The players could go on and win other titles. There would always be another day, another chance for us. But for a team like West Ham to get so close to beating them all – that's a longer journey and never, ever certain. It wasn't the players I felt sorry for that day but the supporters.

A few days later we ran out against Everton at Goodison Park – a bunch of cardboard cut-outs with the heart wrenched from us. Just as if the results had gone the right way, the Hammers would have played with broken legs and played well. So now that the results had delivered a cruel blow, we couldn't have cared less. Second place was at stake between us and Everton. But we didn't give a toss about being runners up. That simply wasn't in our nature.

The game ended in a 3–1 victory to Everton. Gary Lineker scored two goals for the Toffees, like I gave a toss. In my opinion it was the worst we had played all season simply because there was no point anymore. We would have gladly stayed at home, passed on the match. None of us spoke about it but I got a sense that we were all looking down our noses at Lineker, Stevens, Wilkinson and the other blokes in Everton tops. I mean, they were trying to win, like it was important to them. Well, if second best is their bag, then second best they could have. We, on the other hand, finished the game that day with our dignity intact.

The end of the season saw Gary Lineker being named as the winner of the Golden Boot award. Now these kind of prizes usually mean hee-haw to me. Then someone pointed out that when given to a striker the award is usually based on how many goals he had scored. As it happened, Lineker had scored 29 while I had scored 28 goals. Then I'm told that Lineker was the regular penalty-taker for Everton and had netted a clutch of goals the easy way that season. I don't do penalties. And if I really worried about it, I'd fret over those two goals he slotted in against us in that last game of the season, allowing him to beat me to the top spot. But why should I bother? What have I missed out on? Crisp adverts and a game show slot where you smile a lot and pretend your jokes aren't scripted for you by someone else. No loss there, no problem about that one. The only competition worth winning was West Ham for the League.

It had been an eventful year and one that will always be one of the tops in my life. I settled down and began to plan six or seven weeks in the sun during the summer break. Then I got a phone call. Alex Ferguson had picked me for his Scotland squad. I was going to the World Cup Finals in Mexico – now, that would be a hoot.

DOWN MEXICO WAY (1986)

What the hell did I know about Mexico? No more than I had gleaned from a childhood of Western movies and the odd bottle of tequila or five. But what did I care? It could've been Antarctica as far as I was concerned – I'd play anywhere for my country, especially in the World Cup Finals.

Mexico was hot, even I knew that. And many of the venues were high in the mountains where the air was thin. So, for a change, the Scottish Football Association splashed out and footed the bill for a period of acclimatisation. Now, a lot of the squads had booked camps in Mexico but not Scotland. Oh no! To be fair it was maybe because we were so late in qualifying that all the best slots had already been booked by the time we disposed of Australia in the play-offs. Then again maybe the SFA had got a cheaper deal. We were heading to Santa Fe then on to Los Angeles to get ready for the heat. Aye, well I knew what type of heat I was after.

In Santa Fe we were put up in a very smart hotel indeed and the training facilities were good. Alex Ferguson and Walter Smith had us out working to a regime from day one. Light running and passing games to start with and then building up slowly. Normally a few days of this would have bored the ass off me but I forgave it all on the basis of the honour of being picked for the squad.

As ever, the World Cup attracted a great deal of media attention. The Scottish press had picked up fully on my performance in England and were heralding me as the on-form striker, Scotland's number one goal scorer. My approach is to try and ignore such ranting. But it was hard to deny that of the strikers in the squad I had by far the best season and in a league that required me to prove I could score against the best defences. So I was settling into

83

Santa Fe, quietly confident of my position as a likely first-choice striker for the team.

The trouble with being abroad in hot, sunny weather and staying in a hotel is that everything in your experience is screaming that it's all designed for having a good time. Living there must be hell if you hate your job since the weather, the clubs, hotels and beautiful women conspire against any serious effort. But professional footballers have an easy life compared to most. A few hours training, a bit of physiotherapy, analysis of tactics, videos of other teams – I mean you can hardly call it grafting. Fergie made sure we saw a good bit of the area but most of this was through orchestrated team trips. Now, I got on well with a lot of the guys and love exploring any unfamiliar territory but it made me feel a wee bit like a young boy on a school trip. As a matter of fact I didn't like school trips even when I was at school.

It will come as no surprise to be told that the players were also subject to strict night-time curfews. As if that wasn't bad enough, Fergie and Smith had to be told of all our plans and permission granted and requested before we went outside for a beer. All this discipline and control was understandable as the premier football competition in the world was only days away but . . . To be blunt, it cramped my style. I had proven that I could run my legs off and score goals living my own lifestyle which included letting my hair down on a regular basis. A monk's existence doesn't work for me professionally and it certainly doesn't suit me personally. But I suppose Fergie had learned the lessons of past Scotland managers who had to deal with the likes of Jimmy Johnstone getting pissed and going missing on a rowing boat in the Irish Sea to be greeted by Dennis Law on the shore brandishing a bottle of whisky and Willie Johstone caught taking drugs. The point he seemed to have missed is that guys like that still played supremely. A bit of adventure was part of the make-up of Scottish strikers and a good night out was part of mine.

Above A young Frank shows an early ease in front of the camera

Right Frank poses for the expected commemorative fountain outside of Love Street (courtesy *Daily Record*)

"You lookin' at me?", Frank, top left, in a love-in with St Mirren colleagues (courtesy of *Daily Record*)

Top left Bright-eyed, bushy-haired, Frank on his first day at West Ham

Top right You can tell by the way I move my hips … Frank on the prowl (courtesy *Hammers News*)

Left Up and Adams, as Frank outjumps Tony of the Arsenal

Above Barmaid In Heaven: Frank enjoys East End training methods with Gillian Taylforth and Anita Dobson (courtesy *Daily Record*)

Left Cottee in the act: Frank & Tony reunited (courtesy *Hammers News*)

Below Dirty Den makes a play in an attempt to replace Tony Cottee as Frank's scoring partner (courtesy *Daily Record*)

Follow the yellow brick road: Frank scores against Australia to take Scotland to Mexico '86 (courtesy Scottish Media Newspapers Ltd)

Frank McAvennie makes exceedingly good cakes … Charlie Nicholas remains unconvinced (courtesy Scottish Media Newspapers Ltd)

Before ... (courtesy *Daily Record*)

After ... insert your own caption (courtesy *Daily Record*)

I'm a little teapot…(courtesy Nigel McBain)

Above Frank and Jenny Blyth leave *Grease: The Musical* auditions disappointed (courtesy Scottish Media Newspapers Ltd)

Right Bitter Old Firm rivals attempt to out-do each other once again (courtesy *Daily Record*)

Below Mark Reid (left) suffers the Mo' better blues as he realises he's not invited out with Frank and Maurice Johnston (right) (courtesy Scottish Media Newspapers Ltd)

If you think I'm
sexy and you
want my body …
(courtesy
Popperfoto)

Of an evening in the hotel, Alex Ferguson and Walter Smith were in the habit of going to their rooms for long spells, I suppose to take the pressure off the players from feeling like they were being watched all the time. The two of them would emerge now and then and check up that all was going well, that all the squad were present and then disappear again. When some of the boys started champing at the bit for a slice of freedom, I reckoned I had an escape plan well sussed.

Waiting till Ferguson and Smith had gone to their separate hotel rooms on the same floor, some of us went to the basement and loaded the service elevator with team hampers. Now these hampers weighed a ton, being filled with strips, spare footballs, goals and other paraphernalia. Once on the management team's floor we shuffled the hampers along and built up a barricade against Ferguson's door. Once that was achieved, the same trick was applied to Smith's door.

Several hours later, Ferguson found us in a local bar, quietly drinking and playing cards. There was a stack of us in there and it was just a joke after all. If we really had been in the mind to let loose we would've ended up in one of the strip joints or chicken farms – an American euphemism for brothels – that were all around the place. But Fergie's face was wearing its petted lip and somehow I got the impression that he thought it had all been my idea. Is it the way I grin, I wonder?

A short while later we de-camped to Los Angeles. When an open invitation came in to the whole team to have dinner at Rod Stewart's house in LA we were all champing at the bit. Rod had been a big musical favourite of mine for years and I'd managed to catch many of his concerts including the Baby Jane Tour while I was with St Mirren. Trouble is that Rod Stewart may have been a fanatical Scotland supporter but he was also infamous for his consumption of the booze. Just my kind of guy, but not Alex Ferguson's. He wasn't impressed that Rod's party had been to celebrate his team, the Los Angeles Exiles, winning the League that year or that he had postponed the party for a week to coincide with the Scotland team being in LA. We were all banned from going to dinner with Rod. Charlie Nicholas and I were particularly pissed off so we devised an alternative plan.

A couple of days later, some of the Scotland squad were due to play an exhibition match in LA. As soon as the game was over we headed to the bar where we had already arranged to meet up with Rod Stewart. We arrived early at this place – as we do – and ordered beers. Soon, Rod's pal Ricky Simpson found us and took us to the part of the bar where Rod was.

As soon as I met him, Rod came over, took the beer from my hand, drank from it and said, 'We'll have to get you a better drink than that, Frank.' And he did. The action and the sentiment put me at my ease right away and I took to the bloke immediately. He might have been some multi-millionaire superstar but it was like drinking with a pal back in an east end London bar or a pub in Glasgow's city centre.

Now, in certain circles, Rod is reputed to be a mean bugger. Let me tell you it simply isn't true. Even in the company of guys not short of a few bob, he wouldn't let us buy anything. Graeme Souness was there and was repeatedly trying to buy drinks and failing. There can't be many people who tell Souness what to do. From memory – but you'll forgive me for being a little hazy on this one – aside from Souness there was also Alan Rough, Graeme Sharpe and Charlie, of course. That is some team, and I mean drinking team, but Rod Stewart was well up to speed.

Every five minutes, glitzy, stunning women with never-ending legs and perfect tans would come and speak with Rod, ask him for an autograph, slip him a phone number. He even had his own cocktail mix called something like Rod's Brew served in dinky little glasses. God knows what was in them. All I can remember is drinking as many as I could get. The man was like royalty. I felt like an awkward adolescent next to him.

It was the blast out we needed. Don't ask me how the

night ended because I haven't a clue. All I recall is feeling great, sitting in some wonderful club in some of the most talented and beautiful company I've ever been privileged to share. It was late at night and Rod and his entourage were planning to move on to some club. Charlie and I were flying without wings, absolutely legless and insisting on going too, in spite of all the players being under an 11 pm curfew. Eventually Rod and Graeme Souness pulled rank and said no. Either they were deciding we were too drunk or protecting us from Fergie's wrath, knowing we were already on the sharp end of several verbal warnings. Apparently, I'd stood up out of the sunroof of the limo driving the players back to the hotel and regaled the population of Los Angeles with my favourite songs and not so witty patter at top volume. The great thing about Scots abroad is that no one can understand a thing we say. Just as well really.

The next I know it was morning and I came to on the floor of Eamon Bannon's room back at the Scotland team's hotel. Now Eamon is a good guy and a cool player but he almost choked when he discovered me sprawled at his bedside. All I could do was grunt some apology and creep back to my own room hoping that I wouldn't bump into Ferguson or Smith. Fat fucking chance.

Ferguson and Smith sussed of course. I'll say this for Fergie he doesn't miss much. To be fair he didn't make a song and dance about it which is just as well. Believe me, a swift hanging is preferable to Alex Ferguson on your case – any day of the week – especially when you have the king and queen of hangovers.

As of then, I behaved myself, more or less, and buckled down to all demands. The way I looked on it was that I had met all of Ferguson's expectations with the exception of that night on the town. It was a good night, it was now out of my system and I was looking forward to taking on the rest of the world.

We moved to our Mexican base a few days before our first game. The time in LA had prepared us quite well and

I felt fit and keen in the heat. We were up against West Germany, Denmark and Uruguay – one of the hardest sections in the finals. West Germany, with one of the best records in the World Cup, were listed as favourites. Denmark was no mean team but we were expected to beat them. The hardmen of Uruguay were another matter. All South American football was of an incredibly high standard. Uruguay had done well in the competition in the past but were not reckoned to be as good as their predecessors. So to stand any chance of going through we had to get results against the Danes and the South Americans. At least in these finals there were no so-called minnows of Zaire or Costa Rica to come a cropper against as we had in the past but we would have to play at our best.

Training was going well for me. In spite of the hard-fought season, being with Scotland in Mexico had given me a new boost of energy and my enthusiasm was always high. I had never been in better shape and was confident of a starting place in the line-up.

On the day of the first game against Denmark, I was gutted to be left on the bench. Ferguson gave no explanation, as no manager is obliged to. Giving him the benefit of the doubt I put it down to his tactical sense, which he had proven time and again in taking Aberdeen to the top in Scotland and Europe. It was no consolation when I was brought on as a substitute for Paul Sturrock late on in the game. The pattern of the match was well set and it was impossible to make a difference as Denmark won by one goal to nil.

Four days later it was the big one against West Germany. Some commentators believed that the German style of football was similar to that played in England. If nothing else I had proven myself capable of scoring against the best in England. Still, I was dumped on the subs bench again and guys like Steve Archibald, then with Barcelona, were given the strip. Mind, I was in good company being one of two substitutes eventually used along with Davie Cooper, one of the most skilful ball players I ever met. As the game was going against Scotland Davie and I were thrown on the pitch, in my case for Steve Nicol of Liverpool. Again it was all too late, with the West Germans winning 2–1.

It's difficult to describe how bloody frustrating it is to be all kitted up, sitting in the dug out, watching your team going down. Everything in your spirit is kicking the ball, judging the moves, your feet itching to get out there and show them how. My arrogance? I don't think so. As a footballer I needed to play football. Watching is fine but that's for Frank McAvennie the supporter. The old me. Ferguson would have been kinder to leave me at home.

Scotland's slim hopes now all depended on the Uruguay game. If we won by a decent score there was still hope that we could go through as runners-up. The South Americans had fast gained the reputation as the bad guys of the finals. They kicked, spat and gouged at any opposition who came near them. Ferguson and Smith spent the next few days contemplating their tactics, though shared little of their debate with the squad. The media also speculated as they focused on the match – Scotland's last stand, one more make and break chance – yet again.

The press debate was about meeting the Uruguay team head-on at their own game, using players like Graeme Souness who were no slouches when it came to dishing the weight about. That theme dictated that Scotland should also throw on their skilful players from the off and the two names touted were Davie Cooper and Frank McAvennie. I just tried to ignore it all and concentrate on my training, feel positive and be ready for the kick-off.

I shouldn't have wasted my time. This time I wasn't even used. The big controversy was Ferguson leaving out Graeme Souness all together. Souness was world-class – having played at the top with Liverpool and Italian side, Sampdoria. I'd play Souness any time. Obviously, Ferguson suspected that Souness's take-no-prisoners style would attract the attention of the referee and the red card. Maybe that's why I was left out as well – who knows? All I kept reading was that there we were in the World Cup finals and hadn't given their on-form striker a full game. I can't disagree with that and simply know if I'd been given a proper run I would have scored goals no matter how hard they kicked me.

The Uruguay team were up to their old tricks and had a man sent off within minutes of the kick-off. That didn't stop them kicking and spitting their way through the ninety minutes and it didn't help us score. The game finished a bleak 0–0 draw and Scotland were out of the World Cup in the first round proper yet again.

Not being played when you are at the peak of form is a very personal letdown. But let me be clear, if Scotland had won through to the second round I would have saluted Ferguson and the players big time. Swallowed my anger, stuffed my pride in my pocket and kept training and trying harder. As it was, Ferguson demoted me from number one choice striker in May, to last choice striker by June. What had happened? Was it payback for barricading him in his room? For a night out on the piss with Rod Stewart? Well if it was, Ferguson obviously doesn't have time for individual spirits and maybe doesn't understand human psychology quite as well as he should. That was Charlie and I being our delinquent, fun-loving selves and that was as much part of our game as slotting the ball in the back of the net.

From the high of going to the World Cup finals to the ignominy of defeat and not even used for a full match. Seems now that I was really pissed off about it but I wasn't. I'd learned that life rarely was straightforward for me. Sometimes I hit the heights when all looked lost. And other times I would score zero when everything seemed right. It was a lesson well learned and is the pattern of my life still.

I just shrugged, had a few beers and planned a holiday away with Anita before the new season started. That was bound to be one of continuing success for West Ham, or so I thought. Right there and then I couldn't wait for the new season, although I didn't realise just then why it would be so significant for me.

LOST IN THE JUNGLE (1986/87)

I was off to the Netherlands with the team for pre-season warm-up games. For someone who had hardly been out of Glasgow in his life I was certainly getting around now. But as they say you can take the boy out of Glasgow but . . .

Staying in the Hague, John Lyall had set an 11 pm curfew on all the squad. We had gone out for the early evening and returned to our hotel when required, as good boys do. But as I say, a few drinks are never enough for me. So sitting around chatting, five other guys – Cottee, Ward, Martin, Gale and Walford – agreed we should sample the nightlife. The mistake John Lyall made was to trust us. So, when he had gone off to bed we sneaked out a side door of the hotel, jumped into a taxi and off to the clubs. It was all a bit disappointing for a continental city – either that or we weren't looking in the right places. We couldn't find a strip joint or lap dancing bar so ended up sitting and boozing in some pub till dawn. Well it beat the hell out of an early night.

Lyall found out, of course, and went ballistic. The next morning he convened the whole team and read us the riot act. Then he demanded we pay a fine of £50 each or else he would resign. Now, I admire John Lyall and like him as a person. He has to be one of the two top managers I experienced in my career and no doubt. But that was over-doing it a bit. I don't mean the fine – the night on the tiles was worth £50 – but the resignation threat. Maybe it wasn't caused by some of us going out on the razzle. Maybe he was more aware of the difficulties West Ham faced in competing with the bigger clubs. Either way, he had been deadly serious, as he related in his own book years later when he labelled us The West Ham Six. It makes us sound like mass murders, freedom campaigners or some bad-assed gang. It was only a few drinks for Christ's sake.

In spite of the wee fallout with the manager during the summer tour, the 1986/87 season started much the way we had finished the season before. We had more or less the same team and there was no reason to believe our form would not remain as good. What's more, we now had the cocky arrogance to go with the form. In our first two games we disposed of Coventry City then Manchester United, now managed by Alex Ferguson – always an achievement and a pleasure to rub Fergie's nose in it. Things were looking excellent and I was having a ball.

My social life was taking off too. Now a regular customer at Stringfellows I was meeting a whole heap of interesting people. Through Margot Mitchell I had been introduced to a professional gambler. This guy, Renes, was a big time card player but would bet on almost anything if he could work out the odds and the form. He was obviously good at it, being loaded. He had a Rolls-Royce and refused to walk anywhere. As a result, he would take this beautiful car, drive 300 yards up the road and park in front of the hotel he was going to. Gambling has never been my thing, always preferring to spend my money on a good time. But the guy was great company and generous with his time and his knowledge. As a result, I was introduced to all the top gambling spots around the city. Being a good Scot according to some of the racial stereotypes I would take to going to the casinos after training. Now there's a story that wasn't printed for a change.

Macca Addicted to Gambling.

Which is just as well because I wasn't. The visits to the casinos were to scoff lunch in a comfortable setting and, of course, all the food was free. Also, being members only, I was well out of the way of any trailing reporters who were now a regular feature in my life. Most of the time I wasn't bothered by these folks but it's good to eat your lunch in peace now and then.

I'd met a bloke called Henry Bradman, one of the city's top lawyers. Henry always seemed to be at parties, openings and in the clubs and he was a very popular man for one good reason – he had contacts with all the best-looking women. Don't ask me how, all I know is that if you were throwing a bash and wanted the place stacked with gorgeous models, you invited Henry. He never let anyone down. When I'd moved to London I remember thinking how everywhere I went there were just so many stunning women – as if all London women were that beautiful. They put the good-lookers of the Glasgow scene to shame somehow, not only by their looks but they seemed classier. Though they definitely were a lot more expensive. But money didn't matter to me, so what the hell.

One good friend I'd met through Henry was the page three model Maria Whittacker. She would always arrive with two or three equally stunning female friends. I'd sit with them in Stringfellows quite often and just sit and drink till they left – no matter how late they stayed. It was the boy from Glasgow, his tongue hanging out, just getting one huge buzz from being in the company of such gorgeous talent. I mean who would leave, eh?

Maria was just a good platonic friend but pictures started appearing in the tabloids of me sitting next to her in Stringfellows or Brown's suggesting that she and I were lovers. Most times, the picture didn't show that Anita Blue was there in the club with us. Like I'm bold but I'm not bloody stupid. I just let the papers write what they wanted. I mean how much of a problem is it for there to be rumours that you're sleeping with an incredibly beautiful woman? Didn't bother me at all, funnily enough.

Anita and I were nest-building. Before I had gone off to the World Cup we had bought a three-bedroom bungalow with a converted loft in Guidea Park, Romford. It was a great area. Alvin Martin stayed across the road and stacks of West Ham supporters were all around us. It was a home, not a house and I loved that place. To complete the scene, we got a Doberman for my birthday. My Mum had been frightened of dogs and I was never allowed one as a child. We christened him Ziggy – a huge beast with a puppy's personality he was spoiled rotten and worth every bit of effort. Ziggy didn't have his kennel, he had his own bedroom. When Anita and I fancied a few days away or a visit back to Glasgow Ziggy would come with us, flying of course. Where I went, Ziggy went – take it or leave it.

West Ham's form began to slip and my scoring record with it. At the time, it was really difficult to see what was going wrong. Looking back we had a run of injuries, as most clubs do, losing Alan Devonshire, Alvin Martin and Ray Stewart for great slices of the season. But West Ham's pool of players wasn't nearly as extensive as that of the Liverpools and Manchester Uniteds of the world. In the 1986/87 season hardly anyone had been out through extended injury – an exceptional experience for any top team. John Lyall hadn't been able to afford to bring in big names in the right positions over the summer. That's the difference between the family clubs like West Ham and the commercial conglomerates that most football teams have become. Money rules. Simple as that.

The other problem for me might have been that other teams had worked out the supply of the ball. I realised by the end of season 1986/87 that Lyall had deliberately signed Mark Ward as a good winger to cross the ball at me. Though I'm not the tallest guy, I'm good in the air as well as on the ground. This caught a hell of a lot of top-class defenders napping in the previous season. Now they were cutting off this route and I was having to dig back in more of the time. That kind of work often meant I was the supplier and not the scorer. I wouldn't have minded at all if West Ham had been getting the results. Trouble is we were getting beaten too often. Now that I didn't enjoy.

A low point for me had come when Newcastle beat us 4–0 in front of the TV cameras. That was the same team we had put eight goals past just the season before. While

94

it didn't bother me at the time, Newcastle also signed West Ham's Paul Goddard, the striker who had been injured in the first game of the previous season and allowed me to move up front. I could understand Paul's position. He was far too good to be warming up the subs' bench as Tony Cottee and I hung on to the first team slots. Some would say that when Paul left so did the threat of any serious competition to myself and Tony. They'd say that was a bad move. They may be right, who knows? All I can say is that I ran my legs off and Tony was no slouch. Maybe it would have worked with Paul Goddard. It could have been that if he hadn't been injured the season before we might have won the League title. Though so much had gone right that season it's hard to believe it could have been better. I would certainly have been happy to keep playing in the hole, behind the strikers in the role John Lyall had bought me to fill – if we had got the results.

Because I wasn't scoring as many goals – and that's what the press noticed – I went to see John Lyall. If West Ham were unhappy with my form I wanted to know it out straight. The manager understood why I was there in his office but wasn't worried at all. He knew I was having to dig back more, do more work and in his view I was playing my best football since joining the club. Intuitively, that's what I had believed but it was good to have the guy selecting me every week confirm it.

The season rolled on with some good results and too many bad results. We didn't get a decent run in the cup and, at best, we looked set to land a spot in the middle of the table. It's not a situation I enjoy. But that old magic stopped me worrying about the implications. Every time I stepped on to the pitch it was a brand-new contest. League positions didn't matter, nothing bothered me – just show me the ball.

Anita and I were growing apart at that time. Sad but inevitable given what we both wanted from life. There was no big deal, no affairs, no page three girls waiting for me in some Mayfair flat. It was just Anita and I discovering that our lives had stopped taking the same path. We separated amicably and without fuss or publicity. To this day, Anita has never gone to the media and sold them stories about me. She has never worked out her anger and hurt by throwing muck my way and let's face it, who would've blamed her? She's a good woman that Anita Blue.

As a single man again, I took full advantage, believe you me. Maria Whittacker had introduced me to another page three girl, Sam Fox. Yet again, the tabloids suggested that I was having an affair with Sam and it simply wasn't true. There were plenty of others though, so many I can hardly remember some of their names. But not Maria or Sam. In their company, there was usually a load of models including my favourite page three girl of that time – Jenny Blyth. Jenny was just someone I fancied but nothing came of it for a while. I mean how lucky do you want to be, socialising with your favourite topless model?

I first met Jenny one night at the Phoenix Appollo at a West Ham boys' night out. The Phoenix Appollo was the regular venue for these sessions, so much so that the team had decided all other guests would be women only and there was a room kept upstairs simply as a shagging pad. Contrary to stories which have been published since, I didn't take Jenny to the shagging pad that first night or for a good while later. To start with she was just someone I liked and, all right, fancied. But then that applied to a lot of women in those days. She seemed to like my company too though later revealed she couldn't understand a word I said. So what has that got to do with anything? Did she want me to converse with it?

The weekend of a Scotland versus England international match at Wembley, I was in Stringfellows with some of the team – Graeme Souness, Charlie Nicholas, Ally McCoist, Bill McMurdo and Roy Aitken from memory. I hadn't been available for the squad because of some West Ham fixture issue. As a result I had been drinking all day and was well pissed when we met up at Wembley.

We couldn't get a taxi at the stadium for love nor money so we all trucked down to the tube. There we were, several million pounds' worth of footballers sitting on trains packed with football supporters. McCoist in particular was looking decidedly edgy, I suppose in case any of the English supporters recognised us. At one station a bunch of heavy-looking guys got on and McCoist tried to hide his face in his shirt and his knees were clenched together tight. Me, I couldn't see the problem having had to deal with that every day. So being a happy drunk I got up and joined the blokes, all of whom knew exactly who I was being Millwall supporters and the like. They were good guys, good company. It seemed to me less threatening than Glasgow's George Square after a Rangers and Celtic match but, then again, Ally is an out-of-towner from Polo Mint City, East Kilbride, so maybe he hadn't been allowed into Glasgow on those days as a boy. He really should've been let out more, you know.

We had gone to Blondes for a meal and then on to Stringfellows where we were all sitting at the bar as usual. Rita Stewart, the young woman from back in Glasgow who had tricked me into dancing to some song from Grease, had looked me up. Rita was now an air hostess, doing well and looking great. Without warning, Jenny Blyth, who had been in our company, waltzed over and perched on my knee, throwing an arm around my neck. From out of nowhere a photographer appeared and took aim. Big Roy Aitken, the only sober one in the company, stepped in front of the guy and said politely,

'Click that camera, pal, and it goes up yer arse – the sharp end first.' Needless to say no picture was taken. Would you argue with big Roy?

Was it a set-up? Some cheap publicity for Jenny posing on my knee surrounded by other top footballers? Who knows? Who cares? I was too sozzled to bother and, besides, I enjoyed her on my knee. A few months later Jenny Blyth and I started going out together now and then – just casual like, no ties, nothing serious. She was still living with a bloke, Neil Turley, and they shared a house together. Whatever, she always seemed to be out on the town on her own and available so it didn't get in the way. Jenny Blyth was great fun – in the beginning. Well, imagine screwing your favourite actress or model or TV star. Of course I had a good time.

West Ham had always told me that I was the highest paid player at the club and I had no reason to doubt their word. Certainly my salary of £1,000 per week was a damn sight more than the £350 I had started on little over a year before. Then I learned by accident that one of the players earned more than me. Tony Cottee was worth every penny he earned. He was an ace striker and more. Tony was also a good businessman with his head screwed on. I now realise that he took the initiative, knocked on the boss's door and asked for more dosh whenever he thought it appropriate. Most of the rest of us expected the salary hikes to be gifted and it simply didn't work that way.

When I found out that I'd been misled about being the highest paid player that was motivation enough to ask for more dough even though we hadn't had the best of seasons. After a friendly chat more than a negotiation, I was offered a hike of £500 per week. That would bring my salary up to £1,500 more than I ever dreamed I'd earn. So I didn't quibble and accepted the deal. But I did ask for a signing-on fee. This was standard at many clubs when a player signed a new contract. With every hike in wages, I had to sign a new contract which always added another year on to my commitment. That meant I was tying myself down to West Ham for better or worse, while if I'd moved I would have received a whacking big lump sum as well as an increase in wages. Unfortunately, the club had a policy forbidding existing players from getting a signing-on fee and there was no room for manoeuvre. While I felt

I'd been let down, I accepted the situation and got on with life.

Only a few days later on a Friday, the day after a £10k kitchen re-fit in my new house had just been completed, I got a call from Ray Stewart. It wasn't unusual for us to chat to each other away from the club but this time he had a sense of urgency in his voice.

'You have to meet John at Heathrow, Frank,' said Ray.

'What? Am I catching a plane? I asked.

'Better take a suit with you,' is all Ray said and the message was received loud and clear. In short I didn't have a scooby-doo what was going on but I knew something important was going down. Why else the suit?

At the Holiday Inn at Heathrow Airport I was met by John Lyall and Eddie Bailley from the Hammers and Billy McNeil, the manager of Celtic, and some of his board. No disrespect is meant to the Celtic board and business people. It's just that McNeil is yet another Lisbon Lion and a hero of mine. I knew he was only there with one thing in mind – to sign me. After that clicked, nothing much else registered. Bill McMurdo was in my corner and the chat got going.

This was my kind of heaven or my kind of hell – I couldn't make my mind up which. Celtic, the team of my childhood and the team I'd still be supporting in the old folks' home if I was ever lucky enough to live that long – wanted to sign me. West Ham – my adopted team, the team I grew to love and identify so much with all their supporters – was what I would lose. The question that was in all their minds was would I sign? These guys weren't fools and had worked out my psyche. They knew that if something didn't suit I'd tell them all to fuck off and worry about the consequences later. Aye, maybe. But Celtic had come in for me offering big money. The rumours had been circulating in the press about them trying to sign back Charlie Nicholas from Arsenal. Instead they had come for me.

While they hedged around on broken shards of glass

broaching the subject, I reckon that old headmaster John Lyall had remembered a conversation with me a couple of years before, a few months after I had joined West Ham. Homesick and blue, I asked to go home. Worried that I would go, he had asked who I would leave for and I had answered truthfully. There was only one team I would leave West Ham for – Celtic. What kid doesn't dream of playing for the team he supports? And there's enough of the child in me still. It is the ultimate. So screw the business side, I was leading with my heart. As much as it pained me to leave West Ham, of course I would sign for Celtic – I just had to.

Bill McMurdo had sussed immediately that I was going to go at any cost. It was his job to take care of me. The transfer fee was quickly settled at £750,000 – now for the details. When I easily agreed the wages offered by Celtic – £1,000 a week that was a drop of £500 per week – he spun into action. He asked for a signing-on fee, standard procedure in those days, and it was agreed. Bill then asked that it be tax free otherwise it would be costing me around £75,000 to transfer. The Celtic team hummed and hawed and munched their gums.

'We don't see how that can be done,' was the answer we eventually received.

'Oh there's different ways of doing it,' replied the cool-as-ice Bill McMurdo and I sat and listened in admiration as he showed the men who ran one of the biggest supported football teams in the world at least five ways to achieve this minor request. They nodded and found no contradiction to his spiel. So, they agreed.

While Celtic had brought down a ready prepared contract – they must have been really sure I was going to transfer – an amendment had to be prepared covering the tax free signing-on fee. So it was drafted on a Holiday Inn napkin by Bill McMurdo and duly signed by all the key players. That done, I phoned Ray Stewart and asked him to look after Ziggy, bade John Lyall and Eddie Bailley a warm farewell, slung my suit bag over my shoulder and headed out to the departure lounge with Billy McNeil.

It was late on a Friday and the very next afternoon my childhood dream would come true. I was playing for the Celtic the next day. That was it, I had reached the pinnacle. Surely things could only go right after that? Well we would see.

Arriving in Glasgow, I was driven to a hotel. My phone was red hot breaking the news to my family and friends. Some of them thought I was having them on and, in truth, I can't blame them. That afternoon I was happy and settled in West Ham, finishing off a new kitchen in a house I loved that was situated in a community I felt part of. By that night I was a fully signed up Celtic player, back in Glasgow and waiting to play my debut the next day. Of course they thought I was taking the piss. I was beginning to wonder myself as I passed on the news.

The next morning was simply unreal. Arriving at Parkhead where I had spent so much of my life as a supporter and marching in through the players' entrance rather than the turnstiles. The welcome from Billy McNeil and being introduced to players I would otherwise have been paying to watch. The sense of history under the main stand where all those men in hoops had prepared for big battles on the pitch. I went about my business, an automaton in a dream.

As the teams got ready to run out, Billy McNeil reached out and gripped my arm, letting the others run ahead. The chanting of the crowd swelled and filled the stadium as I stood and waited. It must have been only for seconds but the time dragged by, long nervous minutes.

'Right, son, off you go,' said big McNeil with a clap on my shoulder. I jogged out towards the green of the grass and the rumble of the crowd.

I swear I felt the blast of the roar as I ran on to the pitch. The times I had been at Parkhead and now, standing near the centre circle, looked entirely different. Standing still, unsure what to do with myself, I slowly moved towards The Jungle where the hardcore supporters stood, where I had always watched the matches, where my pals and relatives would be and, most important of all, where my Dad was standing watching his boy. Maybe he was thinking of the times when he lifted his youngest son over the turnstiles to see his heroes. The crowd roared again, chanting my name. I waved and their one voice boomed out again and again. Scanning The Jungle I tried to pick out my father and my friends. I could see exactly where I liked to stand and knew they would be close by. Could I see a thing? Not a chance, just a sea of faces and they were all on my side. My people, lost in the jungle.

If I was a crying man I would have shed tears. All I'll admit to was a lump in my throat soon dispelled by the joy of the occasion. What had I to be sad about? This was a celebration for Christ's sake. I grinned and laughed and waved back.

So many days and nights I'd stood up there on the terracing howling my views, telling the Celtic what to do, where they were going wrong, celebrating when they played it right. Now it was my turn. It was as if some Saturday afternoon one of the players had pulled me out of The Jungle and said,

'So you think you can do better, wee man. Well show us how.' In the middle of the park there was no hiding place now. I bloody loved it.

There was nothing, absolutely nothing, compared to that day. I had reached the top – where would it go from here?

ONE HUNDRED YEARS OF PRIDE
(1987/88)

This wasn't just any old year to be signed by Celtic. This was the club's centenary year and the fans fired up by the media had been going on and on for months that Celtic had to win something that year of all years. And they were quite right too.

The most worrying alternative was that arch rivals Rangers won everything. The way Rangers were modernising it seemed it could just happen. Chairman David Murray had invested millions in the club and had brought in Graeme Souness as player/manager. Souness in turn signed Terry Butcher, then England's captain, and other top-class English players like Graham Roberts, the goalkeeper Chris Woods, Trevor Francis and so on. This was reversing the trend when successful Scottish players would head south to earn a decent wage. Now Rangers had proven themselves capable and willing to pay enough to attract such talent to Glasgow. They were a threat all right and the pressure was on Celtic.

To understand a team like Celtic you have to understand the supporters. Imagine this. A packed stadium, the home team down by two goals and five minutes to go. All right? What do you see – home supporters trailing out through the exit gates to their buses and cars? At Parkhead you'll find them there to a man, woman and child. Green and white scarves being waved around their heads, the chants roaring to lift the clouds, urging the team on. The beauty is, they are also precisely like that when Celtic are three nil up with minutes to go.

Supporters like that you can't buy or make. They are born. And they expect a price for their loyalty – exciting football and regular trophies. Especially in the centenary year. Did I feel any pressure? Did I what. I would have felt the same way as a supporter. Only now I was on the park and maybe able to do something about winning a couple of titles. It was put up or shut up time.

My first game had ended in a disappointing 0–0 draw against Hibernian. The team would have to do better than that. Celtic's form was not impressive and for a while it looked as if we were going to be lucky to be in the reckoning at all. The Celtic board was infamous for running the club from a biscuit tin full of coins. It was seen as the tradition of the club which had been formed by a priest a hundred years ago to raise money for the poor of the east end. Many of the supporters felt that the club hadn't moved on a lot since then. Others, the thinkers, reckon it had deteriorated.

Earlier that year they had brought in Billy McNeil as manager. One of the legends of the Lisbon Lions, McNeil clearly had a good football head and had shown it at other clubs. The combination of an old boy – or should that be bhoy – with a track record was exactly Celtic's style. Before they appointed McNeil the club had had something like six managers in total in a hundred years. Even before the modern merry-go-round approach to football managers, that was stable beyond belief. McNeil had a lot to prove – the pressure was on him.

On the personal front, I was glad to see my Mum and Dad more often, catching up with old acquaintances and making some new ones. Celtic had tried to make it difficult for me by dumping me in a hotel out in Moodiesburn, miles away from Glasgow. It was a nice enough hotel, just inconvenient for the nightlife.

Yet to start with it didn't matter that much. I had determined to behave during my return to Glasgow. Though well used to the city's major rivalries between Protestant and Catholic, Rangers and Celtic, that experience was based entirely on me as a supporter or a player for another team, St Mirren. Now I was a Celtic player and it might be a different matter. I had always got on well with people whatever their allegiance but on both sides there were fanatics who took the banter to violent levels. With my blond hair, good time lifestyle and the fact that I wasn't exactly a wilting lily – I wasn't going to be mistaken for just another guy at the bar. That was okay but I didn't want to be marked. So I took it cautiously to start with, feeling my way back into the territory cagily. It was ground I knew well and all the more intimidating for it.

But the hotel wouldn't do for too long. Not only did I know I was going to get itchy feet to start hitting the bars again but there was also Ziggy to consider. Ray Stewart had been kind enough to look after the big guy then Anita had moved back into our house to take care of him. He was in good company but I doted on that dog and was always unhappy when he wasn't around. I'd need to get sorted with a house and while I was at it, might as well move closer to the nightlife.

I got on the blower pronto to Bill McMurdo who was also Mo Johnston's agent. Mo was playing for Nantes in France and had a smashing house in Mount Vernon which was lying empty. How did he fancy a tenant? It was a done deal. Sometimes when Mo was back in Scotland we would toss a coin for the rent. It turned out to be cheap living for me some of the time.

Along with the house came a good pal of Mo's, Frank Graham. Frank was a great guy nicknamed Heart Attack after an unfortunate incident. He had in fact suffered a heart attack and was rushed into hospital. Lying there in intensive care, wired up to monitors, tubes in his arm and every orifice, his wife came rushing to visit him, followed swiftly to the bedside by Frank's girlfriend. As soon as the two women clicked and began to have a go at each other, Frank promptly had another heart seizure right there on the spot. Now that was either careless or unfortunate. Either way, he fortunately survived though I think both the women were goners.

Frank Graham always knew what was going on. Any party, any opening, new pubs and clubs – he knew the score. Within a week he had me at a models' do held at the Scottish Exhibition Centre. A whole hall filled with the most gorgeous women – the man knew my tastes.

My social life opened up immediately I moved into Mo's house. But still I wanted to be a wee bit cautious, feel the temperature of the air. Frank Graham's advice was to head to the Cotton Club owned by Colin Barr. It was the top club in town at the time and likely to be a safer option than some of my old haunts. On the first night I ventured there I soon realised it was a great place, on a par with anything in London. Colin Barr had a knack of running really good clubs. Better than that I met some old friends – Ally McCoist and Ian Durrant. Now these two were good time guys extraordinaire. Just because they played for Rangers and I played for Celtic meant nothing at all. The Celtic and Rangers players have always been friendly regardless of high feeling on the city streets. Ally and Ian were my kind of people and we spent some good times at the Cotton Club and later elsewhere.

An old pal turned up, Charlie Nicholas. Charlie was always drifting in and out. You just couldn't be sure when you'd see him, just that you would see him. Charlie would just take it in his head to fly to Glasgow, stay a couple of nights and bugger off back to London where he was still playing with Arsenal. But Charlie was just plain crazy. Always up for a laugh, getting pissed, calling people's characters to their faces, chancing his arm with the most unavailable women as their menfolk sat right next to them. All of that I loved in the guy, but Ziggy, well that's another matter.

Charlie had a habit of wearing these ankle-length coats, often black leather. Given Ziggy's size most people were wary of him at first till they got to know his gentle character. Not Charlie. He just lifted up his long coat into a batman-type cloak and ran whooping at the dog. Ziggy looked for a second and then took to his heels yelping for help. Ziggy was far from stupid and every time Charlie walked in wearing that type of coat he'd take to his heels. There were times in London, Charlie and I would walk Ziggy late at night. We would chat quietly about this and that as the dog calmly did his business for the last time of the day. Then suddenly Charlie would be off.

'BATMAN!' and running after my pal. Ziggy would be galloping through the dark lanes and back streets of Essex like some runaway horse, yelping for his life, pursued by mad Charlie Nicholas whooping and laughing. Just as well the newspapers didn't get hold of that.

It was a great move to Mount Vernon and a wonderful house equipped with its own sauna and bar but a house that I was to pay a price for in unexpected ways. Before leaving for France, Mo had been busy on the socialising front. Any time I picked up a woman and suggested she come back to my place, as soon as they heard the address it was NO GO. I've had them with their tongues stuck down my throat and their pants dangling from one ankle in the back of a taxi till we pulled up outside Mo's house then it was 'not on your life'. Some of them looked terrified. Others just plain sick. It didn't matter that Mo was away in France, they refused to step over the threshold of that bloody house. They were willing to go to a hotel, go back to their place, do the business in the taxi, anywhere, but not in there. God only knows what Mo had been getting up to.

Early on there were a couple of small matters to be dealt with at Celtic Park though. To start with, the club said I was too heavy and unfit. News to me given the very active role I'd been playing at West Ham. But the Celtic paid my wages now so it was extra training – back to endless bloody running. The second, most pressing point, was that a certain Mick McCarthy had been signed by Celtic a while before me. It was our first meeting since I'd busted his nose down in England and I didn't fancy sharing the same dressing

107

room with him at all. Those first few weeks I avoided him at every call and, when we had to be together, made sure that there was always at least one unsuspecting body between us. Thankfully, one of the hardest men in the game didn't bare grudges at all – well, not against team mates. Now I had the joy of watching McCarthy boot other players up and down the park. Old Mick hadn't lost his insensitive touch.

My first goal for Celtic was more memorable for what happened elsewhere than on the field of play. Obviously it chuffed the hell out of me and I sensed it was the start of a good run. But down at Upton Park, West Ham were taking on Charlton Athletic. Both teams had hit a difficult patch and there were murmurings that both managers were in danger of losing their jobs. Come half-time, over the tannoy, the speaker announced that I had just scored my first goal for Celtic. Apparently it got the biggest cheer of the game and the biggest laugh. It was about all they had to cheer and laugh about that day as the teams fought out a 1–1 draw. Still they took the time to acknowledge an old boy. Other clubs turn against favourites who dare move away. Not West Ham. Once a Hammer, always a Hammer, whoever you are playing for.

Meanwhile I had lost a few pounds, was fit as hell and my game was picking up. I was linking well with my new striking partner, Andy Walker, a whippet of a bloke and a sound finisher. Andy did a lot of running as well as being sharp in the six-yard box. We were shaping up to be a swift striking force. We were at the front of a team who liked to go forward, it was great fun to play for and I'll bet good entertainment to watch.

McNeil had also splashed out for a young Chris Morris who was proving to be a find. Also, young guys were emerging from the Celtic squad like Derek Whyte and Anton Rogan. The most notable had to be Paul McStay then only 19-years old. Paul was a very straight young guy whose life was as well ordered as the V-necked jumpers and corduroy jeans he used to wear. With his careful ways and polite manner he looked, sounded and behaved more like an off-duty Sunday school teacher than a top-class footballer. But he did his talking on the field. McStay could read a game better than almost anyone I have ever played with and his passing was out of this world. The wonder is that he was already demonstrating all that as a teenager and kept on doing so consistently for the rest of his career. All that Paul ever wanted to do was play football for one club – Celtic. That was his high. No wonder he was so bloody quiet for the rest of his life.

In goal we had Allen McKnight who became a good friend but more of him later. Also Paddy Bonner. A big, genial giant whose career didn't seem to go anywhere till he arrived at Celtic. Bonner was simply tremendous at that time and was about to play a major part in a Republic of Ireland team that were going to shake the big boys of the international game. Bonner reminded me a bit of Ronnie Simpson, the Lisbon Lions keeper. Both seem to have had good though not sparkling careers till they arrived at Celtic where they took off to the heights. Like Simpson, Paddy also seemed a lot older than his years. Unlike Simpson, Paddy didn't look it. He had the fresh face and square haircut of a Jehovah's Witness knocking on folks' doors. Then again, you have be some kind of mental to be a half-decent keeper.

In the squad you had tried and trusted players like Billy Stark who had done the business with Aberdeen. Then again there was Tommy Burns, one of the most respected footballers in the game. Tommy's bad eyesight and carrot red hair made him appear more like a half-pissed supporter than an athlete. But could he play. Tommy was the total professional who kept to the game plan perfectly. But like so many of the squad, he was also a supporter of Celtic. So when the going got rough Tommy went Crazy Horse. It didn't matter if we were getting a doing and the game was beyond hope. Tommy would hare up and down the pitch, trying everything for that last saving grace, screaming white gobs of spit at any of his colleagues who weren't trying as hard in his opinion. If Tommy Burns hadn't been in the green and white hoops he would have been up in The Jungle waving his scarf around his head. My kind of man.

As captain, of course, we had the one and only Roy Aitken. Still sober, still totally off his nut. The guy had the wildest sense of humour I have ever met first thing in the morning and no wacky baccy. Big Roy just didn't stop having a go, throwing wisecracks, taking the piss. Though as a captain you didn't argue with Roy Aitken, as a person and a player he had a particular fondness for the traditional Scottish striker – the guys who hit the booze, whose personal lives were in confused disarray, got into trouble frequently and scored goals for a profession. Guys like Mo Johnston, Charlie Nicholas and me. It was a funny trait because superficially we seemed so much at odds with Roy's own lifestyle yet mentally we were entirely on a par. Whatever it was that gave Roy Aitken that buzz I wouldn't mind finding out. It would have saved me a fortune in bar bills over the years.

By October 1987, Hearts were at the top of the league table, neck and neck with Aberdeen, while Celtic were trailing by three or more points. The pundits forewarned that it was Souness's Rangers who would emerge as victors and not Celtic. Celtic were going to win sod all or so they predicted. Not a great feeling to be going into one of the greatest spectacles in sport.

The Old Firm game. The fixture that leaves all other derbies trailing in its wake. The match all football supporters know about even when clueless about where Glasgow is. The contest that produced as much bloodshed on the streets as it did rivalry on the field. The one where skill didn't matter but winning always did. It was to be my first Celtic versus Rangers match. The fantasy of every young supporter. I was going to show them and I would. I just didn't know exactly how dramatic the game would turn out to be.

MY FIRST AND THE FIRST
(IBROX, 17 OCTOBER 1987)

I prepared for the high ritual that is Celtic playing Rangers in my usual way. Not out on the perpetual sauce as some journalists would have it but taking it easy, drinking tea and getting to my bed early – for two whole nights. Normally cool under such circumstances even I could feel the buzz. To understand what this game means you have to be Glaswegian or a supporter of one of the clubs or, at least, hang around the city as the kick-off draws closer.

It's a slow build-up, staring with a pinkish-red flag warning in the press. Moving on to determined chats in the pubs, the buses, betting shops and the Clockwork Orange of the underground with everyone an expert. Then it's sprinkled with rumours about key players being injured, fallouts in the squads, last-minute transfers being rushed through. Slowly but perceptibly the tempo rises, voices grow louder, more and more people start wearing team colours in the street: till on match day, the city becomes a temple to the game with every punter a worshipper, a fanatic and you do not get in their way. Just my kind of game really.

Rangers hadn't just been modernising under Souness they had also been bringing in key players. While Celtic has always had a tradition (sadly now long gone) of signing local men, Rangers have always been prepared to spend money on talent from the outside. As an incredibly wealthy club there was a time they had a habit of buying a player just because he had a good game against them. One example in point was Davie Cooper who helped lowly Clydebank give the Rangers a right run around in a cup competition only to be bought by them. But now, Souness with his in-depth experience of the English game was bringing in top talent from down south. Terry Butcher, captain of England, Chris Woods, an England goalkeeper, and Graham Roberts, a former star for Tottenham Hotspur and a fellow who thought he was one of the hardest players in the game. All good talent and Rangers' buying power, underwritten by chairman David Murray, was awesome. Celtic buying me was like pissing in the wind compared with that. And it was just the start.

Souness himself was no slouch, being one of the best players Scotland had produced in recent times. Graeme had stated his case in his first game for Rangers when he was promptly sent off against Hibs for a challenge that belonged in a pub brawl. That year, including the end of the previous season, Rangers' players had got into a wee bit of bother. Graham Roberts and Ian Durrant were both sent off in a league game against Hamilton Athletic. Souness was sent packing again against Aberdeen. Mental Graham Roberts lost the place in a bloody friendly of all things and against the Israel B team, getting dismissed for his tantrum. While at the start of the 1987/88 season, Souness again got a five-match ban after having a right go at a referee who had the audacity to send him off. They were certainly blaring out a message loud and clear. If we can't buy our way to the top we'll kick our way to the top. They didn't spook me. I'd had the hardest guys in the English game boot me expertly and repeatedly and I still scored.

The game was at Ibrox which brought back memories of appearing there with St Mirren. In the early 1980s, visiting teams were not allowed to go on to the Ibrox turf to warm up. Most of the St Mirren boys came from Catholic and Celtic-supporting backgrounds. In football terms that naturally sets you resenting the big money of Ibrox. So, we couldn't see the fairness in that rule. There was the important principle that, while you can warm up your muscles in the changing rooms, it was crucial to test your studs in the grass. Fail to do so properly and you could end up sliding and skittering through the game, ripping tendons or worse till you were allowed to sort them out. Fuck it, we just ran out.

Trouble is that some sick Rangers supporters sitting overlooking the players' tunnel would gob down on you. If you ran on to the track and got too close to the fans on the terracing they would spit out at you. We would run back in to get ready for the game with our hair and track-suits smeared in their filth. Then, kitted up in our black and white strip and running out for the kick-off, the filthy bastards would repeat the process. Well, screw that. Fuck the studs. By my Celtic days I had already adopted my preferred approach of warming up in the dressing room anyway. Football boots had been developed a great deal and stud testing wasn't so crucial. Even though Rangers had since been forced to allow other teams on to the pitch to warm up, I wasn't going out there till it was time for the whistle to blow.

So I prepared my first Old Firm match sitting on my own in the Ibrox visiting team's dressing room. Lonely? No way. The ghosts of every Celtic v. Rangers game were in there with me. Of every conversation I had had with my Dad, analysing the result after the games. Celebrating or commiserating. Whichever it was it was felt strong and hard. More than spectres would be watching this game. My father, my mother, brothers, sister, my pals, cousins, every Celtic and Rangers supporter, all the football supporters in the country and abroad, as well as those who didn't usually watch the game who would be eyeing us as TV footage was sold round the globe. An Old Firm game is as big as it gets and I was going to be right in the thick of it. Only winning could be contemplated and I was deter-mined to do my best.

Come the call to run out for the match, I found myself ducking at the point where the main stand ends and the tunnel starts. But there was no shower of gob. Seems the Ibrox board had also cleared a couple rows of seats around

113

the tunnel and added a retracting plastic funnel through which the players ran right out on to the pitch. So the old Rangers' greeting was no longer allowed. Maybe it was more than the management and the squad this modernisation was about?

Ibrox is a large stadium but was moving to be all-seated. Somehow the changes made the crowd higher as if they were looking down on you. The new buildings had created a partial roof and when the roar of 44,000 supporters went up – it was like hearing it in a tin dustbin. What a row. There is nothing that compares with the racket and clamour of an Old Firm crowd.

Then the kick-off was taken and the game was on. Celtic immediately served their intent and had a go as a ball was sent in on Rangers' goalkeeper Chris Woods. In every game I like to get an early, heavy challenge in on the goalkeeper. Get right up close, nudge him a bit, rattle his poise and see if he fancies coming out the next time I'm charging down on him. The first minute is best since how often do you see someone being booked in those early seconds? This ball was perfect and I hassled Chris Woods right into his net. Big Chris wasn't too pleased about it especially as I ran away with a grin on my face, no booking being made. The Rangers' support howled their anger and I was happy that I'd got off to the right start. As a Celtic striker it would be an entirely bad reference to have the Rangers' fans on my side.

The game got off to a frenetic pace as is often the case in Old Firm clashes. Professional as every one of the players might be, you can't help but be infected by the crazed sense of urgency zooming in at you from every angle. Win or lose, the players are desperate to try their hardest, to be seen to be going that extra mile and at full pelt. Fast games suit my style and my temperament. I had a growing optimism that this was going to be a good match for me.

Then another ball went through on Chris Woods and I pounced on him. He clutched the ball and stood up, still obviously furious over our first minute clash. Holding his forearm out in front of his chest he rammed me. I put up my hand and he pushed me hard sending me staggering back a couple of steps. Then Graham Roberts flew in and punched me a weak one and shoved me back. Before I could react big Terry Butcher was right in front of me shoving me out of the way. Behind him, the smaller Roberts was making a show of trying to get at me but couldn't. I decided that this was in danger of getting out of hand so hit the deck. If they decided to mix it with me while I was down then I would have got straight back on my feet and not been responsible for my actions. As it was, I thought it was all handbags at ten paces. A simple hot spot in a game simmering with passion. Nothing to fret about. The type of thing that happens in every game.

Jim Duncan, the referee, didn't agree. After a lot of running around trying to calm things down, he summoned me over, I reckoned for a severe ticking off and nothing more. The red card was out and the black arm pointed towards the dressing room. I was off and I was totally devastated. They say the blue-draped crowd was howling for blood. Can't say I noticed. They had been making so much noise since an hour before the kick-off it seemed impossible that they could shout any louder. That walk back, I can't remember a thing about it. Even watching video recordings after the event, it means nothing to me. All I can remember is a pain in my chest and lead-filled feet. I'd let everyone down.

They say in the records that I was sent off after 17 minutes. That might well be accurate but the incident happened at 14 minutes. My first Old Firm match and I lasted 14 minutes. Not even quarter of an hour. Some hero, eh? I felt like a complete failure.

Sitting in the Celtic dressing room under the Ibrox main stand, the physio Brian Scott came to check I was all right physically. After a few rudimentary tests he concurred I was fine and left to join the others in the dug out. Of course

I was physically well. That punch from Roberts hadn't even bothered my jaw. I've had plenty of harder smacks from women. Everything had been blown out of proportion but I sat there, slumped and bowed, knowing fine well that that's not how the media would see it nor the fans feel it. Giving your all in this game was entirely expected but getting sent off was going too far. Leaving your team one man down against the Rangers was suicidal, unacceptable. A few minutes after I had reached the dressing room I heard an enormous roar. I just assumed that the crowd was approving or disapproving something. What I didn't know then was that Rangers' goalkeeper Chris Woods had been sent off for the same incident. For the remainder of the first half I sat in blissful ignorance, dreading the half-time result, believing that Celtic were one man down and it was all my bloody fault.

Slapper Graham Roberts had taken over in goal from Chris Woods. Well, maybe he was a better goalie than a boxer. The game continued apace. Celtic had been further weakened by young Paul McStay having to come off in the first half through injury. But Rangers being without their goalkeeper was a major weakness. The Rangers support considered the match as some sort of last stand Alamo and started singing all those old sectarian songs as if they were hymns – battle hymns. Graham Roberts took it upon himself to conduct the fans' singing of The Sash throughout the game. It was the most traditional of all their songs, the one most easily identified as coming from that historical Protestant roots of Rangers. But he had to conduct, of course, because recent arrival and Englishman Roberts wouldn't have known any of the words. For the same reasons, half of the Rangers' team would have been clueless about those lyrics. On the other hand I knew every verse, having had the song sung at me as some effort at provocation so many times.

In the second half, Celtic were 2–1 up but backs-to-the-wall Rangers were making a fight of it. One of Celtic's goals had been an own goal by Terry Butcher though Celtic's Peter Grant had tried to claim it – as you do. Now Terry is a fine player and a good guy but he tends to take things a mite too personally. When he went up and challenged our goalie of the day, Allen McKnight, he followed through and had a go. Thankfully he was almost as bad a boxer as Graham Roberts and would later be proven to be more adept at booting holes in doors. But Jim Duncan, the referee, was a brave soul and marched straight up and sent Butcher off. Believe me, in that stadium, in that atmosphere, with Celtic the opposition, it takes a referee with huge balls and iron principles of fairness to dismiss the Rangers' captain. Fair play to Jim Duncan.

In spite of the upheaval and the controversy, Celtic should have won. But a last gasp goal by that ever trying Richard Gough for Rangers secured a 2–2 draw. The one thing you learn as a Scottish football supporter is that nine times out of ten Old Firm games don't go as everyone predicts they will. Form is overturned, runaway victories achieved by the weaker team and a ten man side can scrape out a draw. It's like there's some She Bitch in the Sky looking down, disapproving of the importance so many people attach to this one particular game. So every now and then she just jumbles up the fortunes and sits up there laughing at our disbelieving phizogs. Serve us right I'd say, but I wouldn't have it any other way.

That night I had planned on a celebration. Now all I felt like was licking my wounds. Though I'd intended to stay in Glasgow, I jumped the 6.15 pm shuttle to Heathrow and was back in my own house in Romford before 8 o'clock. A few quiet drinks in my local, The Ship, where no one talked about the game against Rangers, just greeted me as a regular, then home and to bed. It was the quietest weekend I think I've ever spent in my entire adult life.

Back in Glasgow the following week for training, I realised the newspapers had been filled with talk of the incidents at Ibrox being subject to a police report as possible criminal offences. The whole affair seemed exaggerated to me. There wasn't even any more crowd trouble than usual with around 60 people being arrested in the ground – pretty standard for an Old Firm match. I just dismissed it as the usual hysteria that followed these games, fuelled in particular by three red cards.

Then that week, Strathclyde Police announced they were going to investigate the issue. I couldn't believe all this hype. The police asked Scottish Television who had covered the game for a copy of their film. The management at STV obviously shared my views and told the cops to get stuffed. If they wanted the film they would have to get a formal order. Bugger me but they did and marched away with the film of the match.

Still I didn't think it would come to anything. In those years there had been a lot of publicly expressed concern about violence surrounding football. Too often politicians would jump on a bandwagon demanding this and that action – totally useless proposals – but it ensured the talking heads appeared in the media. It was bound to be just some more of that kind of banner-waving was my view and I just buckled down and got on with my life.

One Saturday a few weeks later, I was in the mood for playing the game of life again and was having a party. It was a great party, lasting into the early hours of the morning. When the phone went a couple of hours after I had fallen asleep I thought it was some bad dream. And it was. Billy McNeil was on the line telling me that I was being charged with conduct likely to cause breach of the peace and I had to report to the police. For those unfamiliar with the Scottish legal system, breach of the peace is a kind of affray and alarm. In short, Strathclyde Police reckoned that what we did on the football field was likely to cause a riot to occur even if that was raged by other people. In the fug of the booze I was shaking my skull trying to jar some reality back into my brain. But it was Billy McNeil all right and he wouldn't be joking about such matters.

A shave and a shower later, I was picked up by Bill McMurdo, which is just as well as I was still too drunk to drive. We travelled to Bellahouston Hotel near Ibrox stadium where we met up with Billy McNeil and two lawyers. Bill McMurdo had retained a bloke called Len Murray who just happened to be one of the finest lawyers in the country. The trouble is, Len Murray had also been retained by Rangers on behalf of Terry Butcher, Chris Woods and Graham Roberts who were all being hit with the same charge. Even half-drunk and in a twilight world of disbelief, it did occur to me that Rangers the club had hired the best lawyer for their players but it was my agent and therefore my chequebook that would be paying for my legal representation. That wasn't important at the time. Len had raised the issue of him representing both the Rangers' and Celtic players. I didn't have a problem with that nor did Bill McMurdo whose attitude was that it was really essential that the two clubs be seen to be fighting this as one. In short, the charges were a heap of crap.

I had to report to Govan Police Station in Orkney Street to be charged, as had the Rangers' guys. Len explained that it wouldn't be diplomatic for him to be seen to be accompanying all four of us in with the police. Would it be okay if his associate Peter Watson accompanied me? No problem. All that Peter had to do was to ensure that the procedure went according to the book and the police didn't get up to any tricks. A bit of a basic job for a bloke who went on to be a Sheriff, a type of judge in Scotland.

When we drove down to Govan Police Station, the road outside was jam-packed with TV cameras, reporters, microphones on long poles, photographers and reporters jabbing tape recorders in our faces. God knows who called them but this was becoming as big news as it was a farce. Billy McNeil, Peter Watson and I went into the police station, leaving Bill McMurdo at the wheel of the car, revving the accelerator, ready for a swift getaway.

The charges were read out, I was allowed to leave and

within ten minutes it had happened. It was the first time in British history that footballers had been charged with a criminal offence for actions on the field of play. By evening it was national and international news. All sorts of people came out to condemn it, including Gordon Taylor in England. Criminal law had no place in sport, they argued. It would be the start of the end of all contact games, they predicted. It was a first but wouldn't be a last, they howled. This couldn't be allowed, they demanded. Oh no?

LAGER LEGS, THE POSSIL BOYS AND MR MAGOO (1987/88)

The farce of being charged with criminal offences for play on the park didn't bother me much. I'd grown up in an area where guys constantly got into scrapes with the law. While I had never been in trouble that was mainly because I was swift on my feet. But I had learned a bit about how the police behaved and I believed they had charged me and the Rangers' players as an act of bravado, a bit of show, politics. Confident that the whole sorry saga would come to nothing I simply got on with my life.

The draw against Rangers had meant that Celtic were still trailing in the league with Aberdeen on top and Hearts on their tail. The bhoys would have to string together some decent results and we started to but knew it wasn't going to be easy. After 12 games I had scored 10 goals and was happy I had recovered the scoring touch. Life was going well and I was going to live it.

I began to stretch my legs socially again, reasoning that if Strathclyde Police wanted to splash my mugshot all over the media as some kind of bad guy I'd face it down and be seen for myself in public. Any concerns of a nasty reaction to the press coverage were soon wiped away. The average Glaswegian saw through the kind of political posturing that was now featuring regularly in the media. What the paper-shuffling bureaucrats seem to have missed is that the Rangers and Celtic match had been great entertainment regardless of where folks' allegiance lay. Even for those of strong persuasion either way, the match ending in a draw had probably helped.

Imagine the worst case scenario – that Chris Woods and I were having a serious set-to and Terry Butcher had tried to lynch Allen McKnight – your average punter had been there and done it and most people love a schoolyard rammy. They probably admired us for being just like them. I am just like them but didn't have a go at Chris and he had hardly touched me. As for Graham Roberts I had no idea why he had been charged at all. It couldn't have been for swinging his handbag in my direction. Maybe his conducting of the massed choir of Blue hadn't been up to scratch. No, the man and woman on the street were fine to me and they were absolutely ace as far as I was concerned.

Out and about of a night, I met some wonderful women like good friends Liz Hynds and Sandra Porter. Whenever we met we had a wee ritual of having a tequila slammer. A nice way to say hello. I introduced Sandra to Stevie Murray and they got hitched. Macca the Matchmaker, eh. But there were other women who I had a carnal interest in and I can't even remember the names of some of them. Well the brief drunken nature of our relationship might mean they can't remember my name either. It doesn't bother me one way or another.

One I do remember but I'm not going to name her. God knows she might be a stable pillar of her community and a granny by now. A granny maybe but stable? I doubt it. She was a model and was featured on Tenants lager cans and promotions. So she was definitely good-looking with long legs. I had met her at some club, we got drunk together and she came back to my place. We repeated the tryst one more time a week or so later. It was good, no-strings fun and we parted with no arrangement to meet again.

A week or so later I'm in the Cotton Club with Ally McCoist and some other friends, including a few women. Next I know Lager Legs taps me on the shoulder and starts howling at me. The gist of what she is saying is that I have betrayed her by going out with other women and that she is going to batter me.

Now, I've been slapped a few times in my life but usually without warning. There was no agreement between us and half of what she was saying was pure gobbledegook. That and a glazed look in her eyes spooked the hell out of me and I backed off. Fuck me but she chased me, intent on bloodshed. I skipped around a bit and headed away. Next I know she is scurrying after me, chasing me, screaming for bloodshed and I had to take refuge in the only place I could think of – the Gents. The only time in my life I've hidden in the bogs and I was chased there by a woman. Not great for the reputation but in my defence I'll say that she was totally demented. I had to hide in there for bloody ages, check that she wasn't around and then headed for the exit door and home pronto. Probably that was another night some punters thought I was hanging round the toilets doing lines of charlie. Take it from me it doesn't take that long and leaves you feeling better not worse.

A few weeks later in one of my usual haunts, this bloke collars me. He claims that I've been sleeping with his long-term fiancée and he doesn't like it. I'm standing there ravelling through my brain to work out who the hell he might mean when he comes up with her name. It's Lager Legs, of course. So one minute I have betrayed her because I'm seeing other women, the next she's getting the bloke she's been engaged to for years to sort me out.

I've never been one to seek a fight in my life. If I'm hassled by somebody or attacked I can take care of myself but all this square-go nonsense is just not my scene. This bloke had a team of five or six guys with him and he wasn't out to set the record straight but to give me a gang kicking. Reasoning with the guy would have been a waste of breath.

'Okay,' I said as calm as I could muster. 'Let's go outside and sort this out.' He nodded and his mates began to follow us. My plan was clear. If we made it on to the pavement I would take to my heels and by the look of the beer bellies on his crew they wouldn't have seen me for dust.

As we headed for the exit, a group of guys I'd noticed earlier stepped over. These men seemed vaguely familiar

123

but I couldn't quite place them. They stood between me and the pursuing vigilantes and held up a hand. Bottom line was that they had been listening to my conversation with Lager Legs' so-called fiancé and didn't like it one bit. Fair enough there was an issue to settle but going team-handed up against me on my own was not on. To even things up a bit, they would come outside too and if they had to leave their drinks they would be far from happy chappies. In fact they would be bloody furious and need to take it out on someone. Like the bunch of wankers they were talking to.

Somehow Lager Legs' honour didn't seem so important after that. Turns out I had recognised my personal cavalry from my teenage years. The guys who had rescued me were from Possil, the neighbouring area to Milton where I had grown up. Milton and Possil boys regularly waged war against each other and that's where I had seen these guys before – when we had been battling each other as kids. Now that we had reached adulthood all that was forgotten and had turned into some bond of allegiance, thank Christ. Stacks of my friends now come from areas I saw as hostile when I was 14-years old. The Possil team were clearly street players, carried something of a reputation and had scared my potential assailants shitless. Needless to say I never heard from or saw Lager Legs again, thank God.

In November, Billy McNeil splashed out on a new signing, Joe Millar from Aberdeen. Just like John Lyall before him, Billy had realised that I could take the ball in the air as well as on the ground. So, Joe was signed as one of the most gifted wingers in Scotland at that time. I had seen Joe all kitted out in the red strip of Aberdeen but in civvies he could so easily have been mistaken for a schoolboy who had wandered into Parkhead looking for autographs. Even now when I think of Joe I imagine him dressed in a school uniform, with braid round his blazer, striped tie, a satchel slung over his shoulder and a big lollipop in his mitt.

Though he was only 19-years old Joe had played in the Aberdeen first team for a couple of seasons and had established a good reputation in a team that was doing really well then. Among other top teams, Kenny Dalglish at Liverpool had been interested in signing Joe and the Celtic buy was seen as a coup. Joe had another thing in his favour, he was a lifelong Celtic supporter. The media were heralding his signing as part of Celtic's counter-offensive on the Rangers' spending spree. It was worth a go and it worked fine. The Celtic were now scoring regularly and looked like title challengers. In December I went out and scored all the goals in a 4–0 win over bottom club Greenock Morton. That's the type of game I enjoyed.

There was one embarrassing incident with wee Joe Millar. At some club social affair, he introduced me to his girlfriend. I almost choked on my drink. One look at the petite, good-looking woman and it all came flooding back. While at West Ham I had been asked to play in a benefit match for John McMaster, a wonderfully skilful player and great stalwart of Aberdeen. I was delighted to play.

Too many guys in football at that time and before gave great service but were never paid enough to avoid being on the threshold of poverty when they retired – still young in life but with no other skills. A benefit match can set a former player up with a tidy nest egg to help them get by. So, no problem at all. It was also a chance to see my old St Mirren mate, Frank McDougall, who had transferred up to Aberdeen. Frank was a great scorer of goals. In one week he had scored seven goals against Rangers and Celtic for Aberdeen. These days, he would be anointed as a football deity for that feat. But Frank's career was cruelly curtailed when he suffered a bad injury to his spine. He would leave Aberdeen and football with something like a £3,000 pay-off, poor reward for all the pleasure he gave folk. I keep in touch with Frank who is now living in England. Last time we met he had gone back to the tools of the trade he had served before football beckoned. He's a scaffolder or some such thing. What a bloody waste of talent.

After the match for John McMaster there were the usual drinks. Aberdeen was the oil capital of Europe, had prospered greatly and so had the nightlife and the talent. I was cornered by a beautiful young woman who propositioned me within minutes of meeting. Next to me her pal made the same offer to another player who was soon to sign for Celtic, though we didn't know about it at the time. The four of us slipped though the back and performed a whole repertoire of tricks in a room half full of beer kegs. I never saw the woman I was with again till that night shortly after Joe Miller signed for Celtic.

'Frank, this is my girl friend,' said Joe, obviously as proud as punch of his beautiful partner. Standing behind Joe, the other player from the night among the beer kegs with mock horror silently mouthed, 'OH FOR FUCK'S SAKE,' as he also recognised the free and easy young doll. I thought better than to reply, 'But we've met before.' Life is life and that was in the past. We should all be lucky enough not to have to relive our histories for better or worse unless we choose to. I hope wee Joe had a good time. Eventually he split up with his girlfriend and took to calling her Mad Cow's Disease, don't ask me why.

In December 1988 I heard that we had a date set for court on the crazy charges from Ibrox. So far, not much had been happening in preparation at Parkhead. Len Murray, the solicitor, recalls how Rangers' approach to the whole saga had been extremely professional and supportive of their players while Celtic just didn't seem interested in what could happen to me. Bill McMurdo was obviously right alongside me and we ascertained that the Celtic board had decided that if we did have to go to court one of the board, Jimmy Farrell, a lawyer by trade, would represent me. Now I was really beginning to panic.

Jimmy Farrell was nicknamed Mr Magoo by all the Celtic players for obvious reasons. On games abroad he would be found wandering around airports, passport clutched in his paw looking for the squad, seemingly without a clue where he was or where he was going. He had been involved in the signing of diminutive winger, Joe Miller, and when they first met at Parkhead, Jimmy said, 'Welcome to Celtic, Willie, hope you'll be happy here.' He apparently confused Joe with Willie Miller, the hardman sweeper and captain of Aberdeen who could've eaten Joe for breakfast and still be hungry. It gave the team some laughs where during games we would call Joe 'Willie' and say that he seemed too far up the park for a sweeper. To this day I wonder if Jimmy Farrell thought he signed Willie Miller. Funny, aye, but not such a laugh when you were going to be represented by Mr Magoo in a criminal court. Now that wasn't funny at all.

Somehow, Graeme Souness, Rangers' player/manager, had heard that Farrell was to represent me. Graeme sought me out one day and asked if this was true. When I confirmed such he shook his head in that stern 'I'm really pissed off' sort of look that he has, then offered that Rangers would hire me a top legal representative, an advocate known as a QC, just as they were doing for their guys.

Souness's offer really moved me. It was such a warm act of camaraderie. I thanked him but refused. In fact he had given me all the ammunition I needed. I quietly let Billy McNeil know that Rangers were going to hire me a QC. Suddenly the Celtic board woke up and agreed to hire a top QC for my defence. The board were clearly more motivated by the potential public embarrassment for them rather than with ensuring I had the best lawyer. Thank you, Graeme Souness, for shaking some money out of that old biscuit tin.

On 5 January 1988 I appeared in Glasgow Sheriff Court and pled not guilty to the charges as did Butcher, Woods and Roberts. I couldn't believe it but now there would be a trial. Though now annoyed by this waste of time and money, I was confident that it would go okay for me. Len

Murray – a good Celtic man by the way – was still retained by both teams and obtained a video of the match. I watched the action relevant to me several times – well I was only actually on the field for 17 minutes. Whatever way I looked at it I had behaved within the law and one angle showed clearly that I hadn't slapped Chris Woods. The police and the procurator fiscal – the prosecuting agent in Scotland – had watched exactly the same film. So why were they proceeding with charges?

A trial date was set for April, Len Murray briefed a team of QCs and it was all a matter of waiting. In the meantime, Celtic had a league to fight, I had a life to live and I was about to receive an unexpected offer of foreign travel. Maybe I should have just stayed abroad?

SAND IN MY EYES
(JANUARY/FEBRUARY 1988)

Football wasn't all going Celtic's way. While we were at the top of the league, lowly Stranraer – then second bottom of the Scottish Second Division – didn't seem to be awed too much about that. In the Scottish Cup at Parkhead they should have seen us off in style.

When I scored a goal in four minutes it looked as if the predicted landside was going to happen. More chances came our way but myself and Andy Walker seemed to have lost our touch in front of goal. In the second half, Stranraer were awarded a penalty. This was shaping up to be embarrassing. Stranraer's striker, Bruce Cleland, stood up to take it. I'd seen enough of the bloke in open play to reckon he would hammer a mean shot. He did but big Paddy Bonner saved and parried the ball sending it straight back to Cleland's feet who promptly thumped it over the cross bar.

Poor guy, I knew exactly how he felt. Celtic continued to play as if we had weights on our legs and Stranraer looked more likely to score. A few minutes before the final whistle, Cleland was gifted the ball yards from our empty goal. Poor bugger smashed the ball against the post.

We won all right but hardly convincingly. If I had been standing up in The Jungle I would have been bemoaning a total lack of confidence that we could win the cup let alone the League. Poor Bruce Cleland, it was probably the biggest day of his life and he'd screwed up. But I warmed to him when I heard him quoted as saying that night after the match he had phoned the Samaritans but they were engaged – it had been one of those days. Any bloke who can keep his sense of humour in the face of such a public humiliation in the middle of a packed football ground gets my vote. I heard a rumour that soon afterwards the same

Bruce Cleland emigrated to Australia. Now I think that was going too far. Me, I just headed south.

London seemed the centre of all things joyous to me then. Every chance I could get I would travel back down and hit the town. The nightclubs in the West End had me propping up their bars so often they probably hadn't noticed that I'd signed for Celtic and moved to Glasgow. A habit was to catch the 6.15 pm shuttle from Glasgow to Heathrow on a Saturday after each game. By 8 o'clock I was out on the town and having a great time.

On 13 February – lucky for some – I scored Celtic's winner against Dundee, then headed to London. I'd gone along to Brown's, met up with a few friends and hooked up with a stunning woman. My plan had been to move on from Brown's but somehow the night raged on. At some time near dawn, the woman and I had gone to Videnzi's and partied there till after six in the morning. Eventually around 7.30 am we made it back to this suite I had hired in some swish Mayfair hotel, I forget which one. Not wanting the night to end abruptly, I ordered a bottle of champagne, popped the cork and settled down beside my new friend.

My arse had hardly hit the sofa when the phone rang. Next to no one knew I was staying at that hotel so I answered the phone assuming it would be the hotel staff checking that everything was all right with the bubbly. I'd tell them as soon as I'd managed to put the glass to my lips.

'Hello,' I said into the mouthpiece.

'Hello, Frank, how are you doing?' said this cheerful, unfamiliar male voice.

'Who is this?' I asked not unreasonably.

'Andy.'

'Andy who?'

'Andy Roxburgh.' It was the current Scotland manager. 'We were hoping . . .'

'Right. This is a fucking joke.' And I slammed down the phone.

There had been some debate in the media about why I hadn't been picked for Scotland since Mexico, particularly given my good form. There were also the jokes about exactly what Ferguson had caught me up to in Mexico. I could imagine Charlie Nicholas, up in his house in Glasgow, just back from a night on the tiles getting some mate of his to phone me to take the piss. Well, I'd better things to do and turned my attention to the blonde, who had kicked her shoes off. The phone went again.

'What?' I was getting annoyed now.

'Frank, Frank, please don't hang up,' spluttered the same male voice. 'It IS Andy Roxburgh. Honest.' Fair enough. The voice did sound like that middle-class Scots English that Roxburgh spoke. The kind of voice I associate with the school headmaster that he used to be. In my opinion he should have stayed in his original academic calling. Would have saved a lot of Scotland supporters a lot of grief.

'So tell me,' I replied, 'how many call-offs have you had this morning?' He ignored my question.

'I was hoping you'd join us on the trip to Saudi.'

'Not a chance,' and I hung up again.

By now Andy Roxburgh had so pissed me off that I was hardly paying any attention at all to the woman and hadn't sipped the champagne. I sat there and fumed a bit and she stroked my hand, sussing my state of mind. Scotland were playing a game against Saudi Arabia on the Wednesday and here we were on Sunday morning. All the players chosen for the national squad who had picked up injuries the day before or in the pubs the previous night were calling the manager to withdraw from the squad. I was sitting there in that hotel running through the names of other strikers that Roxburgh might well have phoned before me. What was I? Fourth, fifth or sixth choice? He could stuff it. Then the phone rang again.

It was Bill McMurdo. Roxburgh had contacted him for help in persuading me to play. Bill was his usual calm self

131

saying neither go or stay. He knew it would be my shout at the end of the day and just wanted to give me a chance to talk things through with someone I knew for sure was on my side. Poor Bill. I gave him the lot about Roxburgh's style of teams being defensive shite. That the man hadn't kicked a ball at the highest level himself and it showed. How he always went with the safe players and ended up with safe teams. Boring in other words. His tactical nous meant that Scotland rarely conceded many goals but were as exciting as grey paint drying on a grey wall. Bill didn't agree or disagree, he just listened. The best agents are part businessmen, part PR and a big part therapist.

We hung up and I turned my attention back to the very patient lady and the champagne sitting in a bucket of now fast melting ice. She was gorgeous and the champagne would still be nicely chilled. This would suit me. Much better than a pointless trip to a meaningless football match. Then the phone went again.

'Frankie, how you doing?' It was Mo Johnston phoning me from France.

'Mo, how are you?'

'Same as you, I'll bet,' Mo chuckled at the other end of the line and I could just imagine him sitting in his house across the Channel, half drunk and in the company of a good-looking woman. 'Frank, it'll be a laugh.'

'What will?'

'The Scotland game.' Who had put him up to this? Roxburgh? 'Listen, we'll have a hoot. I'll catch a flight and meet you at Heathrow. Travel up the gether. Have a good time.' I knew he'd be right. That the pair of us could turn a simple journey into a bundle of delinquent trips. But still I wasn't for shifting. Mo harangued me in his good-natured way for a half hour and we hung up with me conceding that I'd at least think about playing. Back to blue eyes on the sofa and maybe a glass of fizz at last. Bloody phone went again. This time it was Andy Roxburgh and this time I agreed to travel after a few hours sleep. It was crucial that I be in Glasgow that afternoon for an important meeting according to Roxburgh. Fair enough. Whatever I thought of him as a manager, I was proud to play for my country.

A couple of hours later, still bleary-eyed and not quite sober, I was meeting up with Bill McMurdo and Mo at Glasgow Airport and going to meet Roxburgh at the hotel there. This had better be worth it, was my view, since I had left both the blonde and the champagne untouched. Some sacrifice. Roxburgh took half an hour to tell us that there was to be a meeting the next day. That was it? A bloody meeting to tell me there was a meeting? Arsehole.

On the flight out to Saudi, once in the air, Roxburgh went up the aisle sticking cocktail sticks into the back of the seats. I pulled some out and saw that each stick was marked with One Div, Two Divs and so on. Now I was flummoxed so asked Roxburgh what these were for. We were all to play cards later apparently – no one was to opt out – and the sticks were for the betting. Was the guy all right in the head? Did he think that playing cards was a good way of building team morale? If so, let's get the green backs out and play for real. But I couldn't hold a grudge. Imagining Andy Roxburgh and his wife sitting at the kitchen table all night marking each stick individually – just split me up. Thanks for that one laugh, Andy.

In Riyadh the next day we set up training in the blistering heat. Just light ball movements to get used to the surface and stretch our travel-weary limbs. In spite of the rude awakening on Sunday I was feeling fit. The beauty of a country like Saudi Arabia is that it is difficult to find booze. So even if I had been tempted I wouldn't have had the time to make the right connections. But I was happy to behave myself as I did before every game. Maybe I didn't think much of Roxburgh as a manager but I fully intended to go out and play so well he wouldn't dream of not picking me in future.

On the training pitch, Roxburgh called me over and I

assumed that he would want a quiet chat about my role in the game and maybe a couple of pointers about the Saudi players.

'Turn your bib round the proper way, Frank,' he instructed.

'What?' The bib was a device that slipped over your head and was tied at the side. They were useful in training for distinguishing the forwards from the defenders or one team against another in a scratch game.

'And pull your socks up, eh?' He wasn't telling me to try harder. He literally meant that I should pull my socks up. At training I preferred them round my ankles and the bib flying loose. Always had.

'Why?' I had to ask. Roxburgh looked at both sides as if checking some spy wasn't listening to this crucial dialogue.

'So you can see UMBRO. They'll give us hell if you end up in the papers and their name's not showing.' And he was off, walking round the pitch, looking the very part in his UMBRO outfit. The wise man surveying his talent. Yeah, right, the man more concerned about his sponsor than the comfort and performance of his team.

I realised there and then that I would never get on with Andy Roxburgh. Bad enough dealing with real football people like Billy McNeil and John Lyall, as well as grumpy buggers like Alex Ferguson when I stretched the rules. But I could just imagine the paroxysms of Mr Roxburgh, the school teacher, when he discovered I was truanting and seven sheets to the wind in some bar. No, I couldn't work with some guy who seemed to care more about a sponsor than the game itself.

The match was a bugger. On from the start I soon realised that Mo Johnston had a cold and it was slowing him down in the heat. His legs were gone, he was slow to every ball and his usual pace in the box was blunted. Mo was not himself and simply should not have been playing. The bold fellow kept apologising to me that I had to be doing more running to compensate for his illness. A couple of times I felt like pulling him aside and saying, 'You bloody talked me into this, you bastard.' But it was just Mo and he was doing his best under difficult conditions. In fact he scored our first goal to draw level with a Saudi team showing remarkable enterprise. One of the Saudi Royal Family was mad keen on football and they had been investing big time in the game. In spite of Scotland's haphazard preparation, I could see our opposition had invested well. It was with some relief that I was substituted in the 64th minute by Robert Connor. The game was a friendly and Roxburgh gave a try out to a good few subs. Strangely he didn't substitute the almost collapsing Mo Johnston. What was he, blind?

On the plane back to Scotland after the 2–2 draw, we could at last relax and have an alcoholic drink. Trouble is Andy Roxburgh banned us. Myself and Mo were having none of that routine so we argued. Eventually he conceded that we could have one small lager. Now I don't like lager and, besides, who did he think he was? The Scottish international match was a one-off and the players were returning to club duty. It was our clubs we were now under obligation to once again, not Scotland. I had an advantage over most others since my manager, Billy McNeil, had come along to the game and was sitting at the front of the plane. Billy had been watching the arguments with his usual silent straight face while sipping a drink himself so I went to speak to him, making sure Roxburgh was close enough to hear.

'Billy, you got any problems with me having a few drinks?'

'Of course not, son,' he replied. 'Get pissed if you want to – your next game's not till Saturday.'

'Cheers, Billy.'

'No problem.' As I headed back up the aisle I could hear Roxburgh shout after me,

'Lager, mind. Just lager.'

Mo and I ordered bottles of champagne. On the flight, they only served half bottles so we bought a couple, then a couple more and then a couple more – the whole way home.

Even before the argument about the booze, I knew I would never play again for Scotland. In total I had five international caps and two of those were as a substitute in the World Cup when it was too late to have any great effect. Not playing for my country more often was a big disappointment but not while Roxburgh was manager. For as long as Roxburgh was in charge then that wouldn't bother me a bit. He continued in his way, choosing teams that would hold out for a dull draw rather than going for glory and style. Among the guys he chose were some great footballers and characters but he insisted on tactics that were geared to hold the opposition rather than destroy them. It's such a bloody shame because there were great Scottish footballers at that time who could've done a lot better if only allowed the freedom to play.

A lot of what Andy Roxburgh was about was behaving in what he saw as the 'right' way. Like the on-board drink saga, it wasn't seemly or moral to be seen drinking when with a Scotland squad. The Umbro sponsorship deal was an agreement so the 'right' thing to do was show their logo. I believe that the supporters I identify with would've been fine about the players relaxing with a few jars after a game, knowing that they do the same after a hard week at work or whenever they want to relax. As for Umbro, they would've been delighted if Scotland played magnificent, exciting football wearing their company name.

As it was, Roxburgh simply didn't have the talent or imagination for any of that. He was reduced to claiming what he thought was the moral high ground. It amused me no end when a few years later he got caught with his pants down having an affair with a young woman. Not the 'right' thing at all, Andy. Nerve of the guy, telling me how to behave. At least I was open and honest about my lifestyle and not the hypocrite he turned out to be.

Anyway, what did I worry about Andy Roxburgh's petted lip? I had a trial coming up facing a judge who might take serious exception to my ways. Now that was becoming a wee bit worrying.

TRIAL OF ERRORS
(APRIL 1988)

The charges rising from that Celtic and Rangers game seemed to be gathering a head of steam. Every week the papers carried some other story about the police charging some other sportsman though usually in the roustabout sports like rugby and football and never for badminton or cricket. Mind you the way the guys in white hurtled those heavy, solid cricket balls at the batsmen was worth at least a severe rap over the knuckles if anything was. But then cricket supporters in England rarely took to fighting each other with Stanley knives and I still believed the whole farce was to make a point to the supporters.

Loads of people agreed. Like the former player, Tony Higgins, now running the Scottish Football Players Association, who predicted that just taking the case to court could spell the end of all contact sport as we knew and loved it. Most of the football commentators and a good few politicians were of a similar mind. It almost seemed that the only people not in agreement were the police and the prosecution. Well, it was all to be decided in court. That didn't fill me with confidence, having known too many guys sent down for offences they didn't commit.

Len Murray had drawn together the top QCs for the four of us – Lord Morton of Shuna, Lord Macaulay of Bragar, Robert E. Henderson QC and Ranald MacLean QC who was appointed to the Supreme Court Bench two years later. The charges were breach of the peace for God's sake. Breach can vary from mobbing and rioting to farting in the street too near a cop though is most often closer to the latter. On a Monday morning the courts in Glasgow, some of the busiest in Europe, are stacked full of guys charged with breach of the peace. Most plead guilty just to end the inconvenience and are landed with a £10 fine. Usually small beer in other words. This must have been the most expensive defence team ever hired for breach of the peace charges.

The trial at Glasgow Sheriff Court in front of Sheriff Archibald McKay started on Wednesday 13 April and looked set to run. Some of the evidence and counter-attacks were interesting. The police had to explain to the court the whole background to Rangers and Celtic. Stuff like: Rangers came from a Protestant base, Celtic from a Catholic one, there's great rivalry between the teams and sometimes the supporters fall out. The Janet and John Guide to the Old Firm. It took me all my time to stop sniggering out loud while this spiel was going on. If the court needed to be told all this basic stuff how the hell were they fit to make a reasonable judgment? When the Assistant Chief Constable of Strathclyde Police pointed out that Old Firm games needed 500 cops to provide security – much more than other football matches in the city – I wanted to call out and ask him if he thought Partick Thistle or Clyde's boards should be sacked for failing to attract decent crowds. It was stuff and nonsense which would have been boring if it hadn't been so serious.

Then this other copper described how we had squared up to each other during the match in such a manner that if we had been on the street he would have had the view that we were about to fight. But we weren't on the street. Our defence was all very polite – as it tends to be – and Terry Butcher's brief put in a bid that he was trying to separate myself and Chris Woods. The court seemed to accept that, though a lot of good it would do him.

The four accused – no one actually called us The Old Firm Four though they probably would these days – would sit quietly in the dock as we listened to tales of how we were dreadful men intent on stirring up the sectarian violence that underpins Celtic and Rangers matches. Now they were touching on my territory. As the only born and bred Glaswegian in the dock – in fact the only Scotsman – I knew all about sectarian violence. With the exception of the Irish, I also knew how difficult it was for people not brought up in this environment to appreciate the issue. Graham Roberts, when he was conducting the Rangers' supporters in singing 'The Sash', had no earthly idea of the undertones of the song. Butcher and Chris Woods likewise. So what the hell had those three to do with sectarian violence? They were just playing football. For my part I was totally opposed to sectarianism – always had been and always will be – and especially when it erupts into violence. Competition between the sides is fine. The difference between values is okay. But there's no need to go hurting each other over them. Then again, nobody asked me about that. Maybe they just all assumed that I really was the Fenian bastard I'd been called thousands of times in my life.

Every day the court was bombarded by the media and lengthy reports appeared in all the newspapers and on the TV. The trial was being covered UK-wide as it had huge implications on sport and the law. This was a world first they kept saying and I hoped it would be a last.

While the stories unfolded, Chris, Terry, Graham and I would pass time together during breaks in the proceedings. We chatted about football, of course, people we knew in common and gossiped – the way friends do. It was ironic that in the same building we were being accused of fighting some ancient war. We were just footballers playing the game in all its senses.

Jim Duncan, the referee, was called to give evidence. He admitted that the match had been arduous and difficult to handle but then so are all passionate derbies. In all fairness to Duncan he said that there was no place for the police on the field of play. That it was his job to keep order among the players and he believed he had. The bloke went as far as to say that if criminal proceedings against footballers for actions on the field became commonplace, he would give up refereeing all together. This man was a top-class referee and the court should have listened to him very carefully.

Len Murray had sought the assistance of a team from Strathclyde University who specialised in working with film. With their help, the video of the game was slowed right down and showed beyond doubt that I had not struck Chris Woods. And I hadn't. In some still photographs it looks like I'm patting him on the cheek, patronising him. I've done that to other players before, usually accompanied by a wide grin, and it's pretty effective in rattling some of them. But not this time. My hand reached out as a reflex to keep him away. The point is, and I could've told anyone at the time, it did not connect. That was the essence of my defence. It was presented thoroughly and expertly and I could only hope now that the court would accept it.

In the middle of the long, drawn out trial, a few of the Celtic board would look in on the courthouse to see how things were going. One day I was sitting there waiting for proceedings to start when board member Jimmy Farrell, Mr Magoo himself, came up to me.

'Don't worry, Patrick,' he said, with his hand placed reassuringly on my shoulder, 'we're going to win this.' He couldn't even remember my name. And this was the guy who Celtic would have been quite happy to let represent me. Yet again I was grateful to Graeme Souness and his offer of an advocate. More grateful than he will ever know.

The trial was taking an inordinate time. Some of the QCs complained about this and made impassioned speeches against the great public cost, never mind the defence fees, squandered on addressing such a trivial matter. While I agree with these points entirely, I couldn't see the point of the defence raising them. What was the sheriff going to do – make them speed up the film clips of the football match? I don't think so.

There's a great deal of debate these days about video evidence being used to investigate incidents during football matches. In essence that is what we were subject to and it didn't prove so straightforward. Viewing the footage of the game as it was shown on TV produced several opinions on what had actually happened even when played back at different angles. It took specialist treatment of the video before a consensus was reached on some incidents, while even that didn't help in others. Though I'm sure film and cameras have improved immeasurably since then, I remain pessimistic that using video evidence would settle all disputes on controversial matters and I reckon Terry Butcher, Chris Woods and Graham Roberts would agree.

That week was one of the most tense and the most boring in my adult life. After a while the court began to ring with what appeared to be the same tune, the same speech. To make matters worse, I had to behave that week, even at night. With all the media publicity it wasn't on for me to go out for a few jars. So, it was nights in front of the TV and early to bed. I prayed the bloody trial wouldn't last too long for the sake of my sanity.

As a result, my time with the Rangers' boys was welcome company. Each day we would lunch together in the court canteen. It was a question of taking turns about who was to buy lunch for everyone. When it was shaping up that the trial would finish by the end of the week I bade my time. On the Friday, it was clearly going to be the last day. All four of us went for lunch as usual and I announced it was my turn to pay. The others asked for their preferences and I went off to get them. Instead of the lasagne or whatever I got all of us fish and chips. They thought nothing of it and ate heartily. As they were munching away I asked them if they knew what they were eating. They looked at me as if I had lost my senses.

'Catholic steaks,' I smiled. It took a minute for the penny to drop then it was the four of us howling with laughter, the Rangers' guys getting the joke. The souls didn't even know about that Catholic tradition, yet yards away they had sat and listened for days about how they apparently were deliberately involved in provoking sectarian hatred and violence.

Shortly thereafter we were called back into court and it was verdict time. I was found not guilty. Terry Butcher was found guilty and fined £250. Chris Woods was found guilty and fined £500. Graham Roberts was found not proven. I explained to Graham after the trial that not proven was a peculiarly Scottish verdict meaning they thought he did it but they couldn't prove it. I don't think he got the joke.

Terry Butcher and Chris Woods both appealed against their sentences and failed. After all the hullabaloo about the four of us being the first to be charged under such circumstances, the day before Chris Kamara of Swindon Town became the first English footballer to be convicted of criminal offences committed on the field of play when he was fined £1,200. The politicians and bureaucrats had their way but what an expensive waste it was to prove to be.

In the aftermath of the trial, FIFA would introduce new rules to the game to try and cut down contact and aggression on the field. But while superficial rules have been altered, the basic laws of football remain unchanged. For example, it is still legal for a player to move in and challenge a goalkeeper as I did with Chris Woods. At the end of the day, I'm left wondering what all that fuss and bother was about. In my view it achieved absolutely nothing. What a waste of money.

At the end of the trial I just sighed a sigh of relief, left the court and started buzzing about the football again. It was the centenary year and Celtic had something to prove by winning a trophy or two. That's football for you – a bit like religion, just more important.

WINNERS, LOSERS AND
PORNO PICS (1988)

B illy McNeil was furious with the players. By failing to
win away at Hearts we had missed an opportunity to
win the title. I knew what he meant. He was a manager
and was being pragmatic. A title championship at all costs
was Billy's rightful priority and he wouldn't have cared if
it had been achieved behind closed doors. But I felt to win
the title that year in particular we should do so in front of
our own fans at home. It simply wouldn't be fair on the
majority of them to be forced to watch the victory on TV.
It's good but just not the same.

For the Celtic players we won the League long before it
was mathematically impossible for us to be stopped. It will
not surprise anyone who is familiar with the Glasgow scene
to know that that was the day we beat Rangers 2–1. Sure,
we could have blown it after that and ended up making
fools of ourselves but that derby game is that important
and, besides, we were confident.

We actually took the championship on 23 April when
we thrashed Dundee 3–0 at home. Young Chris Morris
scored the first goal and our fans showed their joy with a
pitch invasion. There were something like 60,000 people at
that match so no wonder play had to be held up for six
minutes before the park was clear. I celebrated with them
– well, you do as a fan even before the final whistle has
been blown. As a player you're meant to keep your cool
but I knew we were going to lift the trophy.

Looking back, the day we actually won the League can
sound a bit of an anti-climax. You would think that after
all the public pressure for Celtic to win the title in their
centenary year it would be cause for a major celebration. It
was for our supporters and the players felt as if we were

144

walking on the clouds even after the long arduous season. It was my first title ever and winning the Scottish First Division with Celtic had not escaped me, believe you me. But what did the club do – held a celebration get together at Parkhead. Now it's not as bad as it sounds with hospitality provisions behind the scenes better than the pie and Bovril stands on the terracing. But it's not exactly the Hilton.

Maybe the club wanted us to let our hair down away from prying eyes. That would be fair since every sports journalist in the country was trying to get access to us. Then again maybe the biscuit tin's contents didn't stretch to a proper knees-up.

We didn't care much. A few weeks before, Chris Morris had got married and we had a great party. A few months before, in the crowded Celtic changing rooms, I had opened some mail that had arrived for me at Parkhead. Usually it's fan mail from supporters wanting autographs and the like that was sent to players at the club. When I opened this big brown envelope out came porno pics of a woman we'll call Joanne from London. It was more fanny mail than fan mail. I had never met Joanne but one glimpse at the pictures told me I wouldn't mind that privilege one bit. Trouble is all the other players managed to get an ogle of the pics and started making a hullabaloo about her – jealous sods.

Joanne kept writing and sending more pics. Inevitably she arranged to come up to Glasgow and spend some time with me. All the other players were savaging me constantly about her and I'd tell them truthfully I could take it or leave it. Of course, when she did come up I was obliged to introduce her to all the guys standing there with their tongues slabbering out. Well, at least it was only their tongues.

A wee while later it was Chris Morris's stag party. I asked Chris in private one time what he wanted as a wedding present.

'A night with Joanne,' he said.

'You sure?'

'Oh aye.' Couldn't see the fuss really but if that's what the boy wanted. When I told Joanne she was right up for it. So, I booked a swanky hotel room, a few bottles of champagne and told Chris he had a date.

Lost his bottle didn't he, and on his stag party night. Lots of guys get up to a bit of badness that night. And stacks of brides to-be as well, trust me, I know. At least Chris had a bloody good idea what he was getting. Never mind, I just treated myself to Chris Morris's wedding present – and very nice it was too.

Joanne and I split up soon after. The reason I haven't spelled out her full name is that we have kept in touch as friends ever since. In fact, whenever I got into trouble with any woman it would be Joanne I would phone for advice. As you'll imagine, sometimes I've been on the phone to her every bloody day.

Chris's stag night was great and his wedding was one huge blast out, so none of us were too bothered at the subdued celebration on winning the League. Then again there was the small matter of the Scottish Cup Final against Dundee United to come as the last game of the season. Might as well keep in trim since I for one wanted to win that too. After all the times with St Mirren when we made it to the semi-finals only to be knocked out, now I would be going to Hampden in a Cup Final and I didn't want to screw up. I'd waited too long for that.

Cup Final day was wonderful. Hampden was almost packed out with 80,000 supporters. Two good teams up against each other. Dundee United desperate to win the cup having failed for so long in spite of being one of Scotland's top teams in the 1980s. Celtic determined to win the cup and achieve a double in our centenary year. Two fingers up to the sceptics who said we'd win zilch and one finger up to the chequebook of Rangers.

Old Iron Side, Maggie Thatcher, the Conservative prime minister, was present, though God knows why. Here she was at the premier sporting event in Scotland's year in a part of her domain where she was hardly welcome. There were next to no Conservative MPs in Scotland and there were about to be even fewer. Unemployment and poverty still raged north of the Border and few home-based Scots had sampled the prosperity or adopted the dog-eat-dog attitudes that her government pushed. The football supporters showed precisely how they felt about Maggie when tens of thousands suddenly lifted and showed her red cards, sending her off. Typically, she didn't seem to notice.

Dundee United took a 1–0 lead through Kevin Gallacher and things looked bleak for Celtic. Late on in the second half I scored an equaliser. Now there was going to be an additional problem. About half a dozen of us had booked a holiday in Spain and hired a massive villa in Marbella for a few weeks. The flights were scheduled for two days after the final. However, if we remained level at full-time, the replay would not be for a full week. Bugger that – we would miss our holiday. Since Dundee United's Billy McKinlay – known as Badger – was coming along, players on both sides had a commitment to see the matter ended one way or another that day.

As the clock ticked away the last few seconds of proper time, I picked up the ball and slotted it into the back of the net. Perfect timing, giving Dundee United no time to hit back. Perfect moment as the Celtic masses saluted me, one of their own. Perfect end to my first season with my boyhood team. It was just a dream.

Not even Maggie Thatcher presenting the medals put me off. I was so deliriously chuffed, I would have collected the Scottish Cup from bloody Adolf Hitler. Then again maybe no.

A few days later we set off for Spain. There was Derek Whyte, Stevie Murray, both of Celtic, a mate of mine Jim Byrne and Billy McKinlay who just kept muttering, 'How could you?' every time we met. Allen McKnight and I were to travel in style. His father lived over in Spain and we agreed to pick up his Rolls-Royce and drive it over for him. That car was some patter. Passing through Customs on the way to France, you could see the blokes checking the passports, clocking the blond hair and looking up with a wee knowing smile. For the past few years people had assumed I had enormous wealth, the type you associate with Rollers. I had grown tired of telling them that wasn't the case so now I just let them believe what they wanted, turning it into my private joke. While the trip in the Roller had seemed a great idea, Allen and I eventually ended up getting pissed off. We just wanted to get to Spain yesterday and the journey was taking too long, regardless of the smoothness of the ride.

The car delivered and settled into the villa, it was like someone had just let the pressure out of me. Wonderful. I had started the habit of taking long summer breaks during the close season, and I would continue as long as I could. Thomas Cook the travel company had me marked down as a VIP. A month or so before the last game of a season I would go in there with a list of places around the world I wanted to stay in that summer. One year it might be Egypt, Turkey and Brazil, say. There were no ready made packages, of course, so they custom built holidays for me, making sure to book me into the finest accommodation in the best resorts. One year I stayed in Acapulco, in a hotel that is rated one of the five best in the world. Howard Hughes had kept a permanent suite there. Even though I couldn't book that particular floor it tickled me that the boy from Milton was staying where the world's richest man had chosen to relax. But in 1988 it was no fancy itinerary, just chilling out with some mates under the Spanish sun.

We ended up with three villas available to us but used to hang around the pool of the one with the greatest facilities. They were all luxurious but this one came with an extra – a pub next door. Every morning, the bar staff would

148

deliver crates of beer to us, slipping the bottles in the swimming pool to keep cool and remove the empties. Heaven.

After a couple of weeks, Badger had stopped complaining about the Cup Final and we were all feeling very relaxed. I had been in contact with Jenny Blyth who told me that she and a group of models were to be on a photographic shoot close to us in Spain. The guys didn't need convincing – we were up there like a flash. A bunch of topless models and young footballers with time on their hands – you can imagine the party we had. Jenny and I were starting to hit it off and, of course, the other guys noticed.

A short while later I flew back to London for a weekend. Stringfellows' photographer and my close friend, Margot Mitchell, was having a birthday party and I wasn't going to miss it. Jenny was there and we got together again. That weekend she had something to tell me. She had posed for Playboy – nude. It was like she wanted to know if I disapproved or something. Looking back I think she was clearing the way, plotting on us becoming more of a steady item, getting possible skeletons out of the closet. Disapprove? How could I? Some would say I had the sexual morals of an alley cat. I would say I was just having a good time which is okay as long as no one got hurt. The first I saw of Jenny Blyth was her smiling face and beautiful breasts on page three of a newspaper. So what if she showed a bit more – in fact, showed everything – in a magazine? What was the difference? What right did I have to approve or disapprove?

Back in Spain after the weekend in London, I went straight to the villa and down to the pool where I found the boys in their usual location sunning themselves. Their greeting was friendly though muted but I just assumed they were hungover as usual and exhausted by the heat and a lack of sleep the night before. Then something in the water caught my eye. Several things in the water and colourful. Pictures of Jenny, stark naked, her legs splayed wide for all the world to see. The same pictures were littered on the ground, every free sunbed, spread over the floor of the villa, in the bathroom and my bedroom. Just in case I missed them, I guess. The buggers had spotted the magazine in a shop and knew Jenny from the party with her model friends. Assuming I was ignorant about the pictures they just thought they would open my eyes. Sods must have bought a dozen copies of that magazine. Of course, Jenny had already told me and I remained unfazed but I've often wondered how I would have reacted if that was how I found out. Just the same, I reckon.

A couple of days later, my pal, Jim Byrne, was due to fly home.

'What time's your flight?' I asked him. He told me. 'You got your ticket?' I asked, all helpful. He fished it out of his pocket and I promptly snatched it and tore it to shreds. We were having a good time so no pal of mine was leaving. Mind you, three weeks later when I bought him another ticket home, he had some explaining to do to his wife. Somehow she was reluctant to accept it had been all my fault.

Back in Glasgow for pre-season training, I had a small business matter to sort out with the club. The agreement I had signed with them on the Holiday Inn napkin that my signing-on fee would be tax free wasn't being honoured. The fee was for something like £140,000 and was paid in quarterly instalments. This is done deliberately so a player can't get big money on day one then rest on his laurels or cut and run. Trouble is my first payment came in through my salary and was, of course, fully taxed. When I had pointed that out to Billy McNeil he had promised to sort the matter out. But then other payments had been made in the same way and I stood to lose at least £50,000.

While the money was obviously important the principle was raging inside me. I had willingly taken a wage cut to play for Celtic and they had willingly agreed to pay me a tax free signing-on fee. It wasn't going to cost them any extra whichever way they paid the money. It was only me who was losing out on all counts. Their refusal to process the payments in that way had gone without explanation and I can only put it down to gross inefficiency or ill will against me. There are too many people in football who take the prosperity of others personally when it has nothing to do with them, as I was to find out to my cost later in my career. While the centenary campaign had been going on I had decided to concentrate my energies on the football. But now I knew the matter needed sorting out or the biscuit tin board would simply continue as before.

Yet again Billy McNeil said he would make sure it was sorted out. I trusted McNeil and had no reason to doubt him. At the same time I didn't envy him having to cope with the pressures of producing the best football on the park and, at the same time, watch his back from the bunch of sweetie wives that were running Celtic at that time. His life was far from easy. But he was my manager, my contact with the administration and he had to listen to and deal with my grievances.

McNeil was a great football manager, who I rank along-side John Lyall as the best two I have worked with. In my first season with Billy I used to get irritated by the way he would fine me at times for my behaviour away from the game or some minor misdemeanour. He'd hit me for a grand a time, enough to hurt but not deadly serious. Then as we shaped up to play Rangers for the last time in 1987/88, he fined me again. This time he offered me the money back if I played well against them. Luckily I did and the dough was duly returned. All he was doing was motivating me, getting my back up before a game, know-ing I would take it out with extra zest on the park. And he was right though I preferred it when he gave me the loot back. Respecting and trusting Billy McNeil, I left the matter of the tax free signing-on fee with him and concen-trated on the business of football.

A few games into the season it seemed as if history was

repeating itself. With almost exactly the same pool of players, Celtic seemed unable to exert the dominance we had displayed the season before – just as had happened with West Ham. We had lost three games out of five, suffered a whopping great 5–1 thrashing from Rangers and were sent out of the Skol Cup by Dundee United, the team we had beat in the Scottish Cup Final just a few months before. Publicly, McNeil said he was flummoxed and so was I.

In spite of the team's bad run, I was doing okay, playing every game and scoring goals. We went to Hungary in the European Cup and whipped Honved Budapest 4–1 with me scoring a goal. By Christmas 1988, I was the club's leading scorer but the media had somehow made up the story that I was desperate to get back to London. Not true at that time. I was seeing a great deal more of Jenny Blyth but she was only an hour away by air. No distance at all.

I'd fly down to London every chance I got and after every game on a Saturday. There was nothing new in this for me. When with West Ham I'd leave the other guys to catch the coach and fly back from away games in Newcastle just to get out on the town as early as possible. Couldn't see the point of wasting a Saturday night sitting on a bus with a bunch of bears. Jenny was still living with the fellow she had been engaged to, Neil Turley. But they had come to an arrangement to share the house they had bought together though not share the same bed. Or so she said. I would have been quite happy for her to move into my house but she didn't want to. At the start she said it was because she had to share costs with her former boyfriend. Then she revealed that she didn't want that house because I had bought it with Anita. I couldn't see her point – it was just a bloody house and one I had been very happy in.

Jenny came up to Glasgow quite often but she hated it. Too smalltown and far away from London for her she reckoned. I was more of the view that the people were too straight-talking for her. That and the fact that as a Celtic player I was the known face and she wasn't treated with the celebrity status she thought she deserved.

Little things irked her. One night we were in a pub in Glasgow when a nasty fight broke out. Frankie Miller, the singer and actor, was in our company and immediately covered me so I wouldn't get hurt, abandoning Jenny to her own devices. God did that give her a sour grin. But Frankie is a Celtic supporter and the football was as important to him as it was to some unemployed guy living in a crap tenement. Most of these guys had started life in crap tenements anyway. One time on the way to my mother and father's place in Milton with Jenny, we passed a row of tenements. Pointing at one close Jenny said, 'What a terrible place. Can you imagine how horrible it must be to live there?' It had been my childhood home where the family had lived for years. Jenny's little snobbish ways didn't bother me at all. It was all a good laugh as far as I was concerned.

But still the media ranted on about me wanting to move back to the big smoke to be with her. Behind the scenes the Celtic board hadn't moved one inch or even properly responded to my issues about their failure to meet their contractual obligation on the signing-on fee. It was a festering sore that was making me increasingly unhappy. But if the press only knew who else had tried to tempt me away from Celtic they would have had a real story that would have made the front pages. It would have been a move that would have changed my life forever and that of everyone I knew.

HOME FROM HOME (1989)

I like Graeme Souness. As a player he was at the top of his game, as a human he is wise to every trick. People can be deceived by his dogged expression and hard-man eyes. They think the way he looks and the way he plays football sums up the whole man. There's a lot more to him than that.

Souness has a fine grasp of human psychology. In his days in management I've had to smile at his deliberate wind-ups. The latest was in 2002, when his team Blackburn Rovers took on Celtic in the UEFA Cup. There was such a hullaboo when Souness took his team to the Rangers' training ground to prepare. As the press theorised and wrote column inch after column inch of speculation, all I could see was Souness's wry grin, knowing that he'd upset them and rattled the Celtic support while meantime getting the finest facilities for his troops probably free of charge.

When Graeme Souness approached me when I was at West Ham, I thought nothing of it. We had met from time to time, got pissed together a good few times and been part of the same Scotland squad. But what he asked that time staggered me. I looked back at that steely, steady stare and wondered if this was one of his wind-ups. No, he was deadly serious. Would I sign for Rangers?

For those unfamiliar with the scene, there had never been a Catholic sign for Rangers. Ever. What might appear a piece of blatant prejudice now was well established and generally accepted as the status quo back then and would never change according to those who knew. Except Souness was intent on getting rid of all that and he asked me. Not only was he going for the first Catholic Rangers' player he was also targeting a lifelong Celtic fan and one who was well known not just for his football but his approach to life. I knew Souness had balls but this was either the bravest or most stupid plan I'd ever heard.

I thought about his offer very carefully. If I had sat down and drawn up a for and against list the negatives would have far outstretched the positives. In its favour was that Rangers were clearly investing heavily in their squad, having brought in guys like Butch Wilkins and Gary Stevens to add to their growing pool. Souness was already proving as astute a manager as he had been a player. If success had been the only criterion then Rangers made for a very good choice. They also treated their players well, paying top wages, generous bonuses and providing total support – unlike the biscuit tin board at Celtic.

On the negatives – Christ, where do I start? Every Celtic fan in the world would hate me and I mean loathe, not some form of polite dislike. I was likely to lose all my friends, my family wouldn't speak to me, I couldn't dare go to Milton again. My life would be in danger. No more hanging around in Glasgow clubs. I'd need a bodyguard. My address would have to be secret and still require a fool-proof security system. I would be the loneliest man in Glasgow, perhaps the world. At the end of it all I could never play for Celtic again or even live safely or happily in Scotland. It would be a one-way ticket from Parkhead to Ibrox with no turning back.

Huge as those repercussions were there was one more. Could I live with myself? It didn't take much imagination to see me dressed in the blue strip scoring a goal against Celtic. The image made me shiver.

When I met Souness again he was persuasive and insistent. But so far it was theoretical – a chat between the two of us. What would it take to make me sign, he wanted to know. So I told him a £1,000,000 signing-on fee. It was more money than any footballer had ever received and still it wasn't enough for the price I'd pay. It was also a deal-breaker or so I calculated.

When chairman David Murray wouldn't come up with the million quid, I sighed in relief and got on with my game. I had an Old Firm New Year's game to look forward to in January 1989. This was an age old tradition and it was one the supporters looked forward to in shaking the slumbers of the Christmas period out of their system. The game rarely let them down.

Celtic were looking to revenge the 5–1 gubbing earlier in the season. We were out of the Skol Cup, the European Cup and now we had the League to concentrate on. We would never get close if we couldn't beat Rangers. But they hadn't been playing well in recent weeks and were without key players Ally McCoist, Chris Woods and Ian Durrant. The Celtic team were hopeful.

The game started well for Celtic and I was on sharp form. There must have been something about my manner that day since, early in the game, Butch Wilkins suddenly and needlessly barged me to the ground at the edge of their box. Maybe Butch spotted some move that had escaped my attention but I'm grateful nevertheless. Rangers' defensive wall was posted missing and Chris Morris stepped up and thumped the free kick into their net two minutes into the match. One up and we kept going after them.

A short while later, Mark McGhee – a ferocious finisher – was threatening the Rangers' goal as I was going up for a ball out-jumping the Rangers' defence. The move looked promising. In the air, Terry Butcher thumped into me, sending me tumbling head over heels. As I hit the deck all I could see was Butcher's booted foot come crashing down on to my arm. Even before I struggled to my feet I knew I was badly hurt. But I did get to my feet, furious at what Butcher had done and ready to get him. Trouble was my arm was dangling, useless, clearly smashed.

The referee insisted I had to leave the field for treatment. As I headed for the trackside I told Billy McNeil that I'd be fit to play on. With some strapping, the arm was aching, cumbersome and a hindrance but I was going back on to the park. As I sprinted past our captain, Roy Aitken, I roared, 'Keep thumping it high into their half.' Every time the Bear got the ball I'd remind him, 'Loft it straight up.' And he would. As the ball soared upwards I'd run forward and wait a few yards short. 'Come on, you bastard, go for it,' I'd grumble, watching Terry Butcher hover and watch. I just wanted him to go up for the ball as he would normally and I was going to run straight at his body, broken arm or no broken arm. He was obviously totally aware of what he had done to me. He could see I was furious – well, it wasn't difficult – and kept well away from every ball big Roy lofted into the air.

Eventually I realised that I wasn't going to get revenge on Terry Butcher. Moreover, the arm was really aching and screwing up my running. I'd no option but to leave the field. Less than 15 minutes had gone by. Another short appearance at Ibrox. I was going to have to stop that routine.

In the changing room it was blatantly obvious that I had badly fractured my arm and would have to get it fixed promptly. What would you imagine happens in that type of situation? That a top club like Celtic would have a doctor on hand, special transport and rush you to the best private hospital for immediate care and attention? No chance. They asked me if I knew anyone at the game with transport. The only bloke I knew was a mate, John Viola, most of my friends opting to avoid the hassle of parking a car at the busy football stadium. They put a call out for John over the public tannoy. Thank God he wasn't long in arriving and drove me off on my own to get my arm fixed. Pampered footballers? Life has changed a bit in the last decade, eh?

We ended up getting thrashed 4–1 that day. Celtic were clearly not going to win the League with Rangers heading for a championship that would be the first of a long run. Rangers had continued to invest in their squad which was shaping up to match the best teams in Europe – on paper at least. Still the Celtic board was stuck in the Dark Ages with no great commercial strategy evident. In fact no strategy evident at all. They were badly letting down all their players and, worse, the supporters who stuck loyally by them. Game attendances had been vastly increased the year before but had now dwindled to all-time lows. And still, the board had not settled their obligation to me to pay my signing-on fee. Not the most optimistic of times for the team or myself. That's when Souness came for me a second time.

It had to be admitted, Souness was persistent. Stubborn even. Maybe he had sussed that I had learned to be ambitious with West Ham and had been playing in a top soccer flight free from all the old Scottish prejudices. But just as the world is getting smaller, football in Britain is like living in a one room bedsit – always has been. Maybe he thought my style of play and rejection of pompous folk was the kind of Catholic he needed. Then again maybe he thought I was just crazy enough to be the first Catholic to sign for Rangers and to sign for Celtic's oldest rivals in a blaze of controversy. Normally I am but this wasn't one controversy I was willing to take on.

Yet again, when asked, I had told Souness I wanted £1,000,000. But let me explain a bit more. If he had said yes I would have got my agent, Bill McMurdo, on to the case, negotiating in as many other terms and conditions as he could. When Bill then told me that the best possible offer was on the table – I would have sat down and examined the package as weighed against the personal price. Even then I couldn't see me sign for Rangers.

Don't get me wrong. I understand what Graeme Souness was trying to do and admire him for it. Breaking that old No Catholics rule was a crucial step towards less sectarianism. Since Celtic had been happily playing men of any religion for a long time, Rangers doing the same would move football into the domain of sheer competition and free it more from its religious roots in the city. It would also allow Rangers to sign whoever they thought were the best players, full stop. Thus, years after Mo Johnston eventually became the first Catholic to sign for Rangers, they have a big slice of their squad from predominantly Catholic countries like Italy. Graeme Souness saw all of this and deliberately made it happen.

The £1,000,000 fee was a deal-breaker yet again. Thank God.

So here I was in 1989 now determined to resolve the matter with Celtic regarding my signing-on fee. I had been with them almost two seasons and still I was getting nothing but deaf ears back from the board. Inevitably, that resulted in harsh words between myself and Billy McNeil.

Rumours were rife in the press that I had been demanding a transfer back to London. That was simply not true. But it was the case that both Arsenal and West Ham had been showing interest in me. In fact, John Lyall of West Ham had stayed in regular touch with Celtic and asked that he get first refusal if I was ever on the market. Billy McNeil knew all of that of course, and he also read the press who were now well off beam, stating that I wanted to go live with Jenny Blyth in London. Added to my growing anger at being cheated over my signing-on fee, McNeil had just signed striker, Tommy Coyne, from Dundee. Things were bound to come to a head.

Early in March, I was dumped in the reserves and headed for a set-to with McNeil. We ran over all the old issues regarding Celtic's breach of contract and I could feel that no progress was being made. At the end of the meeting, Billy McNeil said that he would raise my complaints as a matter of urgency with the board. I'd heard all of that before. He then asked me not to go to the media. It was a fair request, I thought. Journalists had now fully cottoned on to the fact that there was trouble between us, but not the reasons. If McNeil was to get some progress from the board, it would be ruined by me spilling the beans publicly. I agreed to say nothing to the press and the meeting ended.

The next day, a Friday, the sports pages in all the newspapers were splashed with an interview with Billy McNeil. McNeil claimed that I had repeatedly asked to leave Celtic. That I had made unreasonable demands. That there was some plot to force Celtic to sell me to a London club. That Bill McMurdo, my agent, had orchestrated this plot and I had been faking a lack of fitness. And McNeil's reason for this tirade? Within an hour of our meeting ending, an unnamed London club had phoned him to enquire about me. Yet Billy McNeil was more aware than anybody that West Ham and Arsenal had kept in regular touch with Celtic about wanting to buy me.

It was all lies and I considered myself well and truly stabbed in the back by Celtic. At the time I was furious with Billy McNeil for duping me. Asking me not to got the press then going there himself. Conveniently, there had been no mention of the ongoing dispute which was the real cause of our fallout. At the time I was angry with McNeil but have since realised he was simply trying to keep his job and cope with a board who must have been nigh on impossible to work with. Poor guy. Such a football brain shouldn't have to bother with such petty bureaucrats.

It was the finish between me and Celtic. I was on the way out. But first there was a game to play against Heart of Midlothian in the quarter-finals of the Scottish Cup. McNeil had the nerve to put me on the team sheet. No way could I play. After what he had said to the media, the fans would hate me. On the day, I was picked to go on from the start. No way was I going to play. Then Tommy Craig, assistant manager and a sound man, had a word with me. Tommy was a football man through and through who could so easily imagine how I was feeling.

'The supporters will slaughter me,' I pled.

'Aye, maybe but there's only one place to deal with that. Out there on the park.'

He was right, of course. Football wasn't about contracts, sponsors and self-satisfied gits sitting as board members. It was about the ball, the teams, skill, effort and going for goal. Tommy knew the only place I ever felt safe was on a football field. If I didn't go on to the turf now, I would never be able to go back in front of the green and white ever again. Out I went.

It was bloody awful. The Celtic supporters booed every time I got near the ball, made up chants telling me to fuck off and die – the very group I had belonged to since my earliest memory were disowning me in public, in the very worst place – at a Celtic game. I did the only thing I could do – kept running, kept trying, while failing to block out the messages of hate ringing round the stadium.

It happened gradually. A good move here produced a pitter-pattering of lonely applause there. A shot that rattled the goalkeeper and an expectant moan slipped from gaping mouths as the boys thought the ball was net-bound. A dribble past three defenders and through ball to a teammate and I heard it.

MACCA MUST STAY!

MACCA MUST STAY!

So it rolled on, louder and louder, till the end of the match that we won. When I ran off from what I feared would be my last game for Celtic, I paused and gave the viccies to the main stand. A big FUCK OFF! but not to Billy McNeil – my hero once and still – but to the board members who might have noticed, that is, the ones who could remember my name.

It was not my best game and it was my best game. I hated being forced away from my boyhood team. I loved the bond between me and the terracing. If I had refused to play we would never have made up. But I had to play and I did play, thanks to the wise Tommy Craig. I had never fallen out with Celtic the football team or the support – never could, never would. It would be like turning my back on my family. I had fallen out with the Celtic board of that time. A bunch of tightfisted, shortsighted prats who didn't deserve the Celtic and let down the supporters at every turn.

The following week I met up with John Lyall about transfer talks. It was good to see the man again. John had been showing interest in signing me back for some time – it was wonderful to feel wanted. It reminded me of a suspicion I had when I was transferred from West Ham to Celtic. At the time, there was no obvious reason why that transfer should go ahead. But I believed John Lyall had let me go because he is a football man through and through. He knew that I had been affiliated to Celtic from childhood, that they needed to pull out something special in the centenary year and suspected that I might just play my best football there that year. That's what John craved most – good football. Over a long chat it was clear that I saw no impediment at all to signing for West Ham though they had still to agree a transfer fee with Celtic. As the time drew on I had to end the meeting, explaining I was to go and see someone.

'Who?' John asked.

'Arsenal,' I replied truthfully.

'No,' he almost moaned and his face folded in disappointment.

'Don't worry, John,' I said, 'there's only one team I'll sign for.'

George Graham was then the high-flying manager of Arsenal. I knew about Graham's football career and progress as a manager but had never met him and didn't know what he was like as a person. So, I had phoned a few men who did. Kenny Dalglish, Graeme Souness and Charlie Nicholas – not a bad line-up of football expertise. After they had all given me their spiels I concluded that George Graham had a good tactical brain but couldn't handle characters with a bit of individuality. His team played effective but often boring football and that reflected the manager's approach. More than one of my advisers reckoned that for the first two months I would be George Graham's blue-eyed boy then he'd shit on me from a height. I had had enough of that to last me a lifetime. But I had committed to speak to him so I did.

George Graham spoke with the self-assurance of a man at the top. But at times he overstepped the mark. He told me he had been interested in signing my old West Ham striking partner, Tony Cottee, but the deal fell through because Tony had apparently asked for too much money. Naturally, I asked how much Tony had been after. When George Graham told me, I stood up and headed for the door.

'I'll give you your answer tomorrow George,' I said.

'Where are you going?' he demanded, perturbed that the meeting had ended so abruptly.

'Tramp,' I replied truthfully and waltzed out of the place heading towards the nightclub. No point in coming to London without having a good time.

If I were a hard-headed, pragmatic sort of guy there would have been no choice – Arsenal. They were sitting right at the top of the league, looking likely champions. They had the backing and resources to go far in Europe and sustain a top three position in England for years. West Ham were right at the bottom of the league, heading for relegation and there was very little time to turn around those fortunes. If they did go down they would find it very hard to climb up again, being in competition with some clubs in the Second Division richer than they were.

But I'm not a hard-head. I'm an emotional sort of guy who listens to his heart. The next day, I travelled to Glasgow, packed a case and my boots, and set off south for my new team. I was going home to West Ham. Where else?

HAMMERED (1989)

The week I signed again for West Ham I got engaged to Jenny Blyth. I was on a high, feeling good, looking forward to my return to Upton Park – so, a man gets careless and then things happen.

The trouble is, certain newspapers made a song and dance about the engagement, as if I were in love or even planning to get married. It's my own fault, of course, because I let them. Well, what do you say when a journalist, his tape machine whirring in your face, asks you if a certain woman is the love of your life and that same woman is cuddling your arm and beaming at the world, more dazzling than the diamond ring she's flashing? You say, 'Of course she is,' don't you? You say, 'She's the only woman for me,' and end up letting them write what they want to write. What was I going to say? That I had asked her if she wanted to get engaged but I hadn't asked her if she wanted to get married? That those are two quite separate questions? That I'd been engaged more times than I could precisely remember? Tell the truth? No bloody chance. She would have given me hell and so would the media.

I was back in town. At £1.25 million I was the most expensive signing in the history of West Ham. They were paying me £2,200 per week, my highest pay cheque ever and so it would remain. And they didn't quibble, didn't cheat on any deals. Like the decent folk they were.

I was on the squad for the very next game, against Aston Villa away and we started with a win. But the credit lay with a new player, a young fellow by the name of Paul Ince playing in midfield. The boy took the ball, carried it almost 50 yards and scored. Even in my carefree state I suspected he might have some talent. But it was West Ham's first league win in two months and loads of folk

164

were getting carried away, reading it as an omen of my return. The press seemed to be interviewing me every two minutes and, of course, I agreed with what they were saying, talking up a positive vibe for West Ham's prospects of survival. Well, that's what it sounds like in retrospect but I truly believed we could stay up. There is only one place for the Hammers – in the top flight.

It was good to see a whole heap of familiar faces. Mark Ward, Tony Gale, Alvin Martin and stacks of others. Also Allen McKnight had moved to West Ham from Celtic a while before. So there were loads of friends. There was also a new face apart from Paul Ince. Well not so new really, given his age, but Liam Brady was a charm. While his legs slowed him down, his silky touch and football intelligence were alive and kicking. As was his sense of humour. He had a laugh that started somewhere in his boots and rumbled through his body. Liam was a talent who could show you a thing or two sitting in a wheelbarrow. Well worth the admission fee alone. So in spite of the likes of Tony Cottee moving to Everton for £2,000,000 this squad was looking good. John Lyall had done a great job yet again within his limited finances. It was a puzzle to know why West Ham were lodged at the bottom of the table.

Jenny and I saw a lot more of our favourite friends and places. We visited Maria Whittacker and her boyfriend, Jason Wright, a great deal at their home in an exclusive estate out in Hornchurch, Essex. One day we were there for Sunday lunch or what not. Jenny and I had been talk-ing about buying a house together. In spite of my still having my bungalow she refused to move into it because I had lived there with Anita. The houses in that Hornchurch estate were extortionate but I calculated that a hefty mort-gage would be less expensive and a better investment than all the plush hotel bills I was paying.

After lunch, we spotted that the house opposite Maria and Jason's was empty and had a 'For Sale' sign stuck in the lawn with a 'Sold' label across it. We had been getting major hassle from the press since my return to London and they were particularly keen to know where we were going to live. I had an idea.

One phonecall to a certain bestselling tabloid later and Jenny and I were posing outside the house in Maria and Jason's street. Next day there was a full-page spread about how we had bought a 5-bedroomed love nest in Hornchurch across from Maria Whittacker. I have often wondered how the actual buyers would have felt if they had spotted their brand new home splattered across the newspapers. Hope they didn't mind but it kept the media away from the question of where we were going to live – for a while at least.

A short while later we did buy a £450,000 house in the same estate – just a different one. We moved lock, stock and barrel including Ziggy, of course, and a wolfhound called Spartacus. The two dogs were given their own room – fully decorated, fitted carpet and with comfy sofas. I loved those dogs and they took better care of their room than some famous guests I've had, I tell you.

The West Ham supporters had greeted me back with their usual warm enthusiasm in my first home game when an extra 10,000 came through the gates at Upton Park. They continued to treat me like the prodigal son even though I wasn't scoring a hat trick every game. However, the fight against relegation wasn't working out for West Ham in spite of everybody's best efforts. With seven games to go it looked bleak. The old master, John Lyall, moved defender Julian Dicks into the central midfield with Tony Gale and suddenly we were winning again – four games on the trot and a few positions up the table. When Everton thumped us 3–1 they left us with it all to do. Two games left and we would have to win them both.

The second last game of season 1988/89 was against Nottingham Forrest then third top of the league. Backs against the wall we took them by 2–1. Now it was one game and we had to win it. If we won, West Ham were safe and Aston Villa relegated. If we lost or drew – we were going down. It was all up to us. The She Bitch in the Sky was playing tricks against us once again. Not content to set up a humdinger of a nail-biting finish, she had also dished us up Liverpool for that last game. Not only against title-chasing Liverpool but also in Liverpool. There's nothing like making it hard for yourselves.

Liverpool were still managed by my all-time hero Kenny Dalglish. The same guy who had broken Hammers' hearts by stealing the League title from us in 1986 with one solitary goal. Here we go again.

The first half was even with play moving fast and furious and the score line at 1–1. In spite of Paul Ince being taken off at half-time through injury we believed we could win the game. Liverpool had other ideas and ran out 5–1 winners. That was it – we were down.

After the match, Kenny Dalglish went public, saying that West Ham were a great club and didn't deserve to be relegated. Fine words and well received but in truth we had been masters of our own fate. We left our revival too late and had disappeared for the most important 45 minutes of football we played all season. Do that against Liverpool and they are likely to crucify you – and they did.

Defeat does not sit easily on my shoulders. A one-off, four goal thrashing in a mid-season game is likely to send me hiding at home licking my wounds. But this game was the mother and father of all double whammies, made all the worse by my conviction that we could have – should have – taken Liverpool. What about the Hammers' supporters? Only three years before I felt their buzz of optimism as they believed they could be champions and here they were contemplating the Second Division. Just as the team had lifted them in 1986, we had let them down badly in 1989.

That night, bleak in my thoughts, did I contemplate what life might have been like for me if I had signed for table-topping Arsenal instead of relegated West Ham? Not for one second. Those questions were for the pundits, not for me. There was only one team in England for Frank McAvennie – West Ham – and I would take the rough with the smooth.

I visited Thomas Cook and gave them my summer itinerary. A few weeks in the sun and I'd be back training. We were going to go straight back up to the top next season if I had anything to do with it.

During that break, Jenny and I paid a visit to Mo Johnston, still living and working in France. It was a short visit to take in a Simple Minds concert. Both Mo and myself were good friends with, as well as big fans of, Jim Kerr and the band. It was going to be a great time. A wee incident happened that gives you an idea of Mo the man. As we were all getting ready to go to the concert, I left Jenny in our room to fetch something from outside. There I found Mo crouched down at the window of our bedroom peering in. I'd left Jenny showering and changing so had a good idea what he was looking at.

Jenny might have been a topless model and occasionally gone further but that was work and there was something unacceptable about Mo's behaviour. Just like I would with any girlfriend I didn't want some bloke doing the Peeping Tom on her as she dressed, oblivious to his attention. That was private. The urge went through me to punch his lights out.

'Jesus, Frank,' Mo said, realising I was there, 'she's got a fucking great pair of tits.' And he walked away, casual as you like, back into the house. That was Mo. He just didn't see anything wrong with secretly spying on his mate's girlfriend. Generally accepted boundaries didn't apply to him, or so he thought. You either tolerated his ways or you didn't have him as a friend. On that occasion I decided to let the matter drop.

The Simple Minds concert was superb. The band had reserved us seats right in the centre of the venue where the sound and light men are situated. From there the quality of the music was out of this world – better than any fancy sound system at home. The crowd went crazy for Simple Minds who played numerous encores. The concert ended and we joined the band for drinks. They were so hyped-up, buzzing on the adrenalin, and they reminded me of how I would feel immediately after a hard fought victory when I had played to the top of my ability.

Some time later we all went out to the tour bus. The idea was that we would all travel the 20-minute drive back to Mo's house where we would be joined by a stack of others for a party. The luxury coach was well provided, with fridges full of booze of every description. If they introduced these facilities to public transport I would never drive a car again. About two hours later we still hadn't arrived and somebody asked if the driver knew where he was going. When we checked with him we found him slumped in his seat, totally pissed out of his skull and the bus hadn't moved one inch. Some night – it's the only time I've partied on a bus.

A while later in the summer, I read an announcement that Mo was going to sign for Celtic. The papers were full of articles about Celtic being unhappy at losing the previous season's title to Rangers and at losing my services. News to me. The board could have ensured my continued commitment very easily and I'm sure at less dough than it would cost them for Mo. Just to confirm the move, photographs of Mo fully kitted out in Celtic gear were appearing in every newspaper. It seemed almost the next day that the front pages of the same newspapers carried the headlines that Mo had signed for Rangers. At last they'd found a Celtic player mental enough. Now he'd done it.

Dangerous enough that he became the first Catholic to sign for that team and he had been a former Celtic favourite, but to publicly announce he was signing again for Celtic only to cross the city. It was obvious that whatever had happened behind the scenes, Celtic supporters were going to see his actions as utter betrayal. Under normal circumstances, playing for Rangers or Celtic means that half of Glaswegians think they own you and the other half hate you. These were worse than normal circumstances. Mo Johnston's life was never going to be the same again.

Mo didn't see the big problem. I haven't entirely worked out why he signed for Rangers – aside from money, of course. On reflection, I believe it was for the same reasons that he thought it okay to spy on a mate's girlfriend as she stripped off. Mo just didn't accept any limits to his own behaviour. At the end of the day, Mo Johnston did what he wanted. Full stop.

He and I began to grow away from each other around that time. Apart from anything else, his life was now marked with taking care from vigilante Celtic supporters and hardline Rangers fans, both equally unhappy that he, a Catholic, was playing for Rangers. The freedom that he had taken in his life was now severely restricted because of a liberty he pursued. Ironic and a shame. There were other ways that Graeme Souness could have signed a Catholic player. It didn't have to involve such a well known guy as Mo and raise such feelings of hatred in the East End of Glasgow.

Before I returned for pre-season training I heard the news. West Ham had sacked their loyal servant John Lyall after 15 years. I felt as if a member of my family had died. John was a football man who took a personal interest in the welfare of the most junior as well as the most senior players. He loved the game and would have done the job for nothing just to see football played at its beautiful best. He was also the man who had given me my big breakthrough and hung on in there, wanting me back. You can't lose someone like that and fail to feel grief.

There was a buzz of speculation about who might replace Lyall. Most of the players favoured an internal promotion of someone like Billy Bonds or Tony Carr. I kept an open mind. As long as the club didn't lose its commitment to style and good football, I didn't care who the new boss was to be. Though John Lyall's sacking upset me, you learn fast in football that it's a hard business. One minute someone might be an all-time hero, the next they are out the door. It's harsh but it's the way the game is run. Whoever the club appointed as manager I'd give them my best. Any less would be to cheat myself, the supporters and be disrespectful to guys like John Lyall who had stood by me.

When they announced Lou Macari was to be the new boss of West Ham I thought it was an interesting appointment. Macari had been a top player with Celtic then Manchester United, before becoming manager at Swindon Town. As a player he had been in successful teams who concentrated on skill. Naïvely I assumed that was how he was as a manager.

From the first day of meeting him, I knew there was going to be a problem with Macari. He is a small guy but cocky and confident in himself, willing to take on anyone. Very typical of street guys in Glasgow. The trouble is, I think he had a problem with his ego. What I mean is that he demanded respect instantly. Now respect has to be earned in my book. Listening and watching him deal with the West Ham players I just knew he was heading for deep waters. These guys were used to being managed by a bloke they all respected as a human being, never mind as a manager. The players were used to being spoken with, not at. Now there's this new guy who demands that they just forget all that and bow to him – even though he didn't have a track record worth speaking about.

Macari was a disciplinarian who liked to give orders. Looking back, the West Ham board should have anticipated this. At Swindon Town, Macari had produced not a half-bad team but the emphasis was on fitness and strength. Now here he was at West Ham, the Academy of Football, applying the same values. The boys did not appreciate it one bit. But we buckled down and gave him the benefit of the doubt. There was a football season about to start and a small matter of winning promotion back into the First Division right away.

The first game of season 1989/90 was against Stoke City away and I was looking forward to it. Now I would be part of the West Ham team for a whole campaign, not just a couple of months desperate fight for survival. Looking at the good players in the squad I was confident we could win the championship. I knew the Second Division was going to be harder than it sounded in theory but reckoned we could take Stoke and start our promotion fight with a bang. Travelling to the match I was grinning all the way.

It was a hard-fought game. Not vicious or violent, you understand, just tight, with every ball being contested. When the tackle came I went straight down. Pole-axed. I'd used that phrase before but didn't realise till that day what it really meant. Stoke's Chris Kamara had come straight into me, crumpling me to the ground. It was the same Chris Kamara who had been the first footballer to be found guilty of a criminal offence for actions on the field of play – the day before my own trial ended. As he stood over my prone body, Kamara spat, 'Get up, you Scottish bastard. This is a man's game.' If I could've got up, I would have belted him.

Rob Jenkins, West Ham's old physio, sprinted on to the pitch carrying his bag of tricks. I'm spread out on the grass. There was no pain but I simply couldn't budge. Rob looked at my injured leg and I saw his face go sickly white. He fussed over it a little while then asked, 'Can you get up and walk it off, Frank.' West Ham's George Parris hovering nearby heard and intervened.

'For fuck's sake, Rob,' said George, 'his ankle is hanging the wrong way.' And it was. Dangling loose, like it would fall off any minute.

The stretcher arrived and I was carried off. As they hefted me towards the dressing room I was looking over my shoulder bawling at my team mates, 'Get that bastard,' and jabbing my finger at Chris Kamara. People assumed that I was angry with him because I believed he had deliberately smashed my leg. Not so. I was furious at him for calling me a Scottish bastard and telling me football was a man's game when he knew I couldn't get to my feet to take a pop at him. If I couldn't get back at Kamara my team mates should. I would have, if it was them on the stretcher and not me.

But all that was in the heat of the game and the kind of lip that goes on all the time. You should hear the patter between opposing players as a corner is coming in. Or while a team is setting up a defensive wall as the other is about to take a free kick. It would make a trooper blush.

It's all psychology aimed at upsetting the other team and totally forgotten about after the match. But one look at my leg told me I wouldn't be forgetting about it in a hurry. It looked like it was ruined. Was this the end of my football career?

LOST AND FOUND (1989/90)

As I lay in the dressing room at Stoke, I knew my leg was mashed. The worried faces around me were all the indication I needed. There was no pain, another sure sign that the injuries were extensive. All fairness to the medics of Stoke, I'm sure they are excellent, but I decided that if I was going to have a limp for the rest of my life I was going to be sure I got the best possible treatment.

I got the West Ham backroom boys to strap up the leg and off I set for a private hospital in London. There, they confirmed that my leg was badly broken, my ankle shattered and ligaments torn. Say what you like about Chris Kamara but that was some bloody tackle. The following day I spent on the operating theatre having two plates and a bolt inserted through my ankle, another plate in my leg and various other treatments. When I gathered my senses on the Monday I knew I was starting a long process to mend because the agony had kicked in. There was another pain waiting for me too.

The newspapers were full of reports on the severity of my injuries and a claim that I was about to sue Chris Kamara for damages. Great journalism I don't think since I had been unconscious from Saturday night and had hardly spoken to the doctors let alone the press. Lou Macari though was a different matter and I wonder who had given the story to the media, eh? Funny but I hadn't spoken with Lou Macari either. Did they think he had actually bothered to visit me?

There have been numerous inaccurate articles about me over time but this was one that particularly annoyed me. I had no intention whatsoever of suing Chris Kamara. His tackle was just one of those things that happen in football. It might as well have been him in hospital following a sliding crunch from me. But that story didn't go away. Kamara

174

started being plagued with death threats, presumably from Hammers' supporters. No doubt they were already well pissed off that I was going to be out of the game for months but they had been stirred up even more by reports that I was going to have a go at Kamara, if only through the courts. That story was really irresponsible.

After a week in hospital the doctor's prognosis was more optimistic than I thought. He reckoned I would be out till Christmas, then, with a careful build-up, would get back to football as fit as ever. So off I went homewards, plastered from ankle to arse and determined it wasn't going to stop me having a life.

Four months is a long time and I knew I would get dangerously bored if I didn't do something. I decided that since I couldn't train, I would just treat it as an extended holiday and take care of regaining my fitness when I returned to the football. Almost immediately, Jenny and I hit the nightspots. I was on a cocktail of painkilling and anti-inflammatory pills but didn't see why that should stop me from having a few drinks. It was around this time that I started hitting cocaine.

I'd snorted a few lines of coke before – just one-offs as part of a night out. Almost all the people I associated with from modelling, football, the clubs and the music scene did charlie. My first line was from Jenny but I don't want to make any big deal about it. Most of her friends did cocaine. It was seen as the recreational drug of choice and if you weren't carrying it you weren't up to par. For the previous couple of years I had grown well used to going into the toilets at clubs – most often for a fly cigarette – and chatting with guys whose noses looked like talcum powder dispensers. It was so common it was hardly worth commenting on.

The first few times I tried coke I was playing football for Celtic. But they were one-offs and on nights at least a couple of days away from a match, if not longer. I enjoyed the high of coke, finding it made me more talkative, happier, seeing life in a positive vein. I suppose it was close to the kind of security I always found on a football pitch. The comedown of cocaine I found to be much less severe than a rank, booze-fuelled hangover. Coke seemed safe, almost harmless.

Injured and bored, I was in Brown's one night in the company of a clutch of footballers, female friends of Jenny's and a couple of folk from TV and film. It was a good night. Brown's toilets made it easy for snorting coke with broad, flat surfaces. That's how common cocaine was and still is. Having hobbled to the toilets for an innocent piss – honest – I met this guy who was part of our company, cutting himself a line. At the time he was a professional footballer playing at the top. During his career he played at the highest level in England as well as on the continent and he is now a manager. The man asked me if I wanted a line and I said yes. It was just another one-off line of coke, I thought. But it turned out to be the start of a habit.

Some might say I should name the guy who gave me that line. Why? All that will serve to do is to get him the sack and have his lawyers advising him to sue me. How do you prove that the guy gave me cocaine? It was in a toilet, cram-packed with other men snorting at Olympic standard, one or two of whom write for national newspapers. Not exactly full of willing witnesses. Besides, it is up to him to come out as a coke user. My responsibility is to hold my hands up and tell you about me.

If he hadn't offered me that first lead-on line, someone else would have. On a busy night in a London club I'd be offered coke four or five times at least and very often from strangers who simply recognised me. They were just being friendly. The same is true in other British cities except the scale is smaller. To put it in context, I've known certain football teams where you had half of the players doing coke with no obvious detrimental effect on their playing or the team's success. I know people who protect their fitness by being careful about how much they drink and wouldn't

176

dream of smoking cigarettes but do some coke most weeks. Although not daily, you understand. As I could leave the booze alone a night before a match, so they would take some coke then leave it for many days, sometimes weeks. It's called having a good time but avoiding the pitfalls.

The trouble with having nothing to do, nothing to aim for, is that the pitfalls can creep up on you. My life had taken a strange turn. Jenny and I always received invitations to events through the mail every day. Most of them went straight into the bin. Now that I was injured, had no training and no match days, we started to accept the invites. Before long it was becoming a daily routine and we would go to the opening of an envelope.

Jenny Blyth loved that type of thing. The people who attended these events tended to be from the fashion industry, modelling, agents, photographers and journalists for magazines. She was mixing with people she enjoyed. Now we were going out every night and in a wider circle, the media started getting easier access to us and we received that Golden Couple treatment that used to make me blush. But Jenny loved it and said it was good for her career. What career?

When we had first met, she had told me that she earned £150,000 a year. I hadn't asked her, she just offered the information in some conversation. Given that pictures of her were plastered in all the papers at that time I saw no reason to doubt her word. But when we started living together it became apparent that she earned next to nothing. It seemed that she would earn maybe a grand per photo shoot – not bad for a few hours work even with your kit off – but the consignments would be far and few between. None of that bothered me at the time. I was earning more money than I had ever dreamed I would and money was for one thing – spending. But Jenny was keen on enhancing her career by making the right contacts so I was quite happy to foot the bills and trek along with her to every event we were invited to.

Coke was rife in those circles, of course, and I began to participate more and more. Still not a big user, I had started buying it from the usual high-class dealers who were always around those kind of events. All the dealers seemed to have public school accents and other legitimate jobs. They were a world apart from the gun-carrying heroin dealers who stalked the streets of the East End and every city in the country. The cocaine was bloody expensive, costing a couple of grand a score. I knew this because I had already been subsidising Jenny's coke consumption for quite a while. The thought occurred to me that I might as well get some pleasure out of it, too.

Photographs were now appearing of Jenny and I in the tabloids with greater frequency. Some of my suits I regret now but they were just the ticket back then. Sometimes a picture would appear of me and some model in some nightclub with suggestions of an affair. Invariably they had airbrushed Jenny out to create the effect and make a story out of nothing. Jenny would throw a bloody tantrum every time but I just thought it was a laugh. That was a big difference between us. She took her image as seriously as I did but she was determined that her efforts be seen as widely as possible. All superficial stuff and something I couldn't get too worked up over.

By December I was almost ready to go back to football and I was looking forward to becoming a player again. I started cleaning up my act, cutting back on the nights out and dropping the coke. It was an old routine of getting ready and fit and one I could cope with easily. The doctors said that the plates in my ankle and leg would have to stay there for the rest of my life. I didn't like the sound of that. It made me feel weakened and a dead cert to be pulled up every time I walked through the x-ray machine at airports. I could do without that. So I made arrangements to have them removed at some time in the future and went back to Upton Park, keen to get on with my profession.

My first day back was Christmas Eve, 1989. The doctor

had been clear that I would need to be helped to build up my strength gradually. It was a relief that I was able to walk never mind play again, and I was willing and ready for any long haul. But Lou Macari, West Ham's manager, had other ideas. On my first day back, he ordered me out with him on a run. Just the two of us. An eight-mile run and he pushed and harangued me all the way. Before the end of the circuit, my leg had broken down, of course, and I was set back further than I had been when Chris Kamara had kicked me.

At the time I was angry as hell with Macari. What was it with him? You would think he would have been pleased at the prospects of a top player returning to duty. I reckoned then it was personal and believe I was right. Macari didn't like the pop star treatment the media had been giving me during my injured spell and feared I might be too big for my boots. So right away he was going to show me who was boss. An eight-mile run would do it. And it did. It did for me.

The doctors told me to forget about the rest of the season. If four months had been a long gap this was going to be hell. There's nothing more depressing for a footballer than not being able to kick a ball. The bastard had condemned me to a kind of purgatory. So I took to the bottle big time and even stopped going to the West Ham games because they were leaving me feeling so bereft at not being on the field. If Jenny wanted to be seen in every hot spot I was her man. A magazine want an interview? Sure, what do you want to know? Fancy a line of coke? Here, have some of mine, I always carry. Well, I did from then on in.

As I licked my own wounds I was getting depressed over West Ham's fortunes which were not looking good at all. Thrashed 6–0 by Oldham it seemed that they were doomed. When Lou Macari lost his post in February 1990 there was no great celebration for me. He had been given the reins at a club I loved and failed to achieve sod all. Nothing to cheer about there. West Ham then appointed old boy Billy Bonds as manager and I thought the future looked more cheerful. Bonds had been a magnificent player, a legend of the Hammers and was used to our ways, our standards. The future suddenly seemed brighter for the club and it irked me that I would have to sit it out for so long. That eight-mile run haunted me even more.

I had stopped being a footballer and become an escort and a good time guy. That is all. We even went to Tunisia for some TV holiday programme. That was one of the better deals – being paid to lie in the sun and stay in one of the top hotels. The luvvies from the media world had us marked down as flavour of the month and we were constantly available. So, when they asked we appeared. The more we appeared, the more they asked. It was a hoot looking back but it was also temporary redundancy and dangerous with it, especially for a footballer. Think of great players from the past who went to pieces as soon as they hung up their boots. There are far too many. For me, this injured spell was a version of that effect. In all the newspaper cuttings of the time I look as if I was having a great time and I was, under the circumstances. But the wide grins hid an ache to get my boots back on and onto that park. Upton Park.

As the months wore on I was on the piss seven nights a week. One night on my own in Stringfellows I met Elton John. Elton was a big football supporter and chairman of Watford at that time. After a few drinks a whole group of us went back to his house. To this day I can't remember where that bloody house was but I do remember the sheer luxury of the place. Elton is made out to be some gifted drama queen. Gifted he certainly is but I saw no signs of the famed hysterics that night. Through the early hours of the morning, as the party raged around us, we sat in a corner talking the universal language of football – a welcome break for me given some of the company I had been keeping. Elton was a generous host with drinks of any kind available on demand and lines of the best coke I

Frank confronts Chris Woods and Terry Butcher in his Old Firm debut and suggests they come and have a go if they think they're hard enough … they do. And Frank is grounded (courtesy Scottish Media Newspapers Ltd)

A disconsolate and sent-off Frank is thanked by manager Billy McNeil for his 12-minute contribution to proceedings… while proceedings of another kind follow as Frank is charged with criminal offences committed on the field of play (above left courtesy Scottish Media Newspapers Ltd, above right courtesy *Daily Record*)

We're all off to sunny Spain: Frank celebrates the avoidance of a holiday cancellation. And a Double for Celtic (courtesy *Daily Record*)

The rest of the centenary squad learn about Frank's holiday good fortune (courtesy Scottish Media Newspapers Ltd)

Above The Butcher of Ibrox leaves
Frank on his aria with a broken arm
(courtesy *Daily Record*)

Right Frank and Terry Butcher audition
for It's a Celebrity Knock-Out (courtesy
Scottish Media Newspapers Ltd)

Put your Huns in the air: Frank celebrates a strike against Rangers (courtesy *Daily Record*)

With Laura,
ex-wife and mother
of son Jake (courtesy
Scottish Media
Newspapers Ltd)

Above Frank takes detention at the launch of School Dinners (courtesy Scottish Media Newspapers Ltd)

Right Not to be sniffed at: free scented candle offer... (courtesy *Daily Record*)

Frank signs for life… Karen is happy with the terms

Above You Winstone, you lose some: Frank and Ray try to impress Helen Chamberlain of Sky's Soccer AM

Above right Kerr-ful, that's my wife, Frank tells the Simple Minds frontman

Right I'm A Celebrity, Take My Photo: … with John 'Fash the Bash' Fashanu

Below East End boy meets the lads from Westlife

Above Son Jake with Frank's father Bernard

Above right Wife Karen (courtesy George Wright, geo@wrightmedia.co.uk)

Below The happy family

had ever had. To this day I don't remember getting into his limo. All I can recall is stepping out of it at my front door. Elton John – top host who knows a fair bit about the beautiful game.

The doctor gave me the all clear to go back to football in the summer of 1990 – thank God. As soon as he told me the god news my mindset changed. All at once I was Frank McAvennie footballer again. Sessions on the piss were cut back, training started, the occasional early night in bed and the coke put aside as an occasional treat. I even cut back on the fags.

These changes in my lifestyle irritated Jenny. She had become used to the self-promoting razzle-dazzle circuit we had participated in so enthusiastically and wasn't for giving it up. Too bad. I would still go with her to some of the events and always had nights out at Stringfellows, Brown's or the Hippodrome but I was no longer available for any snapper who asked. Invitations were refused more often than accepted. Magazines couldn't expect to get free access to our home. Jenny didn't like those changes to her lifestyle one bit.

Some night as we left Brown's a photographer from a well known tabloid stepped up and started to take pics. Before the first flash lit the dark pavement Jenny was posing, all teeth and tits and naked thighs, her arm grasping mine.

'No pictures, mate,' I growled at the photographer who hadn't had the manners to ask.

'Oh, come on, Frank,' he pled in a kind of parental, humouring-the-child sort of tone. They had become too used to me saying yes to everything.

'Fuck off!' I blurted, getting suddenly angry. 'I'm a fucking footballer not a model!' And with that I shrugged Jenny from my arm and headed away.

That summed up the change in me she hated most. Now that I was allowed to play again, I was a footballer once more. I needed to see myself as a footballer, think night and day that that's what I was, escape the rigmarole of celebrity poseur and replace it with the preferred choice of striker for West Ham. While I played I knew how I saw the world, with a balance between the serious discipline scattered with the delinquent I am. All I was doing was reverting to type. Jenny hated it.

That night she harangued me on the pavement. Lost the place and stamped her little kitten heel. All I can recall of the conversation was that most her sentences started with, 'I want . . .', 'My career . . .', and 'I need . . .'

Or at least it seemed that way. I don't row in public. Quietly, I waited till we got home and then I spoke out. She could continue with her self-promotion. From time to time I'd go along with her. But as of then I was the same person who she had first met – a footballer who likes a good time. She accused me of being selfish and maybe she was right but we had given a whole year to her type of work and it had produced nothing in the way of new contracts for her. In fact she was working less often. All that had happened is that as a couple we had hogged a slice of the limelight. In sheer earnings, Jenny was taking in less a year after we had set up home together than when we first met so what good had any of our poncing around achieved? She should continue with her career and I'd give her every support.

It was a top-class row that ran on for ages. I thought it had cleared the air and settled matters. God, how wrong I was.

THERE'S EAST THEN THERE'S EAST (1990/93)

My return to West Ham was slow and tenuous. This time there was no hassle with inappropriate runs and my fitness slowly but surely returned. Billy Bonds was still in charge and the team had changed a great deal, building on the close call the season before when they had missed the play-offs for promotion by just a couple of points. By November I was playing close to my old form and scored the only goal against Portsmouth to take West Ham to the top of the Second Division for the first time that season.

At home things were not great. Jenny and I had started to row almost constantly. The standard routine would be for her to start niggling at me while we were in some club. I'd take it, having a real problem about fighting in public but on our own it was an entirely different matter. At first it just felt like a passionate relationship. Fierce rows followed by making up in bed. Jenny would try and take advantage of this sometimes. When we were heading back from the club in the back of a taxi, and I would be letting loose for the bad time she'd been giving me in public, she'd slip her panties off – trying to divert my rage. It worked – in the beginning – but it wouldn't work forever.

Increasingly Jenny was at some do or yet another opening. Fine by me as we had agreed that we should both pursue our separate careers in whatever way necessary. I'd long given up expecting her to actually bring home some dough but she was always full of some optimistic chat about new contracts, TV roles and the like. None of it ever came to much and I had now accepted that most of the time she was just socialising with friends. A 1990s version of ladies who lunch. All show and no substance.

I had taken to going out on my own to a local pub fairly regularly for a drink of a night. Just a few quiet quaffs in a local where they treated me as a human being and not some name. Most nights I'd spot Tony Adams of Arsenal in there. I had known Tony for a while as a competitor and through the usual football circles. He always seemed to disappear shortly after I arrived. I don't know if he was avoiding me or what but it became a bit obvious after a while. Now that we've read his confessions to alcoholism maybe Tony slipping out the side door should be put in context. But he made a bad move.

The guy who owned the hotel knew I loved vodka. He had some source for importing the stuff from all over the world – definitely dodgy. The landlord would invite me out the back after hours for a tasting session. Some of the bottles had a label with just a cockerel on them or a plough – no words, just a picture. Made me worry before the fluid had touched my lips and usually I wish I hadn't since most of the stuff was rank. Powerful, but tasting of bog water mixed with potato peelings. But it was free and new – I could cope with that. If Tony Adams was such a big drinker back then, he could have cut his bar bills down by hanging around in that pub.

Thinking of his confessions to alcoholism, I'm left a bit perplexed. When Tony started out in football he wasn't a great defender. He'd tackle okay and then belt the ball away as hard as he could, not caring too much where it went. It was only over the years – and allegedly through his hard drinking times – that he learned his craft. So too much bevy makes you a better player? Maybe.

When I used to take on big Tony on the park – usually winning the jousts, of course – his breath seemed fine to me. The alcoholics I've known can't get too far out of bed without the help of a bottle. It seems these days you can't be a top footballer without confessing to some type of addiction. It becomes a theme tune with each one singing louder than the other. Like Amoruso of Rangers recently opening his heart to being an alcoholic on a daily intake of Bailey's Irish Cream. That's not a drink, it's a meal.

I don't blame it on the players but their environment. There are too many health fascists in football these days. Too many bloody puritans coaching the teams. So when a player has a drink – it's a problem. Take it from me, boys, it isn't. Like the black stuff from across the water, it's good for you.

One night Jenny and I ended up at a function on this magnificent boat on the Thames. I hate to admit it but it was the launch of The Chippendales, the all-male strip show. You can safely assume that Jenny wanted to go, not me. It was a good night with other entertainment, free drinks and interesting company.

At some point late on in the proceedings, Jenny was up dancing with this guy we didn't know but who had been standing close by to us all night. The bloke starts getting too friendly and his hands are all over Jenny. When her efforts to tell him to cut it out clearly weren't working I jumped in, grabbed him by the collar and threatened to throw him overboard if he didn't stop immediately. All these guys around me starting laughing hysterically. I wondered what the fuck was so funny till I caught a clear look at one. I'd thought I had recognised him earlier but couldn't quite place him. London is like that – too many people moving around. Then it clicked, it was Paul Ferris, the young, baby-faced guy who was credited with running most of the organised crime in Glasgow.

Paul's picture had been on the front page of the newspapers frequently. The guys with him were also beginning to fit into place as members of some of London's top crime families. The bloke who had been taking liberties with Jenny was clearly one of them, was probably carrying a gun and had a profession with something to do with inflicting pain. If I had tried to throw him overboard chances are I'd have ended up wearing the bloody boat.

Fair enough but he wasn't going to mess with my

woman. Thankfully, my stance was appreciated by the guys. That and that most of them were West Ham supporters and young Paul was a lifelong Celtic fan. The buggers had known who I was all along. There was no more hassling of Jenny and we had a good night in the blokes' company. Ever since, I've been on good terms with Paul Ferris coming, across him from time to time. What I couldn't know that night was that it was to prove extremely useful to me in later years.

Round about then Brown's had a little problem. Sitting in there one night it gets raided by the police, big style. There were scores of cops all wearing these flak jackets running round the place with their wee baseball caps on. It was a drugs raid – surprise, surprise. This was a club where they had the best toilets for snorting dope. That wasn't unusual in London. Not only did the police catch the main dealer they also found out that one of the guys in charge had a gun in his desk drawer. Brown's was never the same again.

Season 1990/91 ended with West Ham promoted back to the top division where they belong. A summer in the sun with Jenny and it was time to get ready for the fight for the club to stay up. Life at home had not improved and I was feeling increasingly unhappy at Upton Park. The club had to upgrade the ground to comply with the Taylor Report which was geared to increase safety standards following the Hillsborough disaster. The work was going to cost around £15 million – not cheap. Other clubs were digging deep or selling public shares. West Ham decided they would introduce Hammers Bonds which would cost at least £500 a time and all the investor would get in return was the right to buy a season ticket. Unsurprisingly, the supporters thought they were being conned and, typically, weren't slow to express their views. There were loud protests, demonstrations, pitch invasions, walkouts and even a sit-in on the centre circle. Some of the most faithful supporters in the country were very unhappy and damn few bought the bonds.

The actual football was bloody awful too. Ups and downs all season eventually saw us head for relegation yet again. As all this was going on I became unhappy at how I was being treated. Not played, put aside, back in the team again, brought on into the midfield with little time to have an effect – there was just no clarity in my role, in how the manager saw me. It all added up to me being suspicious of the backroom boys' intent. Then West Ham sent me to a doctor to examine the leg I had injured. I just put it down to one of the many insurance requirements football clubs have to meet. But I was concerned that they sent me to a different specialist from the one who had treated me. This new doctor said that my leg remained badly damaged and I would be unlikely to regain full power ever. Now, he was a highly respected consultant but he had hardly looked at the bloody leg and announced his conclusion after five minutes.

I had been having some pain and was not fully fit. But the business about sending me to a different doctor worried me. So, I made an appointment to see the guy who had treated me after the injury. When I told him what had happened he said I was quite right to come for a second opinion. After a good hour of examinations including a scan as well as an x-ray, he revealed that I had an Achilles heel problem that would mend within three weeks. Hardly a career-threatening injury.

As ever, I was straightforward and blunt about my suspicions with the club's management. Better out than in, I say. Feelings were running high for quite some time but I just sensed that I was right. Eventually, after a heart-to-heart with Billy Bonds, it was agreed that I'd be given a free transfer at the end of the season.

The club refused to honour John Lyall's commitment to give me a testimonial match and offer me a post on the coaching staff when I stopped playing. All that seemed to have been deleted the day John lost his job. Football clubs are like some women I've had the misfortune of meeting

– they only remember what they want to. In the meantime he wanted to be able to use me in the last couple of games of the season. I was sure he wouldn't play me, that I had played my last game for the Hammers.

On the very last day of season 1991/92, West Ham were at home to Nottingham Forrest. My minor injury had cleared up just as my doc had predicted. To my surprise I was named as a substitute. It was commonly known that I had been given a free transfer offer and I reckoned that Bonds wouldn't put me on for a last farewell. Before the game, I shared this view with Mitchell Thomas, a West Ham player and a good guy.

'No, Frank, I think you're wrong. You'll get a run out today,' said Mitchell with conviction. Through a goalless first half I sat on that bench feeling as low as I can get. My last time at Upton Park and I wouldn't even get a kick at the ball. At half-time, I was suddenly told to get stripped and get on for the second half.

'You're replacing Mitchell Thomas,' said Billy Bonds, 'he's taken a knock.' Like hell he had.

I took full advantage of Mitchell's generosity. That day Brian Clough's son, Nigel, was playing centre half for Nottingham Forrest and great things had been predicted for him. I ran rings around him for 45 minutes and scored three goals. The supporters were going wild and chanting my name. I could do no wrong by them and they could do no wrong by me. It was a perfect send-off, a moment to savour for the rest of my life.

A short while later, when officially freed, I was given my files, including my medical file as per procedure. Normally, I wouldn't have opened them, let alone read them. These things tend to bore me easily. But the business about being sent to a different quack was still bugging me so I read the whole lot. There in my medical file was a letter I wasn't supposed to have. It confirmed that West Ham, with the help of their chosen doctor, had intended to officially declare me unfit ever to play again and claim the substantial insurance on me. It was going to be worth a very tidy sum. A lot of money that the club could have used but it would have been curtains for me. Thank God for a suspicious mind sometimes.

All I had to do now was find a team to play for and it wasn't going to be easy. The effect of the Taylor Report at that time meant that there wasn't a lot of money around in England for football players. All the heavy investment was going into football ground development. In a sense, I was a victim of my own success with clubs unable to match or even come near my expected salary. As far as I was concerned, I was fit, was playing as well as ever and was ambitious to keep playing.

Roy Atkinson came for me on a short-term deal with Aston Villa. It was to be a month only, on a week-to-week basis. I enjoyed my time there and appreciated big Ron's style. At the time he was shaping up to spend a lot of money on Dean Saunders. In spite of that he still offered me a long-term contract which I declined. A move had come in for me that was full of eastern promise.

South China sounds like a geographical term most likely found on a map but it was also the top football team in Hong Kong at that time. They offered great money, good terms and a long contract. Sounded ideal – getting paid to play and explore a foreign country at the same time. Perfect.

As the plane swanned through the skyscrapers I was amazed at how close we were to the washing hanging on the lines on the balconies. In the UK, people would start a protest meeting at jumbo jets flying that near to their homes and no one would be keen to live in the flats. In Hong Kong, the folks seemed to think nothing of the noise or the danger and that kind of summed up entirely how I found the people.

Jenny and I collected our luggage and headed for the main foyer of the airport looking for someone with a crude handwritten sign with whatever spelling of McAvennie they had managed to come up with. Ahead of us the place thronged with TV cameras, reporters and rows of cheering faces with that unmistakable mixture of anticipation and excitement carried by young fans. We stopped pushing our luggage trolley and looked behind us. Someone important must have been on the plane and we hadn't noticed. When bouquets of flowers were crammed into our hands it finally clicked that the greeting was for us. That's how we were treated throughout – like stars.

We stayed at one of the best hotels in Hong Kong for the duration, were taxied around everywhere we went and the club picked up the tab for many of our day-to-day expenses. It was great to feel not just wanted but fêted. On the field the standard of football was not great but not nearly as bad as those in Europe assumed at the time. The crowds were appreciative and enthusiastic though not as frenzied as the Hammers or as spirited as the Celtic. It was a good place to be.

The local people thought us off our heads. Bad enough we were a blond couple but we had to go and do things like sunbathe. I didn't care if it was their winter and they felt the chill – a boy from Milton gets his gear off at much lower temperatures than the 80 degrees that it was. Though I picked up next to no language I understood they were calling us mental to our faces on the beach. Well it's a universal concept, isn't it? The one disappointment was the food. Don't get me wrong, it was wonderful but it wasn't your Glasgow carry out. It was different.

The change of environment and climate had cooled things down between Jenny and I for a while. Everything seemed rosy in life apart from one thing. I still felt I had a bit to give to football and wasn't being stretched enough in Hong Kong. I went to the South China management and explained. For a long while they tried to persuade me to stay but with no success. I said that my mind was made up and that I'd leave at the end of the month. They

190

said fine but go now. I'm trying to tell them that it's okay, I'll stay till the agreed period. No, they insisted, we are paying you to leave immediately. A large brown envelope stuffed with cash was pushed across the desk. This one flummoxed me at the time but I realised that it was something to do with their code of honour and keeping face. They couldn't be seen to being left but had to be in control. And when they had made their mind up, it was really made up. It was the first time I had been paid to leave town.

Chased out of Hong Kong with 24 hours' notice. It was more a hassle than dramatic. We had to go straight back to the hotel, pack up, sort out some business issues and catch a flight booked for the next morning. These people didn't mess about.

Once back in the UK, word came through Bill McMurdo that Partick Thistle, the Scottish team that had rejected me all those years ago, were interested in signing me. It wasn't Upton Park or Parkhead but it was a good grade of football and I was interested.

I'd always appreciated the cavalier reputation of Partick Thistle. The chance to gub the bigger teams against the form book made me grin and they were just the boys to perpetrate that sort of impudence. After a good bit of negotiation, the deal was set up. It was a good offer which agreed that I could live on in London, train with a team there and travel up for matches only. Trouble is, when we went to sign the papers, the SFA wouldn't let the contract go ahead. For once, not one of the SFA's petty bureaucrats interfering but me – wanted for offences in Hong Kong.

In the rush to leave Hong Kong, I had omitted to pay my phone bill at the hotel – a matter they took very seriously. This was one of the few expenses the club wasn't covering. As I flew out of the city, the police were being notified of my dastardly deed. As a result, South China FC had held on to my registration as a professional footballer.

Well I wasn't going to go back and collect it, that was for sure. I didn't fancy the jail in Hong Kong. It was only a couple of hundred quid so Partick Thistle had to cough up the dosh before South China would free my registration. A small price but it delayed my signing for Partick for a while.

In the meantime I was invited along to their ground, Firhill, to meet John Lambie, the manager of Partick Thistle. When I arrived I was surprised to find the place heaving with TV crews. I'm wondering what the hell is going on when TV presenter Hazel Irvine comes up and plants a welcome peck on the cheek.

'What's happening, Hazel?' I asked, nodding at the cameras being set up.

'Oh, they're signing somebody,' she replied.

'Who's that then?'

'You, Frank.' I laughed at the whole circus and the unexpected nature of the media presence. 'Great to have you back, Frank,' Hazel smiled. 'You'll keep us in a job for the next few years.'

Everybody seemed to know that there was a publicity event apart from me. But what the hell – I've never been camera shy. I'm dressed up in the Partick strip out there in the centre circle with John Lambie being interviewed. Suddenly my mobile rings and I excuse myself to answer it. I'd recognise that rumble of a laugh anywhere.

'You signed yet?' asked the gentle Irish lilt.

'Eh, no,' I replied, turning my back on the TV crews and John Lambie and moving farther away.

'Do me a favour – don't sign till you talk with me.'

'Okay,' I replied, deliberately keeping my words to a minimum.

'You know where my house is?'

'I'll find it.'

'Good – see you there in an hour.'

'Okay.' I hung up, put my phone away and turned to the TV crews. 'Have you got enough, folks?' I asked. 'It's just I've to go meet someone.' They let me go at that and I left the stadium without saying a word about my phone-call. I was on my way to see Liam Brady, the current manager of Celtic. I was heading east again but this time only as far as the East End of Glasgow.

WEE WOMEN AND WEE MEN
(1992/94)

As Liam Brady and I met at his house to discuss a move to Celtic the TV beamed footage of me in a Partick Thistle top with the commentator declaring I had signed for the Jags. I knew the story would run big in the sports pages of the newspapers the next day. But I hadn't signed for Partick – not yet – and, frankly, there was no competition when Celtic was an option. As I shook hands with Liam on the proposed move to Parkhead I knew there was going to be hell to pay but I simply had no choice. I would have played for the Celtic for free.

Within a couple of days the media had picked up on my move to Parkhead and they were giving me hell as I expected. They had run with the Partick Thistle story too early, probably on the initiative of the club. Okay, I went along with the charade but what would you do if a troop of happy journalists was waiting for you? What the public were never told is that part of the agreed contract with Thistle stipulated that they would let me go if a bigger club came for me. So even if I had signed they would have let me move to Celtic.

I have to admit that much as I love Celtic and admired Liam Brady, I had some problems to sort out in my mind before I finally committed myself. There was the small matter of my unhappy departure a couple of years before and them owing me £50,000 on the breach of contract. That still smarted. Tommy Craig, the Celtic coach who had convinced me to play that last game for the club before I left the last time, was instrumental in getting me back. While the longer-term issues were being sorted out I signed a deal for one month and went about the game.

The media interviewed me about signing for one of the

country's biggest clubs so late in my career. My answer was: 'Well, Mark Hateley's doing really well for Rangers and he's older than me. I think I might have a few goals in me yet.' Big Mark was certainly scoring a stack of goals for table-topping Rangers at the time but he was a good couple of years younger me – he just didn't look it. Obviously, the journalists fully agreed and duly reported the story.

Celtic wouldn't tolerate one of their players living as far away as London so put me up in the Albany Hotel, then one of the best hotels in Glasgow and close to the city's nightlife. I went about taking care of myself and getting as fit as I could. Every week I was travelling down to London to spend time with Jenny, who still refused to come to Glasgow, but things were fast running out of control.

Every time I returned to London some dealer would corner me, telling me I owed them a few grand. The suggestion was made that Jenny had been running up substantial cocaine bills on the strength of my name. I didn't argue. I paid up. It had been going on for years apparently but the bills had crept up to £5,000 and as much as £10,000 a time. A bit hefty for a few weeks' fun and lot more than I was making in wages at Celtic. My top pay cheque in my career was £2,2000 per week at West Ham. We were running through my money quicker than I could earn it. They say that arguments over cash are the biggest reason for the break-up of relationships and I can believe it. In our case it was just one other issue to add to the basketful of problems.

Then there were the minor hassles. Like one time Jenny asked if I could change anything about her what would it be. It's the kind of adolescent chit-chat that adult lovers sometimes fall back into. Jenny was obsessed with her appearance so I knew she wasn't looking for some comment on her education, approach to life or spirituality. She was beautiful, there's no doubt about that, and I had told her more times than I can remember. But she was tiny and I knew she knew and even admitted it. So like some bumbling naïve idiot I said, 'I'd add two inches to your gorgeous legs.' World War Three broke out as the words left my lips. That one raged for bloody weeks. Our relationship couldn't handle even small stuff like that.

Jenny still had the habit of starting rows with me in public. I often drove us to and from nights out at that time, being keen to cut down my drink and curtailing our growing financial difficulties by removing the need for taxis. So, in the early mornings, driving her home from a club, I'd start back at her. The car would rock from side to side with our row. Jenny never seemed to learn that my tolerance level is very high but when pushed over the limit I go spare. Then again maybe she enjoyed the aggro. Who knows?

During this time she had developed an old approach of trying to calm me down. Rather than merely slipping her knickers off she'd slowly strip in the passenger seat as we whizzed up the motorway. The only other traffic on the roads at that time was usually long distance lorries. Some drivers would spot what was going on and draw alongside us, keeping at the same speed, getting a free ogle at Jenny sitting there stark naked. If only one had a decent camcorder or digital camera there would be some interesting evidence of Jenny's little habits. She tried this trick so often, I reckon there were long distance drivers who caught more than one eyeful of her in the scuddy.

With mounting financial pressures as Jenny earned nothing and refused to curtail her expensive habits, the two of us together were a time bomb ticking faster and faster. Being driven home by a friend after a night out in London, the police pulled the car over and charged him with drunk driving. One of the cops was a female and her more senior colleague told her to drive Jenny and me home while others would take our friend to the nick to be charged. This cop didn't like it one bit, I suspect. Maybe she considered being a chauffeuse beneath her calling or maybe she just didn't like folk who have their pictures in the newspapers. Either way she was arrogant as fuck. Talking down to us as if we had just committed some heinous offence rather than having been sitting innocently – though admittedly very pissed – in the back seat of the car. She was asking for trouble.

I can't stand people in authority who push their weight around. Jenny is so full of herself she doesn't like anyone – especially a woman – talking down to her in any way. So we gave the copper lip back and with extras. The cop had another go. We gave her worse. And so it went on, all verbal but increasingly heated till the inevitable happened – we were arrested and hauled off to the station. After a lecture from the desk sergeant and a long delay we were eventually let off with a caution and told to get a taxi home. It was a lucky break. In Scotland I'm sure we would've been done with breach of the peace – especially if the police had been Rangers' supporters. But falling out with the cop was a welcome diversion from being at each other's throats. Welcome, but short-lived.

I've often been asked if any of my girlfriends have had plastic surgery. The answer is only one – Jenny Blyth, when I took her gold credit cards off her. God how she loved those cards and she used them. But we were fast running out of money and she wasn't curtailing her spending – so drastic action was necessary. In fact, the whole affair had ground to a sad end. I told Jenny that we were finished but she didn't seem to want to hear. I was quite happy that she continued living in the Hornchurch house till she found somewhere else but she took that as some kind of licence, a signal that contradicted what my voice was telling her repeatedly and clearly. Jenny Blyth didn't accept no from any one.

The house in Hornchurch was costing around £4,500 per month. But Jenny's spending was eating up all my income and more. I had fallen behind with the house payments and was determined not to lose my home. Negotiations with Celtic were dragging on. I had been signed on a month-to-month contract with eleven games remaining of the season and had scored nine goals. Even on my first game back, against Airdrie in a mud bath at their home ground of Broomfield, Tommy Coyne had scored the winner for Celtic from my header rebounding off the bar. Only away at Partick Thistle was there any awkwardness when they refused to announce my name in the team lists before the game and the supporters spent all their energy booing me. To be expected, I suppose. My play was back on form in all the games they would allow me to participate in – Celtic at that stage having decided to keep me off the list for Rangers games in case trouble erupted once again. Like I would?

But they made me wait all summer before they decided if they would offer me a contract. The break-up with Jenny was so bad I was now avoiding going to London at all. The reception staff at the Albany Hotel were my saving grace. They knew Jenny's voice and sussed I wanted to have nothing to do with her. When she called they'd tell her that I had just gone down to the gym to train or for a swim. Then they would phone my room and warn me. I would speak to Jenny when I wanted to speak to her which wasn't often.

The Albany staff applied the same trick if any of the Celtic management came on the line. But I would talk to them. The media had sussed I was living at the Albany and would float into the foyer trying to catch me up to no good. Around then I was seeing a number of women and wanted to keep that private. Not that there was anything to be ashamed of but I knew the kind of headlines that would appear in the newspapers. Plus, Jenny was busy telling the press that we were still together. It was a recipe for a shock-horror story that would be nine-tenths shite. The Albany crew didn't hesitate. They showed me the way down the stairs to the back door and warned me when the media were hanging around. For months I'd slip out the back, go out on the town, slink back in the same way with some woman and the poor hacks would be sitting all the time, bored out of their skulls, waiting for me to appear.

Around then I met Laura Macarthur at Victoria's in Glasgow – better known locally as Vickies. She was a hairdresser in Glasgow and I wanted to be open about our relationship. But the situation with Jenny and, worse, my continuing financial uncertainty made it difficult to make any plans. If Jenny had found out then about Laura she would have given her the same type of stalking treatment as she was giving me. That was not on. So we spent time together and kept as low a profile as we could.

Finally near the end of the summer, I was offered a long-term deal and a substantial signing-on fee from Celtic. At that stage in my career it should have been unexpected money to put in the bank, invest for the day I couldn't play. But the first thing I had to do was to see the Merchant Bank and pay up £100,000 towards my house in Hornchurch. Almost losing my house was one of many last straws between Jenny Blyth and me. I had been telling her for ages that we were finished, now it was final. I went down to London to talk with her. We had the usual marathon barney in our home and I stayed over. Well, it was my house too.

The next morning, I met Laura and we flew off to the Bahamas together. It was a holiday, long delayed till I had some money. It was only for a week, all the time I had left before the season kicked off. We were two free agents and wanted to spend time together – no problem there. Later, the story would appear in the media that I had spent the weekend shagging Jenny, told her one morning I was going to some business and would be back later in the day only to bugger off with some mystery blonde to the Bahamas for six weeks. It wasn't the media's fault. Jenny had given them this nonsense and she probably got well paid for her exaggerations. It was the first of many, many stories that Jenny flogged to the press.

Over the coming years I would read articles that I was connected to organised crime, carrying holdalls of cocaine wherever I went, and everything else under the sun. All crap from Jenny earning herself a few quid while she took out her vitriol in the only way left for her to get at me. Like I said, not a woman who accepted no from anyone.

The football season started and it was mixed fortunes for Celtic. Liam Brady, a legendary player for Arsenal, Juventus and West Ham, had bitten off one hell of a job. His appointment was the start of some effort by Celtic to catch up with the huge investment in players and facilities at Rangers. It wasn't going to be easy or quick. Liam would need more money and more time. In the meantime, the supporters were getting worked up by the behaviour of the Celtic board and 'Sack the Board' became the most common chant on the terraces of Parkhead. Most days, I felt like joining in. There was confusion and mixed messages about Celtic's ground and the general financial situation at the club. Back in the game, it looked like Rangers were going to win everything going. Not a happy era at Celtic Park.

The time had come to finally settle the business with Jenny. The house had to be sold and all my belongings moved out, including the dogs who were still there. When I appeared at the house Jenny put up the usual show that all wasn't finished. It was now time for calm, clearheaded insistence and I just told her straight for the umpteenth time. But it got too much for me and I decided to get out for a while, clear my head and take refuge in a local pub. Ten minutes after I had ordered my first drink, Jenny arrived wearing a fur coat. Sidling up to me with a smile, she slowly opened the coat, revealing that she was stark naked underneath.

'Am I supposed to be impressed?' I asked, and without waiting for an answer turned to the bar and ordered another drink. She had tried the old trick, a ploy that had worked so often before and now had no effect on me whatsoever.

If I had need of any proof that my feelings for her were dead she had supplied me with the ideal test.

Back at the house she continued to protest that we were still a couple, while blaming me for everything under the sun. It was all getting too much for me. At that point, as I had arranged, a van arrived to take my dog to Heathrow so he could be flown up to live with me in Glasgow. When Jenny realised Ziggy was leaving she knew it was all over and became totally hysterical. All I could do was hitch a lift to the airport with the van driver and get the hell out of there, abandoning a great deal of my stuff. I left, confident that Jenny Blyth would be okay. She was far too selfish to harm herself – and she didn't.

When a long time later Jenny did eventually move out of the house, her friends ripped it bare. I don't mean just removing all the furniture, electrical goods and so on – they tore out the light sockets, broke the taps, smashed the toilet cisterns and sinks. The people who had done this had been both of our friends, or so I thought. One of the guys was repaid with a night in bed with Jenny who made sure I got to hear about it. Like I cared.

In the months after that final separation, many people made sure I got to hear about what Jenny was meant to be up to. According to the rumours she had started working as a call girl. Then I heard she was an enthusiastic member of the lesbian scene. I swore at that one, thinking of all the times when we were together I had tried and failed to talk her into a woman-to-woman romp. Every time a new snippet about Jenny came my way I listened and promptly scrubbed it from my brain. There were too many rumours and I didn't have the time to work out whether any were true. All the while she was going to the media with more and more outlandish stories about me. The media would have sucked up any tittle-tattle I threw them about Jenny but I wouldn't play that game. It just seemed so bloody petty.

I bought a house in Milngavie and Laura came to join

me there. Life was feeling settled, even at Celtic where I was sure Liam Brady would create a great team if given the time and the chance. That season wasn't going to go well for Celtic, that much was obvious. I had some injury to a foot that meant I couldn't play without constant pain-killing injections. An x-ray revealed no damage but the pain was getting worse. A scan showed that I had a broken bone that needed urgent attention. But the team were up against it so for Celtic and for Liam Brady I continued to play on for seven games till we had played Rangers, unfortunately losing. Only then did I go for the treatment.

By October 1993, a defeat by St Johnstone dumped Celtic in fourth bottom place in the League. As an honourable guy, Liam Brady had no alternative but to resign. While that made me sad enough, his replacement was to make me livid. Former bhoy Lou Macari was given the post. Christ, here we go again, I thought.

But football is a business where you can't choose your colleagues. If Macari was the boss I'd give him the benefit of the doubt. Besides he might have learned a bit about man management since his brief spell at West Ham. One thing for sure, I was going on no eight-mile run with him while I had a gammy leg.

Macari brought in loads of new faces. Trouble is, some of them should never have been signed by Celtic, either because they weren't good enough or they simply didn't have the spirit of the club. On the other hand, Macari obviously hadn't read that part of his man management manual about personal grudges being destructive – and he promptly dropped me.

My position had suddenly become uncertain again. But my contract allowed me to leave on a free and in those cash-strapped days that was an attractive option to some clubs. Manchester City came in for me and Bill McMurdo set about negotiating a deal. Celtic were going to let me go and Man City were offering between £3,000 and £4,000 per week. While I was a Celtic boy born and bred, I wasn't going to let Macari treat me like a spare prick in a brothel. Man City were a good team and were offering better wages than I'd ever earned.

One Thursday Macari called me into his office and told me that the Man City deal was on, as if he was breaking news. I had been fully involved in the negotiations all along with Bill McMurdo, of course, and knew more about the offer than Macari. It wasn't his business to know – simply to agree to let me leave which he had already done. Some other matters had to be confirmed so Macari said he would phone that night. No problem, so I stayed in all night but no phonecall was received from him. Next day I went into Parkhead but Macari wasn't there, wouldn't be and couldn't be contacted. Next thing I know I get a call from Bill McMurdo – the Man City deal was off. Lou Macari had been on the phone to Man City and couldn't believe what they had agreed to pay me so he withdrew Celtic's agreement to the move. The vindictive wee shit.

There was no way I could stay on with Lou Macari as manager of Celtic. When in February 1994 Swindon Town, then in what had become the Premiership in England, came for me I was delighted to move. It was a short-term deal till the end of that season. I worked with some really good people like John Gorman, Davie Hay, John Moncur and ended up on the same team as Brian 'Killer' Kilcline who used to give me such doings when he was with Coventry City. Off the park, Brian turned out to be really nice guy, gentle and a good mate – like so many of the truly hard men of football.

Swindon's two main strikers were both out injured and I was brought in as cover. As often happens, the arrival of a new boy – even an old new boy – helped both of them to a sudden, unexpected recovery. But, no problem, I was just put in the midfield. Until, that is, we played against Man United when I was moved up front to spook the hell out of them – given my record of scoring against them. It didn't get us a victory but it was great fun.

203

Another unexpected opportunity was given to me by my time in Swindon when West Ham came to play us. It was weird going out against the claret and the blue, contesting with my old pal Ian Bishop and meeting so many mates. The West Ham supporters were chanting my name like the old days and I wondered how the Swindon supporters felt about that. I felt great. It was my competitive farewell to the Hammers.

I ended that season not knowing if I'd ever play football again and clueless about what to do with my life. I was soon going to be 35-years old, young in human terms but a graveyard age for a footballer. But what else could I do? God, if I only knew what was about to happen . . .

SCHOOL DINNERS AND THE BEST
MOMENT OF MY LIFE (1994/96)

The next season it was back to Scotland and while Falkirk hummed and hawed about signing me, an old comrade came in for me – Jimmy Bone, now manager of St Mirren, the Ralgex Kid himself. My leg had gone and I wouldn't lie to the likes of Jimmy. After it had been smashed at best I might have had 90% fitness, now it was 80% and struggling. I had a daily dose of anti-inflammatory tablets and if I missed them my ankle would swell up like a balloon. So, it was a short-term contract with St Mirren taking every week as it came.

After reaching an agreement, the first task Jimmy asked me to fulfil was a night out for the St Mirren players. Jimmy was a first-class social convener himself and had taught me a great deal about organising nights on the piss when I'd first been at St Mirren – as well as a few things about football. Now was my chance to repay the favour because, as the boss, he couldn't party with the players. The young St Mirren squad were enthusiastic as you'd guess but were all for hitting the high spots in Glasgow. No way. As far as I was concerned Paisley was the team's town and that's where we'd stay. It made me almost nostalgic being back on a bender with the St Mirren squad, out among the Buddies, for the first time for 14 years.

The team's presence in the town attracted some attention from the other revellers, some of whom tried to muscle in on our entertainment. My cousin, Joe Carvill, was acting as custodian, insuring that there were no gatecrashers. A young good-looking woman came to the door of the lounge we were occupying and asked to see me. Joe barred her way.

'But I used to be engaged to him,' she pled her case.

205

'Aye, hen, but who the fuck wasn't,' blurted Joe, finally shutting the door on her face. It turned out it was the lovely Anita Blue and I had been engaged to her. Gorgeous Anita who had been good for me and refused as many offers as she wanted to sell me out to the press. That Joe Carvill is a hard man.

My time with St Mirren didn't last long. It was the end of my playing career and my first team turned out to be my last. I wish I had been fitter, scored more goals and given them more back for the start they gave me. But life doesn't end with football and if I can get any chance to repay St Mirren I certainly will.

Without football I was lost. But I never intended to stay that way. I'd work on TV and radio, commenting on football but got into trouble too often for letting the words move straight from my brain to my lips. On one occasion I said on air that I might never have been picked for Scotland if Jock Stein hadn't died. The next I know the papers are full of stories about me saying that I was glad Stein died when he did so that I could play for Scotland. Not the same at all.

But I was also going to try my hand at business. In London, I was a regular attendee at School Dinners – a club with a difference then. The idea was to replicate the school dinner set-up except you had fully grown waitresses in school uniforms with tiny skirts, stocking tops flashing and blouses unbuttoned to their navels. A headmaster or headmistress would be on hand to keep order and issue instructions. I loved it and so did stacks of the public. It was a moneymaker for sure.

The first club was in London and owned by a guy called John Miller who was a bit of a character. A few years earlier Miller had launched a guerrilla-type expedition to kidnap Ronnie Biggs, the Great Train Robber, from his safe exile in Brazil. While his plot failed, Miller received mega coverage in the media and was soon announcing other plans to find Lord Lucan who had mysteriously disappeared decades before. John claimed to have been a member of the SAS at one time and I used to ask him to prove it. Of course, he couldn't but then neither could anyone actually prove that he hadn't been a member of that crack force. He was a rascal and I knew it. I would say to him that he wouldn't have to search for Lucan long since his shady lordship was probably drinking in one of John's clubs. Yeah, a rogue, but likeable and he knew how to run a club.

Miller had decided to sell franchises to the School Dinner concept allowing others to buy the right to set up clubs in other cities. That was for me. They sold me the franchise for Scotland and the North East of England. Although I reckoned I could have set up in Edinburgh, Newcastle and maybe Aberdeen, I was going to start in Glasgow – where else?

I found some premises on the corner of King Street in Glasgow's city centre and came to a deal with the owners. The School Dinner guys in London were great. We recruited enough good-looking women in Glasgow and then the experienced waitresses and bar staff came up to train them. For the headmaster we had to get someone a bit special. The role wasn't just part of the routine, it was essential to calm things down if serious trouble looked like brewing. I'd had enough experiences of clubs in my life to know that the old-fashioned heavy-handed bruisers of bouncers were the ultimate sanction, to be used only as a last resort. Much better if someone could humour the customers back into line. Eventually, I found a bloke called Willie Johnstone, a gay guy well known on the nightlife scene in Glasgow. This bloke was a character, over the top at times, usually hilarious but scared of nothing and with exactly the right manner. Willie was game as usual and we soon had him kitted out and well into the role.

The next issue was promoting the club. Usually, new ventures would spend a good few quid on advertising but I decided to do it a little differently. We would run two nights only to start with. First there would be a night for the press and media only, free of course. Then there would be a one-off Christmas night for paying punters. Having judged the success of these events we would run regular nights at whatever frequency we believed the interest could sustain.

The first night was a runaway success with the members of the press never slow to take up on a gratis night out, especially with a well stocked bar. The one-off Christmas special was shaping up really well. Word had circulated that I was setting up School Dinners and without trying we had 800 bookings for that first night. This was looking to be an even bigger success than I had hoped. Then the shit hit the fan.

Two days before the Christmas night, the company who owned the building went into liquidation. No warning, no hint, just totally bust. I'm not into panicking but I came close then. There were scores of people who were depending on me for jobs, 800 folk expecting a night out and ten people who had paid big bucks for tickets I'd gifted to some auction to raise funds for Children in Need. Not good.

I went to see the liquidator to try and reach an agreement, quite willing to take a loss just to make School Dinners happen. The guy we met with just listened and shook his head. When we asked an open question about covering the cost of the building he just continued to shake his head. I was offering money to the company to help clear up as much of the building owners' debt as possible. Why the hell weren't they at least listening? I'm sure the creditors would have listened and named a price but not this guy. We were banging our heads against the proverbial shithouse wall. There was no deal discussed and School Dinners wasn't going to happen.

Bad enough that I'd let the future staff down but I wasn't going to allow the ten good folk who'd bought the tickets for Children in Need to go away emptyhanded. If they cared enough then so did I and I booked their flights from Glasgow to London with overnight accommodation at a hotel. In conjunction with School Dinners down south, they had their night out as planned – just a few hundred miles farther away.

One of the prices I've paid for being in the spotlight is that I can't balls up in private. The very factor which meant that everyone knew about School Dinners without much effort from me also meant that the world and his deaf, dumb and blind aunty knew instantly about the cancellation. As usual, people added their own fanciful interpretations to the basic facts and rumours rampaged all over the place – the show was too raunchy, I had been refused a licence, gangsters' money was behind the venture – all pure fantasies and crap. All I could do was tell people the truth whenever they'd let me. Trouble is, rumours are always that bit more interesting.

Still, I persevered and found other suitable premises in Glasgow with the plan to launch School Dinners at a later date. When I met with the police in connection with obtaining a licence, they more or less told me not to open the club. According to the guardians of the law, I was too high-profile and that was bound to attract trouble. Tell me something new, I thought. But I scrapped the idea nevertheless. No point in working on when the cops are shaking their heads long before the off. That would be a recipe for disaster. The whole affair had cost me a bloody fortune and all I had succeeded in doing was giving a free night out to the media. Cheers, folks.

Laura and I had been going steady and, of course, got engaged and the next you know it we were married in St Andrews Cathedral in Glasgow in May 1995. I'm still not sure how that happened or why. Maybe it was all the changes bringing uncertainty into my life and I was looking for something more definite. Maybe it was because I'd always joked that I wouldn't get married till I was 35-years old thinking that was a lifetime away. Now here I was at 35 doing precisely what I had said. But it was only meant to be a bloody joke.

The wedding was a lavish affair, just as Laura wanted. It was the traditional approach whereby the bride's father, in this case stepfather, picks up the bill. Three days before the big day he did a runner to Spain and has never been seen since. Which is just as well because I want a wee word in his shell-like about dumping me with all the costs. But bugger it, I like a party.

On honeymoon, Laura kept putting her feet up and resting though, believe me, she looked fitter than I did. Shortly thereafter she announced she was pregnant.

'I'm not like the others,' she said, a few months into her pregnancy, patting her swelling belly, 'you can't get rid of me now.'

It was a strange way to celebrate a pregnancy but, at the time, I gave her comment little thought. Obviously, Laura was well aware of my reputation. The entire tabloid-reading population of the UK had my number in that respect. So maybe she was only too right to be wary of my history repeating itself. While I had actually made some commitment to her, I was well used to women being concerned I'd be in and out of their lives as well as their bodies. So I just shrugged my shoulders and got on with life as usual. Late night parties, long boozy lunch sessions, leaving an increasingly heavily pregnant Laura at home – I was trying to build up businesses and still leading the life of a lad. Guess that didn't make me a great husband but that's just how I was.

When it was time for Laura to go to hospital I reckoned I'd take it all in my stride. For some reason I was in the company of a friend of mine, a bloke called Matt, a member of the Blue Angels motorcycle gang. A huge hairy guy, he was the muscle for the team and frightening just to look at. Matt had a secret that he shared with most hard men I've known – he doted on kids. When sent out to sort out some dispute, calling at the errant bloke's house, if there were kids in the vicinity he just walked away. When Matt realised it was time for Laura to give birth he just came along too and you didn't say no to Matt.

The hospital had a strict policy of partners only in attendance but when the nurse caught one look at Matt somehow she didn't object. Matt and I were shown into a room to wait for them to carry out some tests on Laura. It was a comfortable room with TV and so on but I couldn't relax. I wanted to be through next door to be sure my baby was going to be okay. I was feeling more tense than I had at any football match ever. Then I looked at big Matt – his face chalk white, huge hands gripped into tightly knit fists and his big jaw working from side to side. He was more nervous than me – more anxious than he had been in any gang fight.

Then I was called into the room with Laura leaving Matt to his worries next door. The birth was long and hard on her and I was there throughout. As the hours dragged by I became frantic. My niece had given birth to a wee boy, Daniel, just a few months before. Accidents during the birth had left the poor soul damaged and disabled. The memory was fresh and sharp and I was getting frantic over my child.

'JUST GET HIM OUT!' I shouted at the fussing midwives as the hours dragged by. 'PLEASE GET HIM OUT NOW!' I pled. God, I must have been a right pain in the ass to those medics. No wonder some of them don't want blokes near the birth. Maybe they would've thrown me right out on my ear if it wasn't for big Matt sitting in the relatives' room next door.

Eventually, the baby was born. A boy. Laura was exhausted after her ordeal and not able to take our son who was howling incessantly. I was standing in the room, my jaw still hanging open and amazed with wonder at how a life enters this world.

'You take him, Frank,' said Laura. A nurse lifted the howling baby and handed him to me. The minute I wrapped him in my arms, the wee fellow stopped crying . . . and I started weeping. I stood and stared into his little wrinkled face, his big bright eyes and felt part of him. Just a few minutes seemed to last forever. We were joined that baby and me. Sharing the same spirit. This was my boy, my son and I was his dad. This was the best moment of my life.

Welcome, Jake, my son. You didn't know it then, you maybe don't even know it now. But you were saving my life right there and then. You were giving me the reason to live that would see me through the hardest times that were just around the corner.

SUNK BY THE TREASURE (1996/97)

Now I had a family to support and I was determined to make a good living. At that time I was involved in a number of business ventures. Earning money from commercial enterprises was something I had had a go at ever since I'd been earning reasonable dough. Way back, along with Bill McMurdo, I had planned to buy a ski slope in the States and develop the area into a major resort. The land and existing facilities were going to cost us $3 million and we easily secured the backing of banks. In the meantime, I met with Richard Branson to explore opening an airport there and with all the major hotel chains who were keen. The interest was high and we reckoned we had a success on our hands.

The day before the deal for the land was to close, another businessman walked into the company and bought the land for cash then promptly offered it to us for $4.5 million. It really annoys me to be gazumped so I told him to stick it where the sun don't shine. Looking back, that was the wrong decision. His asking price was still rock bottom cheap for what we had planned.

Another major venture was working with the banks setting up business contacts, providing letters of introduction and the like. Out of this came many proposals like the Greek families in London who wanted introductions to the right people to import oil. For a while I was the agent of an American, investing his money in business deals in the UK so he could make a profit here. Most of these dealings were paper transactions with no actual cash involved. It was all meeting and greeting, talking and drinking on my part, and I'm a natural at those arts. My eyes had been opened to the world of banking and I wanted to become more fully involved.

213

Part of my lifelong trouble is that I don't stick at anything long enough. That, and my capacity for spending dosh as fast as I lay my hands on it, sometimes faster. I knew I needed to earn a greater amount of cash and an opportunity fell into my lap – or so I thought.

One night in Victoria's in Glasgow this guy, Alan Short, introduced himself to me as a businessman with investment proposals. He was looking for introductions to bankers and private investors. Short was a smooth-talker and chock full of ideas. He was a shark with a sillky tongue, the type of bloke who would sell his granny her own false teeth and not feel embarrassed about it. I had already met a whole string of successful legitimate business people and Alan Short seemed to have all the strengths and qualities required in that bullpen. Just the kind of guy to help me extend my involvement in the banking and investment arena, I reckoned.

Short and I set about forming a company, Gleneagles Worldwide plc, completing all the usual formalities such as memorandum of articles through the usual channels. One of our first ventures was to be £200,000 invested in a ship based in Belgium. My knowledge of ships can be summed up easily – ships go in the water. But money I know a lot more about. As I understood the deal, the ship could be used for a number of commercial tasks worldwide, would be a long-term asset and the projected return figures for every year were very tasty indeed. That's what I needed – a steady income earner to cover my family's needs while the more adventurous projects would be riskier and sometimes losers though, hopefully, more often winners. I paid up my investment of £100,000 to Short in Glasgow and went on to see Laura and Jake.

A sort while later I had been travelling up from London to Glasgow. Stepping off the shuttle from Heathrow and marching through Glasgow Airport I hadn't a care in the world. Then I got stopped by the police and searched. This type of thing happened to me frequently. Just what the cops wanted – to catch a well known name in possession of drugs. But this time I wasn't worried. No drugs on me.

Then they found the coke. For a second I looked at the wrap in the copper's hand and wondered if he had actually planted it in my jacket pocket himself. No, I recognised the package. It was mine all right. A small amount left over from some night out weeks before, forgotten about and left in that pocket. I'd thrown the suit on that morning, totally oblivious to the coke lodged there.

'It's just a wee bit charlie,' I said to the policeman, in a phrase that was to haunt me in the pages of the newspapers. But it was just two lines, if that. Not enough to have a real good time let alone deal in the stuff. Nobody buys two lines of cocaine. Too bad. I was done and duly charged with possession of cocaine and I would be going to court in due course.

On our business venture, the money invested in the ship had to be lodged at Dover by a particular date. Two weeks before I had been told that it was there. Then, out of the blue, I discover that Customs had refused to accept the money since the formal memorandum and articles creating Gleneagles Worldwide plc were not in place. It would only take days but they refused nevertheless. Assuming that the money was still in the bank, I checked up – as you do, over a hundred grand. The money wasn't there either. It had been seized by Customs. The smelly stuff was hitting the fan big time.

I telephoned Customs and said that the money was mine and asked for its return. They asked me for proof. My lawyer said that I wasn't required to give proof since in the previous years I had earned £250,000 from Celtic and other ventures. The income was there to afford £100,000 in other words. Bill McMurdo chipped in that he had recently paid me £42,000 – money owed to me from the usual football-related sources. In other words, it wasn't half-inched.

Interviewed by Customs & Excise I suddenly got a lot more worried. Alan Short had a record of drug-dealing from years before. News to me. They believed this money was headed to Amsterdam to purchase a large consignment of drugs. Then they hit me with a bombshell.

'We don't believe this money is yours,' the Customs guy said.

'I can assure you it is my money,' I insisted.

'Are you sure?' What sort of question was that? Are you sure this £100k is yours? Like you would make a mistake.

'Of course I am. I can prove it.' My bank withdrawal slips, dates and so on matched entirely with the movement of the dough.

'Of the £200,000, Mr Short claims that £100,000 is his.'

'Yeah.'

'But he has now withdrawn that statement.' I couldn't understand what Alan Short was about. If I could get him in a room for ten minutes maybe I'd get the truth.

'I'm only concerned with my £100,000,' I insisted. What Short was up to was his business.

'We think all the money belongs to someone else.'

'Who?'

'Thomas McGraw.'

'WHO?' They had just named one of the biggest gangsters in Scotland according to the newspapers. Probably one of the richest in the UK.

'Thomas McGraw of Glasgow. Commonly known as The Licensee.'

'I know who you mean but I've never met the guy.' And I had not. I could well imagine that I had been at the same football or entertainment event as him at some point – street players mix with all sorts of other folks especially from sport and entertainment. But I had never been introduced to McGraw and never done business with him – legitimate or otherwise.

'We think it's his money and you're fronting a drugs deal.'

'No way. This is an investment in a ship.'

'Can you prove this money is yours?'

216

'Prove it? If I don't get it back I'm going to be bankrupt within a week– will that be proof enough for you then?' And it was true. My affairs had reached such a stage that the £100,000 was the difference between keeping my head above water and sinking. But the interviewer wouldn't believe that. I was Frank McAvennie who had obviously more money than sense. Top footballers don't go broke, do they? You couldn't spend the amount of dough foot-ballers earn. Oh yes you could and I had.

Customs weren't for budging – we were going to have to go to court to get the money back. While attending the court hearing at Dover, I booked into a local hotel. That night, a team of tabloid journalists arrived and started offer-ing the night porter bribes to tell them which was my room. The bloke told them he wasn't a football fan and didn't know who I was.

'Blonde-haired guy, Scottish accent,' they said.

'Oh right, I know who you mean now,' said the porter, duly gave them a room number, then allocated them the room next door. What the journalists didn't know was that they were spying on a blonde-haired Customs officer who had travelled down from Glasgow. All along I was on another floor being very well behaved – not what they were expecting at all. When a member of the hotel staff revealed to me the next day exactly what her colleague had been up to I had a quiet word with the bloke from Customs. Thankfully he had been very well behaved too and his wife back home in Scotland wasn't in for a nasty surprise in the pages of her daily newspaper.

As soon as I walked into the court I knew we were in trouble. The money wasn't there and Alan Short had failed to turn up. I tried to explain our business project to the court but they were more interested in Customs' allega-tions that the money was to be used for drugs.

I had to involve a guy called Joseph Josife who swore that he had recently given me £46,000 for the venture. Josife was a straight guy whose family were well-to-do and connected to people like Margaret Thatcher. It was embarrassing, to say the least, for him to be involved in a court case like this. I had loaned some money to another party who was owed money by Josife. The deal had been to cut out the middleman and Josife paid me direct. The court was not impressed. Worse was to come.

Alan Short had told Customs that the ship in question was to be used to retrieve sunken treasure. When this was announced to the court my jaw hit my chest as other people started smirking. I knew vaguely that one of the functions of the ship in question was to lift salvage from sunken ships. Alan Short also did a spiel to whoever was interested on the money to be made in recovering precious artefacts. Short had claimed that in lifting ancient precious items to the sea's surface they got tarnished and damaged unless they were placed in a decompression chamber. Our investment was to buy such a device for the ship according to Short. First I'd bloody heard of it and it caught me cold sitting there in the court.

So I muttered a few comments about this kind of sunken treasure, trying not to appear as if I was turning on Alan Short. It was important that we appeared to be working together on this. Besides, I had questions to ask about Alan Short but until I got those answers I had no basis to turn against him at all. God, I could just imagine the headlines in the newspapers about pieces of eight and mock-up pictures of me with a parrot on my shoulder, a skull and crossbones hat and a black eye patch. My prediction was absolutely accurate as it turned out. For months I wouldn't be able to go into a pub without somebody cracking a sunken treasure joke.

The court decided that the £100,000 was to be withheld and I was in deep shit financially. But there was a bigger concern than that. My mother had suffered a heart attack and I had to rush back to Glasgow. It was the lowest of times. That case had seemed so bloody frustrating, dragging the last ounce of security from me, and the pressure on my parents was hell. As the world thinks of that time as some sort of Sunken Treasure laugh, I remember it as when I almost lost my mother. Thank God she survived.

Two days after the failed appeal against Customs I was declared bankrupt. It was specifically to do with £10,000 I had loaned to buy a black BMW and I'd fallen £4,000 behind with the payments. Such a small sum but enough to send me over the financial brink.

A week later I was cited to the court on the possession of cocaine charges and fined £750. I was so broke I had to ask for time to pay. With no money in the bank and no quick earners on the horizon it was looking bleak.

What a bloody week. It was surely a week out of hell. Bust, broke, battered where it hurt. My mother ill. I was sinking fast.

After word broke about my bankruptcy, a few people who I used to rate as friends suddenly stopped calling. That didn't bother me much since they were obviously free-loaders anyway and who needs creeps like that. More importantly, a load of people stuck by me – too many to mention. But one had a particular influence, Ray Winstone, the actor. I'd met Ray in the late 1980s and we had been close friends ever since. Ray was a big West Ham supporter and his hard-man swagger, street humour, big heart and supreme loyalty epitomised what I love about the East enders of London and the working class of Glasgow. Ray was filming some place when he heard about all my troubles. He knew better than most what it meant to be broke, having been bankrupt himself twice. He phoned to offer help and support, typical of the man but the most valuable thing he gave me that day was simply something he said, 'It doesn't matter how you go into something, Frank,' he said, referring to my bankruptcy, 'it's how strongly you come out.' And he was right. He had succeeded in hitting the pits twice and still fought back to be one of the most popular and successful actors in the world. In that statement, Ray gave me hope and determination and I would dig his words out and dust them down many times over the next few years.

Laura and I had been drifting apart for a long time. Though we had shared the same house for a few years I think of our marriage as having lasted ten minutes. Now we separated in reality. I have to admit that I wasn't a great father to Jake during that spell. Well, you can't be when you're still out on the sauce, chasing skirts and hardly ever around. But I loved him and he was part of me. Whatever the grief of the marriage at least he was the gift. Though the marriage was over I was determined not to lose Jake.

My finances were not improving. It was like I had simply sunk into my personal gutter of booze and drugs and I couldn't find the way back up on to the pavement. In January 1997 it hit another low point when I was cited to appear at Paisley Sheriff Court for failing to pay the £750 fine for possession of coke. Just a few years before I'd spend that much on a round of drinks without a second thought. If I didn't stump it up then I was heading to jail for 30 days. My only way out was to try and sell my house in Milngavie. It was valued at £175,000 and the relatively high price for that time in Glasgow was going to mean that it wouldn't sell in a hurry. I wasn't flogging the house just to pay the £750 fine since other debts had accrued. But it seemed like I was about to throw away my last valuable possession to pay off much less. It was the type of economic madness that poor poverty-stricken folks fall into. A downward spiral of reducing returns simply because they have no choice.

As those problems lay heavily on me, I went to visit a friend one day, Hugh O'Donnell, who owned the Parkgrove Sauna in Glasgow. It's a very high-class establishment in one of the plushest parts of Glasgow's city centre, ironically just along the road from the headquarters of the Scottish Football Association.

Hugh was out at the time so I said I'd wait. The

receptionist showed me into this waiting area where customers go to choose their girl for the day. Sitting in there already was this guy and across from him a clutch of the most beautiful women. Some were naked, others wearing next to nothing and I admit I was enjoying the view. I must have been sitting in there 20 minutes or so, and chatted with the guy and the women. Nice to be nice. Hugh arrived and I left the room to spend time with him, thinking no more about it.

A few weeks later, the cops pulled me in for an interview. I was expecting an increasing amount of this hassle now that I had a criminal record but not what they wanted to interview me about – a murder investigation.

Glasgow's prostitutes were being targeted by a serial killer, or so some people thought. In 1991, young Diane McInally's battered corpse was found in Pollok Park. She would be the first of several over the next few years. Two years later, Karen McGregor's naked body was found in a car park at the Scottish Exhibition Centre. In June 1995, Leona McGovern was discovered dead in the city centre. A couple of months later, Marjorie Roberts was found floating in the Clyde. Then, in June 1996, Jackie Gallacher's semi-naked corpse was found on waste ground in Bowling a few miles from the city. Now, the cops suspected that 21-year old Tracy Wilde, found dead in her flat, was the sixth victim of the same bloke. Understandably, the police in Glasgow were under enormous pressure to catch and convict the killer. But what the hell had it to do with me?

Since it was prostitutes who were being killed, the cops had been paying close attention to the red light district in the city centre known as The Drag. A high spec black BMW had been spotted in the vicinity several times. A black BMW similar to mine. They didn't have a registration number or even part of one. No description of the driver either. Just a black BMW and they decided to interview me, wanting to know where I had been on certain nights at certain times. The usual stuff.

221

The detectives didn't give me a hard time, having very little to go on. Their palaver was about checking all the owners of such cars around Glasgow – there weren't that many. But they also knew I had been in the Parkgrove sauna recently. Well, they were interviewing every working girl in the city. They seemed hellish curious about the bloke who had been choosing his girl while I waited for Hugh. I had chatted with the guy but that was it. I talk easily with anyone and must have friendly dialogues with scores of folks every day. That day was no different and I couldn't remember what the guy looked like, was wearing or even what his voice sounded like.

To have your name on a list as a possible murder suspect is scary to say the least. My suspicions were multiplied when I approached a bloke who lived close by me who had a black BMW of the same spec as mine. Of course, the cops hadn't interviewed him although they'd probably passed his motor on the way to my place. It was that old double albatross of my name and reputation that had put me on the cops' list. Fuck knows what I'd get dragged into in the future. It was time for a serious review of my position.

A couple of nights later I was rudely awakened around 4 am having just crashed out. Half asleep and fumbling with the key in the front door I fully expected two coppers to be standing on my doorstep. But it was a Good Samaritan. We'll call the guy JD, a well known street player. I wasn't that friendly with JD, in fact he was just someone I had heard of and could recognise. JD had read about my financial plight over the unpaid fine and the bankruptcy in the newspapers but had also somehow sussed the police had been sniffing around me again.

My night-time visitor was of the opinion that I should leave Glasgow promptly for my own safety. He knew better than most how the Glasgow police worked and reckoned they would get me on something else sooner or later – whether I had actually done it or not. JD offered me money, practical help, a place to live elsewhere in what was one of the most generous and spontaneous acts I could imagine. Even more remarkable given that the bloke was a lifelong Rangers supporter, too, though obviously one without a sectarian bone in his body.

Within a few weeks I was out of that house, out of Glasgow and heading south to my other home – London. At least there I didn't stick out like some easy target. In London I got treated like a regular Joe and had many friends. It had been a hellish year and I decided I could use a bit of rest and recreation and London's the ideal location for such therapy. A wee bit of fun and then I'm on my way back up. But it wasn't going to turn out quite the way I planned it. So what's new?

BAD COMPANY (1998/2000)

It wasn't what I needed but it's what I wanted. When you need a good blow out – phone some friends. What I was looking for was one last blast – a chance to lose myself in sex, drugs, booze and whatever else might come around. Before long it was introduced to me in the shape of Nicole, one crazy lady.

The first time I met Nicole I actually wasn't with her. I was to present some prizes at some rugby do being hosted by Michelle Collins. When it was my slot, I was nowhere to be found till Michelle looked in the bar and found me there, as ever. I was well into my cups and forgetting the trouble of the past. Duty done, back in the bar, this young woman slinks up and drapes herself around me. Suddenly cameras were flashing and I was happily posing for Scotland, thinking nothing of it. What I didn't know was that the photographer worked for a newspaper that had interviewed Laura about our separation. She had given a positive story and they wanted better. So, they showed Laura the picture of me and this mystery woman I now knew to be Nicole. It worked a treat and Laura gave them another interview, this time slaughtering me. When that appeared in the press I sussed what had happened. Shit, if I was going to be hung for a dog I might as well enjoy it.

Nicole was a professional singer, still is, so we'll just leave her name like that. She wasn't beautiful but had a wonderful figure and was simply outrageous. Whatever I liked she wanted more of. Keeping up with her was no problem but the combination of the pair of us was just one roller coaster heading towards deep, murky waters.

I'd lost so much I simply stopped caring. If I had over-dosed one night and never woken up it wouldn't have surprised those who knew me. It was a time I was into drugs and booze the heaviest of all as well as the company you need to keep to sustain those habits. People I had considered arseholes all my life could now walk right into my life and I'd welcome them with open arms. But let's get something straight. I wasn't some hopeless cokehead addict. No cries of Poor Wee Me from this corner. I was in control of what I was doing. It's just that I decided to do the lot and then some more.

One night I got a call from a friend in Glasgow. Another mate we'll call Bud had lost it big time. I'd known the guy from my childhood days back in Milton and now he was hitting crack, jellies, blues, booze and whatever else he could get his hands on. He was floating around the city taking what he wanted and didn't mind using violence to get it. Poor guy was losing it and I knew that if he wasn't stopped he'd either end up on a slab or a prison cell. People were frightened of Bud, particularly in this state. They had called me because they knew that I would always face up to him. Trouble was I was so skint I didn't have my fare to travel to Glasgow. The bloke on the phone said he'd sort it. A couple of hours later there's a knock at the door. Standing there is this guy whose mugshot I recognised from crime stories in the London newspapers. He didn't say much but just held out a wad of notes. Not a fortune but enough for an air ticket up north.

When I hit Glasgow the next day I went straight to see Jake. No matter what state I was in I always took every opportunity to see my boy even if, as at that time, Laura and I argued frequently. Laura and I had just been involved in legal action against a newspaper who had run a story about her being a heavy user of cocaine during her pregnancy with Jake. Utter malicious lies provided by some bad bastard. The paper had paid out a substantial sum so I asked Laura for the return of the £2,000 I had paid for her legal fees. After a hot dispute she agreed and handed over the dosh.

When I caught up with Bud he was staggering around the East End looking for trouble, heading to a drug dealer's house. I tagged along with him. In the guy's flat, Bud started ordering crack, grams of coke, jellies by the hundred. He'd no intention of paying but was just taking the drugs and the terrified dealer was handing them over.

'No way,' I butted in, once I saw what was going down. 'You give him nothing . . . right.' The poor dealer didn't know what to do. He knew that if he didn't hand the drugs over Bud would rip him apart. It was also clear that if he persisted he would have me to deal with. In the end I won, insisting all we took were a stack of blues, Valium to you.

With the £2,000 I got from Laura I booked Bud and myself into adjoining rooms in a hotel. Settling him down I gave him a handful of blues, waited till they kicked in and he fell asleep before I headed out. I'd learned enough about drugs to know that to help in the comedown you feed other drugs. So kids still raging with an ecstasy high will smoke a bit of heroin before they fall asleep. Mine was the same principle, just safer.

A few days later Bud was straight and conscious. I'd taken him down through the terrors. Bodily forced him to stay in the room. Fed him sugary drinks and listened to his ranting. Now he was back in control. I couldn't nurse-maid him forever. If he was to stay clear of drugs he had to decide, not me. I gave him a stiff talking to about this being his chance, his call and then I walked away. That might seem hard but it is the only way. No one can fight someone else's addiction for them. All you can do is help and then stand back.

Nicole joined me up in Glasgow. We ended up at a party run by Stevie, the manager of a well known nightclub in the city. Stevie was a good guy, always game for anything. Just a short while before I'd been in his club when propositioned by a young woman. Keen to take advantage I asked Stevie if I could use his office. Trouble is, there was a meeting going on. No problem, he passed me the keys to a broom cupboard. Not the most romantic setting but I enjoyed the visit and she appeared to as well.

As this party spluttered to an end, Stevie suggested looking for more fun. I was game.

'Fancy a sauna?' he asked.

'Sure,' I agreed, knowing there was a choice in the neighbourhood.

'What about Nicole?' he asked, nodding in her direction.

'Don't worry, mate, she'll come with us.' He looked at me sceptically but didn't argue. Stevie had built a reputation for being willing to try anything and everything. So he grinned and we left with Nicole, heading to the nearest sauna.

Glasgow isn't well known for its saunas. For some reason the local council prefer to make it difficult for such premises to run and thereby push most of the working girls on to the streets where they face most risks. So, saunas hadn't developed a great deal and worked to the basic principle of having female workers to serve exclusively male customers.

When we got to the place, I'm sure Stevie was expecting Nicole to laugh and back off at the last minute but she walked right on in with us. The receptionist wasn't fazed with Nicole as a customer but she had to explain there was only one changing room. Still Nicole came along, stood there beside us and stripped off – as I knew she would. The bold Stevie suddenly lost his nerve, threw his clothes back on and headed for the exit.

Nicole and I stayed on. While I had an actual sauna, she preferred to lie about outside, ogling the good-looking women who worked in the place. What I knew and Stevie didn't was that Nicole swung both ways but preferred women. As she licked her lips and eyed up the talent, I lay and mused about how many confident men totally lose their bottle when a woman calls their bluff. That has never been one of my problems, thank God.

Back in London again my life rolled on – downwards.

I was drowning in a sea of booze, drugs and mounting debts. Nothing in my life was organised or under control. No longer did I care about myself or anyone else apart from Jake. Nicole and I broke up as was inevitable and I drifted around, having casual relationships, sleeping at other people's houses, unsure of the day of the week. Then I got an invitation to go to some event up in Gateshead. In spite of my lifestyle I rarely refused any such attendances and usually managed to turn up. A few days out of the city might do me good, I reckoned, so off I trotted.

At a party in Gateshead, I was standing chatting as usual when in walked a right blast from the past. Michael Edward was a Glasgow boy from my youth. Though he had lived in Easterhouse on the city's north-eastern periphery and miles from me, our paths had crossed when we were young. Michael had been a first-class footballer, playing for the highly successful Celtic Boys Club but had not pursued football as a career. I knew he and his first wife had split up years before and his former partner had subsequently been the girlfriend of Paul Ferris, the Glasgow street player who was reputed to take over crime in Scotland. It was hard not to know since Paul had been involved in the longest criminal trial in Scottish history in 1992 but walked free after being found not guilty of murdering godfather Arthur Thompson's son and a host of other serious charges. The whole affair was front page news for years and Paul Ferris still got that kind of attention.

In spite of not seeing him for years, I heard someone tell Michael that Macca was here and he was over immediately, giving me a warm greeting that only old friends can genuinely muster. It was good to see Michael. Touching base with someone from my life when things were more certain, more predictable and more optimistic was an absolute tonic.

We got chatting. He told me about moving to Newcastle and it sounded bliss. I filled in the pieces between the headlines of what had been going on with me since I quit football and fully confessed to the awful bloody state I had allowed my life to dip into. Michael Edward sympathised but didn't stop there. On the spot, he invited me to go and live with him for a while, get my life sorted out. When I thanked him and politely said no – why would I want to impose my mess on others? – he then insisted. Within the hour I had agreed to move in with Michael Edward and his family.

That move possibly saved my life. God knows how far I might have stooped if I'd failed to get out of the London scene and away from my self-destructive routine. The Newcastle set-up was great. I was beginning to be able to hold on to some of the money I earned through the media and the like, could visit Jake in Glasgow much easier and more frequently and I was fighting fit.

At one point I agreed to go away for a short holiday with some guys to Belgium. It was a boys' trip away with a lot of boozing, carousing and chasing the women. We drove there in one car, catching the ferry at Hull. One night, after a bellyful of vodka, I was shacked up with a woman in my hotel room. It was that type of holiday. In the morning I woke up to discover that she was gone and my wallet with my cash and passport with her. After cursing and swearing for a while, I settled down and told the other guys. Money was all right – they would take care of that. I would have to apply for a temporary passport locally though. It would take three to four days to obtain. No problem, we could travel back whenever we wanted.

On the way to find the office where I'd have to apply for a passport, I stopped at a call box and phoned my parents in Glasgow to see how they were. My mother was unwell and had been rushed into hospital with another suspected heart attack. Screw the passport, I had to go home and now.

I had no need to explain much more to my friends. We quickly packed the car and headed off. As we approached the ferry terminal they pulled in to a layby. Rearranging the cases and shoving one into the back seat, I climbed into the boot and lay as comfortably as I could. There was a high risk that we would get stopped by passport control and Customs so I really appreciated the risks my friends were taking. What was the penalty for smuggling a human being?

The next I knew, the boot was being opened and a familiar smiling face beamed down at me. We were in the hold of the ferry and part one of the journey had passed without trouble. It was an overnight journey and we had booked two cabins so I spent the rest of the night in comfort though in the confines of the room. Next morning I was loaded into the car boot again and off we set.

My friends let me out of the boot when we had safely passed through passport control. With me now sitting in the back seat we headed off. Customs stopped us before we left the terminal. We knew this might happen but if they did anything it would be to check the luggage and the boot and it was as well not to have me grinning up at them. They did check the boot then asked for our bloody passports. It was confession time. After I had to tell them three times about how my passport had been nicked they were chuckling and laughing at my expense. I still thought I was going to be arrested and held in custody and started to plead my case about my ill mother.

'No, no. Don't worry,' said one of the Customs guys. 'You've made it back in Britain now. Besides – we know who you are.'

After signing a few autographs for their kids and sisters, they waved us on through. For once, my reputation and lifestyle had served me up some benefit. By that afternoon I was in Glasgow at my mother's bedside. She was well and would be fine but the fear of losing her still ached through me. I spent a few nights at home with my Dad and visited the hospital every day. That and spending some time with Jake was all I got up to. It was one of my quietest trips home and I did a lot of thinking. This was what was important to me. My Mum, my Dad and my son. I had almost lost them all through my own behaviour. That wasn't going to happen again. And it won't.

Around that time, I was at a Newcastle United match with Michael Edward. It amused me to be going along as a spectator to the Newcastle games and how welcome all their supporters made me feel. As a player with West Ham they used to give me a hell of a time – usually because I regularly scored goals against their team. Now I was fast becoming an adopted Geordie and I liked it. At the game we met Mick Galloway, the seasoned footballer, who fancied a night on the town. Michael Edward wasn't keen but I went out on the razzle with Mick and expected a good time if he was up to his usual form. He was but it wasn't the drinking exploits that were of any significance that night, for a change.

After a few drinks, Mick announced he was trying to sell his house and had to go and meet someone interested in buying it. I thought I recognised the potential purchaser Tina, though we'd never met. We got chatting but I was looking past her at her pal, Karen Lamberti. Now her I really fancied. By the next day, I knew Karen was a bit special and thankfully she felt the same about me. What was it about her? Beautiful? Absolutely, but not just that. Karen had had a life and didn't judge me for mine. Didn't make me feel like she thought I'd run out on her any second. Didn't make me feel that I was on my guard. She had had children herself and understood entirely how I felt about Jake – an essential requirement of any woman I was going to attach myself to.

Some time after we started going out I took Karen on her first visit to Glasgow. She loved my Mum and Dad and got on well with my son. She even got on well with Laura, with no sign of jealousy or rivalry coming from either side. Karen was a match and more for me and I was beginning to realise I was falling for her.

But on that trip back to Glasgow her eyes were opened a wee bit as to who exactly she had been knocking about with. We took the chance to go along to a concert raising funds on behalf of Kosovo. There were stacks of big groups playing – just my scene – and other entertainment. As we arrived at the venue Karen commented on how everybody in the city seemed to know me. This was my life and it had been happening for so long I no longer noticed. Then, in a break in the music one of the other acts came on to rapturous applause from the audience. It was Jonathan Watson, the comedian, acting out a character from his TV show *Only An Excuse*. One of his most popular characters – me. It took Karen two seconds then her mouth fell open. She simply hadn't a clue that my infamy had reached the heights of becoming a joke TV character. Not a clue. Thank God it didn't put her off me.

Before long I had moved in with Karen. I was settled and happy as I have never been before. At last I'd found some peace, some joy and didn't feel I was running at a hundred miles an hour all the time. There's no need to, when what you want is what you've got and she's right by your side. The days of bad company were well behind me, I thought, and we started planning for a bright future.

Then I went to play a round of golf and the whole lot came smashing down on my head again.

GIVE A DOG A BAD NAME (2000)

It was the rain that caused it. Not just a shower but a bloody downpour. I had been a keen golfer for years but was a fair weather kind of guy, preferring the smell of newly cut grass in the summer sun to the crackle of waterproof clothes as the rain batters against you. No way were Michael Edward and I going to play golf in that rain. I wish to hell I had.

Michael agreed when he turned up at the house I shared with Karen. After sitting and chatting for a while over a cup of tea and biscuits, Michael said he had some business to do in the Newcastle. Not having anything else on myself I said I'd tag along for the ride, keep him company.

At the main station in Newcastle, Michael's mobile goes. A little later he greets somebody and I hear him say, 'Macca's here.'

It was a close friend of his, Vinnie Wallace. Now I knew Vinnie Wallace. He owned The Life of Reilly pub in Glasgow's city centre and I used to get him signed Celtic strips and the like for charity raffles. A good guy, as far as I was concerned. I was a bit puzzled at Vinnie suddenly turning up in Newcastle but didn't think it my business to start grilling Michael. After all Vinnie might have been coming to Newcastle for his own reasons and thought he might as well give his old mate Michael a call while he was in the area. These were friends, almost family, with Vinnie being godfather to one of Michael's sons. You don't subject friends to the third degree.

We picked Vinnie up and the chat was good. Michael drove to a place in Newcastle where he said he had to go. Giving us no explanation, Michael parked and left the car. Vinnie was in the front passenger seat and I was in

233

the rear. The back doors had child locks on them so I wound down the window, crawled out, got into the driver's seat and moved the car about 100 yards up the road. Childish? Sure but just a prank and one I carried out with great caution, being a banned driver at the time. I'm a real big time villain, eh?

Michael emerged from the place and, of course, found the car. Cursing at me for the joke, Michael drove to another place where he and Vinnie got out to go to some shops leaving me in the back seat of the car. I sat there, kind of bored, having a cigarette and reading some newspapers and magazines. It was just killing time, getting through another dull morning.

A while later we were to drop Vinnie off at the station. The traffic out front was busy, so we pulled in and Vinnie climbed out sharpish. Short and sweet and I guessed that Vinnie was going to catch a train back to Glasgow. Guessed, but didn't know.

Vinnie was away and Michael and I were still at a loose end. The discussion turned to what we would do next and the prospect of going to a lap dancing bar came up. Okay by me since Karen was out that night at a hen party or some such event. The trouble is, neither of us had been planning an expensive day so we both checked how much cash we had on us. They would tell me later that between us Michael and I had £146 in our possession. Hardly a fortune yet I hadn't finished counting it before we were surrounded by police and arrested.

Down at the cop shop they had me in an interview room chatting about this and that. So far they hadn't explained why we had been lifted and I was having a real problem taking any of it seriously. The tape of the interview has me laughing and joking, pulling the old wisecrack routines with the cops. Then they tell me I've been lifted for dealing in drugs.

'YOU'RE A FUCKING LIAR!' I roared, my mood suddenly turning.

'Along with Michael Edward you have set up a drug dealing operation between here and Glasgow,' said the cop, or as close as damn it.

'What are you talking about?' I hit back. 'This is total bollocks.'

'No it's not.'

It wasn't. By the end of the day the Scottish Drugs Enforcement Agency had arrested Vinnie at Queen Street station in Glasgow, alleging he had 5,000 ecstasy tablets and five kilos of amphetamine paste. I realised that the police had been tracking this case for a while and it was a joint operation between the drug agency up north and the National Crime Squad in England. These were serious players, the charge was heavy and I was right in the mire.

To make matters worse I had some cocaine in my possession. Just a few lines, a bit of personal and no big deal compared with the other charges. But it was an offence, though not significant enough to hold me in custody. I was found fair and square with my own coke and put my hands up to that but no way did I know anything about the other business.

Now the cops grilled me, taking me over and over the events of the day. They claimed that Michael had brought the drugs in a carrier bag out of that house we had parked in front of, the time I had moved the car as a joke. Well I didn't see any carrier bag but they weren't having any of that. They also claimed that when Vinnie had got out the car in front of Newcastle station I had also jumped out of the car and handed him a bag – implying that I was handing over the drugs. Well, I didn't and the traffic had been so busy all we could do was pull the car in briefly to let Vinnie out. The cops were adamant and I was getting too worried to be bothered by the frustration welling up in my guts.

At one point they suggested that there might be some gear at my house or a load of money stashed. Without being obliged to, on two consecutive days I gave them the keys to my place knowing that Karen wouldn't be in. There were no drugs there and as far as I was concerned I wanted to be as open as I could, clear this matter up and get the hell out of that cop shop. Later I was to be told that the police drove at high speed to my home, lights flashing, sirens blaring. What the fuck was all that about? A wee message – 'Hey look who's in trouble again.' A lot of show for sod all because that's what they found. Zilch.

I cooperated in every way. Showed them my bankbooks that spelled out I was £30 overdrawn. Big drug dealer me. But still they weren't satisfied and grilled me over the whole rigmarole yet again.

'How long have you known Arthur Burke?'

'Arthur who?'

'You visited his house earlier today.'

'No I bloody didn't.'

'Yes, you did in West Denton.' The penny dropped. That's where Michael had gone when I had hidden the car from him.

'If that house belongs to an Arthur Burke then it's the first I've heard of it or him.'

On and bloody on, an endless stream of questions that repeated themselves on a never ending tape. Still, I knew I had nothing to do with the drugs. Even as they were pounding me over and over, I was more concerned that they had noticed me driving the car 100 yards. Now that had been an offence and I didn't want to be without my licence any longer than necessary.

Eventually I knew that the cops' time limit was running out. They had to charge me or let me go. I was knackered, fed up and felt like I hadn't washed in a week. All I wanted was to get the hell out of the place and get into a shower. I reckoned that's where I was going – home.

With one minute to go of their legal time limit, the police formally charged me with conspiracy to supply Class A and B drugs. That was me well fucked. Held in cells overnight all I could hope for was that the court would release me on bail to await the trial.

Having been charged on a weekend I was allocated a duty solicitor who duly applied for bail on Saturday morning. Being ignorant of the criminal justice scene, I didn't know that bail could only be allocated by three magistrates and on Saturdays only one sat in the court. Bail applications would all be knocked back in other words and I would lose one life, one hearing, one chance to go home. I didn't know that but neither did the bloody lawyer. On the Monday morning when I appeared in court he failed to turn up till noon, hours late. No surprise then that the judge remanded me in custody. I was going to jail for the first time in my life.

I'd driven in a few blacked-out limousines in my time but this was by far the most memorable. The bus smelled of a mixture of disinfectant and sweat, a bit like football changing rooms on a bad day. On the rumbling, slow journey I wondered how the hell my name and fame were going to affect me in this place. I'd known a few guys who had done jail time and they'd told tales of how folk who were well known were singled out for a bad time by bitter screws or mental prisoners. What about my association with Celtic? Just because this was England there were still bound to be people who took exception to that. I sat there and feared the worse then we were there – the gates of Durham Jail.

Being processed through the place was demeaning. Standing bollock naked in front of men has never been a problem to me in football changing rooms but in the jail they made you feel vulnerable, despised, downtrodden. Bending over, being ordered to pull your arse cheeks apart as some warden shines a powerful light on the spot so the medics can get a good look without getting too close. Any second you expect a sharp pole to be shoved up your hole. By the time I'd been processed, dressed in their crap, over-large clothes and shown into my grubby little cell I was beginning to think, 'Fuck you. If that's how you want to play it – fine. Come ahead.' No wonder so many prisoners resort to violence.

I reckon the cell was about 15 feet by 10 feet and accommodated two people. Against one wall there was a short partition that barely managed to hide your dignity as you pissed and shit in the crude crapper. To start with, it was a 23-hour lock-up every day. When one of the cellmates went for a shit the stench hung around, coating your teeth, filling your nostrils for hours.

Michael shared the cell with me and, naturally, we talked on and on and on about the arrest and charges. I was spitting teeth saying that when this business was cleared up I was going to sue somebody big time. Michael agreed, was equally angry and all the time declared he had sod all to do with the drugs. Two friends caught in the same unjust trap – that's how it felt.

When eventually released for association with other prisoners I was on my guard. This was the time when I'd find out how the other prisoners and the wardens would treat me. The screws were all bustle and bullshit. Marching around, roaring at the top of their voices, demanding to be called sir or boss. This was the easy part. Years of dealing with football managers made the term 'boss' fall easily from my lips and made orders easy to follow. I just imagined this was the training session from hell and put up with it.

One particular senior screw, a gruff Scot, was hell on legs. One infringement and he landed you right bang in trouble. Most of the other, more experienced cons were frightened of him – always a bad sign. Early on he cornered me and I expected the worst.

'See you McAvennie,' he started, as if reminding me of my name.

'Yes, boss,' I replied, wanting to give him no excuse to take a dislike to me.

'My wee boy once asked you for your autograph.' Fuck's

sake, was he one of these kids at the back of a huddle that I didn't spot? 'Lucky for you you fucking well gave it to him, eh?' End of conversation. Off he marched, yelling at everybody for any reason. But that was his way of telling me that I was all right by him. And he was true to his word. In fact, all the staff were fine to me, good-humoured and fair. No complaints there. But the prisoners might be another kettle of fish.

My first day circulating with the others, I moved around carefully watching my step.

'You're in for drugs, Macca,' said this other prisoner, an obvious conversation-starter since my arrest had been spread all over the newspapers and on the TV for days.

'Yeah, but I didn't do it,' I replied.

'No. I'm sure you didn't,' he nodded sympathetically, though a wee bit dismissively. I'm sure he was well used to prisoners saying that they were innocent.

'How about you?' I asked. 'What you in for?'

'Murder,' he replied and without explanation strolled off. He was an ordinary, innocuous-looking, little bloke – not half as fierce as some of the heavies. Yet he was in for murder. Was Durham Prison full of murderers? Was I locked up with guys who would go the full way on you if they were slightly irritated? It wasn't a reassuring start.

The other cons were fine. The first comforting sign I had was the number of people sporting Celtic tattoos. But no one gave me hassle. Most seemed to enjoy having a guy they had heard of in their midst. Especially when they realised I could take a joke – even if I was the butt – and dish it right back. Prison was being locked up with guys with a joint purpose. In the main they all believed they were on the same side. They could help each other get through this or they could make life hell.

As part of the general chit-chat with staff and prisoners, I would tell them this was my first time in prison and I knew no one else in the system. Then my first letter arrived.

239

On the back, for all to see, was the sender's name and address:

Paul Ferris
PD 1510
HM Prison Frankland
Brasside
Durham DH1 5YD

Everybody had heard of Paul. Not only had he grabbed the headlines in Scotland for years as, allegedly, the man who ran most of organised crime, he had also been nabbed for gunrunning in London and was serving a sentence in the top secure jail nearby. Aye, not connected, my arse.

The letters were opened of course, and read. Paul is a small, fresh-faced, smart kind of guy who looks nothing like a gangster. Thankfully, he writes the same way, being articulate and polite and he was just sending his support and some good advice about how to keep strong in myself to get through the jail time. So whatever the screws were expecting they didn't get. What I didn't know till a long time later, Paul had put the signal out through the prison grapevine that I was an okay guy who was a friend of his. So maybe there had been one or two folk in Durham Jail who fancied a pop at me but thought better. Who knows?

As well as enormous support from friends, the other letters were a bit more outrageous. Lifelong Celtic or West Ham supporters who talked of killing the screws and bombing the courts. Lonely women who wanted to have my babies. People who offered to convert me to some religious sects, others wishing me in Hell and every nutter in between. At least they would have brightened up the prison censor's day.

My first prison job was making football nets. I suspected the prison staff were taking the piss. It certainly gave the other cons a good laugh. Then I was moved to cleaner. Sounds demeaning and is but in jail it was a gift. It meant that my cell door was open most of the time and I could get to the phone whenever I wanted. Apart from the usual calls to the lawyers, it meant I could keep in daily touch with Karen, reassure my parents I was okay and phone my boy Jake. That's when I discovered that Laura had suddenly, without warning, taken Jake off to Spain for an alleged holiday. It wasn't a holiday but a house-hunting trip and Laura planned to move out there, taking my boy with her.

Talk about hitting a man when he is down. The punishment of prison is in how helpless you feel. It's not just about not being able to see someone when you want, go to the pub when you choose or wee things like deciding on your own what you would like to watch on TV instead of putting it to a vote with 30 other guys. The deep punishment is how bloody useless you feel in tackling any problems in the outside world. If your kid is being bullied at school or your partner has some financial problems or your mother is suddenly ill – you are simply unable to do anything. In my case my son had suddenly disappeared and there was sod all I could do. If I had been free I would have been over in Spain hunting for him. Now all I could do was fret and worry myself sick. Alone in your prison cell you start to fear the worst. I wondered if I'd ever see Jake again.

I made another phone call this time, thinking of the future. When I got through to the renowned PR agent Max Clifford's office, he wasn't available. I left a detailed message with his secretary and explained that I would phone back in ten minutes. You can't receive incoming calls in a jail, of course, so can spend days failing to contact people. To be fair to Max he took the call right away. I had one question for him.

'I'm innocent but mud sticks. When I get out of this what will it take to get back my good name?'

'It's going to be difficult,' Max replied, 'perhaps impossible.' I liked his bluntness. 'It will need an orchestrated campaign over a lengthy period and still it might not work.'

'But if I wanted to have a go, what would it take?' He didn't hesitate.

'£60,000.'

I didn't have £600 let alone the balance. I thanked him for his time and for telling me the hard truth and hung up. Looked like I was stuck with whatever name they wanted to give this dog.

Of course, I changed my lawyer. Not only did the first guy screw up my application for bail, he also thought he could do everything himself. I knew I needed a barrister to represent me to be sure that my innocence was proven. That and the more pressing issue of getting me bail and out of jail.

Dave Singleton was my new lawyer. He took a different tack entirely from the first guy and I was beginning to feel a bit of confidence and optimism at last. Soon he had fixed me up with a top barrister, Richard Bloomfield. When we first met they listened to my account of events. I was beginning to feel I had been repeating the same endless story over and over in my own nightmarish version of *Groundhog Day*. They thought differently.

'I know you're innocent because of the way you're talking,' said Bloomfield, the barrister. 'This case stinks.'

My new legal team's belief in me and their skill paid dividends when I was released from jail on bail after one month. Walking away from the police into Karen's arms I felt like I had been reprieved from the death sentence. I was so bloody happy I was in tears.

We drove home and locked the door to celebrate in privacy for what would be days. But I wasn't reprieved. It was only a postponement and I would still have to face a trial on serious drugs charges. Having got all this back I could soon lose it again.

PASS GO (2000)

S ome people will step into your spotlight any chance they get. My arrest and jail brought a whole stack of these rabbits out of the woods to stand transfixed in the headlamps. Trouble is, they talked crap at the same time. One of the funniest was Emma Padfield, a former Miss Great Britain contender.

While I had still been safely locked up in jail, Emma padded around trying to flog a story about me. Or at least about the two of us. Emma Padfield is a self-confessed football groupie. Apparently she spent her young life trying to get top footballers into bed and claimed she was successful. Having seen pictures of the lady I can well believe her. Then she made a lot of dough by selling her story to the newspapers, claiming to have spent one night with me in the Moat House Hotel in Covent Garden, London.

I have stayed at that hotel a number of times. In fact on one visit there I met with another woman who was a star of a late night soft porn TV programme made in Italy – Tootie Fruity, or some such. People phoned in and if they got a question right they chose which of a bevy of models would take off an item of clothing. Strange programme but needless to say I used to watch it. When I actually met up with one of the models – well it was just too tempting. This woman was stunning, full-figured and as ripe as the name of the TV show suggested. She had turned up at the Moat House wearing a figure-clinging, plastic dress that just about covered her buttocks. Now that I remembered vividly, but Emma Padfield?

Emma claimed to have slept with 27 footballers and rated me the second best between the sheets. Now forgive me but that was just too good for my ego so I let her tell the story unchallenged. She has told it numerous times

243

since, often saying I was the best. Keep up the good work, Emma, whoever you are.

Some particular friends are worth a mention. You have to realise that the newspapers had hung me out to dry. Although the law says you are innocent till proven guilty, lead writers took a different view. In public image terms I was not just the golden boy fallen from grace I was a dirty drug dealer – not the kind of character to be seen associating with, if you ever wanted to work again. But right by my side were footballers Charlie Nicholas and John Fashanu, actor Ray Winstone and football commentator and character, Chick Young. Special friends. Brave buggers.

At the same time, for a number of years, comedian Jonathan Watson had kept running an impersonation of me in the TV show *Only an Excuse* parodying people from football, particularly Scottish football. As these guys do he had given me a catch phrase, 'Where's the burdz?' True to form it's something I never say. Apparently Jonathan had been thinking of taking my character out of the show till he realised I was too popular. So the Macca character stayed – in fact is still in the show – and Watson continued making some dough out of my foibles. Good for him. I was glad somebody was earning for what I was going through but, let me tell you, sitting where I was at the time I felt far from popular.

Waiting for my trial I heard the worst of news. My father was diagnosed as having cancer and had emergency surgery to remove one lung and a kidney. He was now 76-years old and had been fit as a fiddle for his age up till then. One minute he was working away at a wee job, the next he was on death's door. My whole anxiety was exacerbated by my bail conditions that stipulated I was not allowed to leave Gateshead and had to report to the local police station every day. It is no good arguing with the State that your dear old dad is ill. That you need to see him. That he is the man in your life. The one you owe it

244

all to and the one man you love. The authorities simply turn deaf. Life deals cruel hands sometimes.

Another restriction of my bail meant that I could not take up any sort of work. With no money coming in, for the first time since my early teens I had to sign on as unemployed. Standing in that queue at the dole made me wonder what had become of me. Was this the same guy who had spent £50,000 on champagne in one club in a matter of months? Absolutely the same man.

The DSS had a problem with me. They would not accept that I had no money. No matter how hard I tried, what documentation I provided, they simply refused to pay out. Some of the bureaucrats actually said, 'But you can't be broke – you're Frank McAvennie.' As if the name held some guarantee to riches.

Now I was destitute, totally reliant on Karen, reporting to the cops every day, stuck in Gateshead and banned from travelling to see my dreadfully ill father. Surely life had to get better? It got worse. Laura took Jake away to Spain to live against my wishes and it was time for the trial.

The affair was a farce from beginning to end. The prosecutor called up his witnesses, mainly police from the National Crime Squad and the Scottish Drugs Enforcement Agency. In spite of this being a high-powered surveillance exercise involving two of the most powerful agencies in the UK, there was no complete log of events and no effective video of events – standard procedure in such operations. Also the CCTV cameras outside the station in Newcastle had mysteriously gone down for the key hour around the time of our arrest. The police had supplied some sort of film but the quality was so poor that even a technical expert we hired couldn't get a clear picture. Then on the day of the trial, the prosecution suddenly without warning produced a much better quality of film.

Let me make it clear that most of the police recounted events exactly as they happened. But two of their colleagues seemed to have been in a different city on a

245

different day. One described me as having been on look out when I was sitting waiting for Vinnie and Michael in the back of their car. Yet all the others had described me as relaxed, reading a magazine, smoking a fag. When he was pushed by my barrister he had to admit that that was what I was doing and I was sitting in the back seat – hardly ready for a quick getaway.

The next thing that was revealed was that at Arthur Burke's house, where Michael had allegedly picked up the ecstasy and the amphetamine paste, drugs were found, as I had been told. But there was no trace of ecstasy or amphetamine in Burke's home, just cannabis resin. So there was no forensic evidence supporting the charges against me at all.

The carrier bag full of drugs that Michael is alleged to have taken from Burke's house was described as a C&A bag, then another type, then a third type. One cop insisted I got out of the car outside Newcastle station and handed Vinnie a bag, while the evidence of others contradicted this claim.

Another copper, this one was from Scotland, was caught out about where he was at the time Vinnie had got out of Michael's car to catch the train. What he had described simply wasn't possible because of a queue of taxis. The Scottish cops had no log and changed their story several times. I knew that they had tried to have me brought up to Glasgow to face trial there but had failed. Thank Christ, since they surely planned to crucify me.

One of the points that worried me was that before the trial Michael Edward had gone very silent. He had turned up in court with me and pled not guilty but was being tried separately and suddenly he was saying nothing. Vinnie was being tried up in Glasgow and I'd heard that he also intended to plead not guilty.

Then it was my turn to take the stand. My lawyer had proposed to give me some coaching before the trial but I had refused, saying that I knew the truth and that's all I had to tell – so what else was there to prepare for?

When it was the prosecution's turn, I was waiting for the difficult questions. They never came. As the grilling went on, it became clear he was asking the same questions in different ways over and over. It got so that I started answering before had finished asking. The judge told me off several times but I think he had some sympathy with my line that the bloke kept asking the same things. After an hour or so the prosecutor began to sweat and stumble over his words. I knew the signs – he was a man losing a battle and had run out of options. He had no other questions to ask. There were no tricks. He was using the same old tired routine again and again because it was all he had.

Then it was over and the jury were sent off to make their minds up. It was lunchtime but I had no appetite. Only that morning I had been told that if found guilty, I faced nine years in jail. That's what was being debated in the jury room – nine years of my life. Other thoughts kept running through my mind. Like the lawyers who had said long before the trial that they knew I was innocent and so did the police. But still they had proceeded. Why? Why had the Scottish cops wanted me up in Glasgow so badly? Why were there no complete logs? What was going on with Michael? Nine bloody years of my life and the jury had sat down to lunch first. Christ, I just wanted it over with.

One hour and twenty minutes later the jury was back. Given that they had had an hour for their lunch and comfort break they had only met for 20 minutes. What could they decide in that time? That they were of a split mind and needed the judge's permission for a majority verdict to stand? Surely they couldn't have made a decision already? They weren't going to jail me for nine years after 20 minutes chat, were they?

When the foreman announced 'Not Guilty', Karen let out a scream of relief and I unashamedly burst into tears. Released from the dock, the media pack listened to my constant, excited gibbering as I puffed hard on cigarette after cigarette. All the time I held Karen tightly to me. I didn't want to lose her now. In all my life I couldn't think of one other female who would have stood by me through this. Karen was there for me every day all the way and she was the one person I knew who had always believed in my innocence. She was special. For the first time in my life I wanted to get married for no other reason than I wanted to be with her forever. Thankfully, so did she. I was never going to lose her again.

After spending a week in bed together, Karen and I set about planning to get married. We had discussed it before but I always felt I was too broke – what had I to offer her after all? That spell in jail and brush with long-term detention woke me right up. Money isn't marriage. People are. Rich or skint I just wanted to be with her.

For the next seven months I found myself terrified to go out of the house. It hit me by surprise one night soon after the trial when I went to collect a carry out meal. I sat in the car in the street watching the people inside the restaurant through the large glass windows – and froze. They were just ordinary punters picking up some food and I was scared to be among them or any other folk apart from Karen. All the time I was sure the police would just swoop right down on me again and whisk me away to jail on some other made-up charges. Macca the party animal had turned into Frank McAvennie agoraphobic. For me it was a state of limbo in the doorway of hell.

I did go out to one place – to see my son Jake in Spain, as soon as Laura would allow me. Somehow I'd managed to scrape up £500 and that was enough for the flights and a few days' keep. To get the cheapest flight I was flying in and out of Liverpool. I had a great time with my boy and I was reluctant to leave him. On my last day I stayed on with Jake much longer than I should have and was forced to change my flights which cost me a good few quid. Since I was arriving late at night I'd been booked into the Adelphi Hotel which is great but not exactly the most expensive place in town. Trouble is, the extra money for the change of flight had left me with £30 to my name – not enough for the room.

When I arrived I had to swallow my pride and simply own up to the manager. He didn't hesitate. He took £25 off me – well short of the real cost – left me with £5 for cigarettes and showed me to one of the best rooms in the place. A kind man. A real Samaritan.

But the incident brought it all home to me. A few years before I'd spent more on one bottle of fizz than the best hotel room in Liverpool costs and thought sod all about it. All my life I had loved people and felt confident, cocky even, playing to an audience. Now I was stony broke and timid of people. The only way was up.

Karen helped me through and gradually edged me back into mixing with people. Now, I'm pleased to report I'm more than fully recovered. What would I do without her? More than ever I wanted to sort out my finances, take good care of her and give her the life she deserved. That's when a business proposal came up from an unexpected quarter. The bold Alan Short contacted me again.

FANTASIES AND FATALITIES
(2000/01)

Since the Sunken Treasure episode, Alan had been busy. He had been sentenced to two years for drug offences in Belgium though it would only be served if he ever returned to that country. The newspapers tracked him for a while and claims were made that shortly before that trial he had bought a house in Scotland, paying cash on the deal. With that and his previous conviction for drugs no wonder he hadn't been upfront with me.

Some might wonder why I didn't tell Alan Short to piss off after all that had gone down between us. I wonder myself. But I thought I now had the man's number and it's always easier to deal with people when you know what they are capable of. Short also made a lot of money from legitimate enterprises as well as whatever else he was up to. He was one of those natural talkers who could sell anyone anything and so much of business is based on precisely that quality and little else. So he always had projects on the go that were perfectly legal and highly profitable. All that and he had a proposal that had my name on it.

The Fantasy Bar in Edinburgh was at that time a strip joint, a lap dancing bar kind of place. According to Short the then owner wasn't paying rent and other debts on the property. He had backers who wanted to take it over but he wanted me to front the place, use my name as a promotion. There was no investment needed from me – which is just as well – all he was doing was offering me a job. It was perfect, especially given what I had been through. Thinking back to my plans to open School Dinners, all the promotion we needed for that new project was word on the street that I was behind it. Why should it be so different for the Fantasy Bar?

Karen and I discussed Short's proposal. She had had great experience in running businesses whereas I was naïve as far as that was concerned. Would she manage it while I did the talking and fronting act, the old meeting and greeting routine? Would she be willing to move to Edinburgh with me? She wanted some reassurances, primarily about what sort of club the Fantasy Bar was. We had recently been passed a video of an old associate – Dodgy Dave Courtney going the whole hog in a porn film. Now if he wanted to go that far in his self-promotion then fine for him. But Karen didn't want us associated with porn or prostitution and I had to agree. I reassured her that in clubs like the Fantasy Bar the essential rule is that no one is allowed to touch the women.

'You sure?' she asked.

'Absolutely – no touching or the customer is out through the door.'

A short while later, after the whole package was set up, Karen gave up her job and we travelled to Edinburgh. When we arrived at the Fantasy Bar we were treated like royalty, all the staff already knowing we were going to be the new managers. We had a look round the club then I went to join the group of men who were described as the new financial backers, leaving Karen to stroll about, suss out how the place was organised and come up with any immediate changes she thought necessary.

I was in the middle of chatting with these blokes when Karen came up and whispered in my ear,

'Rule one is no touching the women, right?'

'Yeah, that's right.'

'C'm'ere,' and she pulled my sleeve. I apologised to the company and followed her upstairs to the rooms that could be hired for private shows. There on the floor were two naked women, their heads buried between each others' legs, too preoccupied to notice they had company. An hour of close observation later I still hadn't worked out if they were two workers, a worker and a customer or what.

Downstairs we said nothing of the little scene we had stumbled on, finished the meeting and left for the night.

Two days later we turned up for a meeting with Alan Short. This was the formal handover that would be sealed by the signing of contracts and him giving us a significant sum of money. It took me an hour to realise that he wasn't coming. In fact I've never seen him since. God knows what all that was about. Twice bitten, I realised that the press had picked up on my proposed role in the Fantasy Bar. If nothing else they had gained free national publicity at our expense. There may have been other issues too with some financial shenanigans in the background. Who knows? All I knew was that I wouldn't be working with Alan Short again – wherever he is.

In the meantime I had to attend as a defence witness at Vinnie Wallace's trial in Glasgow for allegedly dealing in ecstasy and amphetamine. Michael Edward had suddenly changed his plea to guilty at his own trial and been sentenced to five years. I had been visiting Michael in prison since my own release and all along the way he had consistently protested his innocence. When I heard that he had changed his plea I was totally flummoxed as to what was going on. I still am.

It seemed to me that the police had to have some solid evidence against Vinnie as being in possession of the drugs or else how could they have charged anyone. But the trial collapsed in confusion over the evidence provided by the police – some of whom had been witnesses at my trial. Vinnie Wallace was found Not Proven and walked from the court a free man. All I had done was tell the details of the day as I recalled them just as I had at my own trial. Afterwards I was delighted that the media had picked up my comments from the court branding some of the cops involved as bent, incompetent or born liars. And they were. They had to be. What a bloody farce.

A woman from my life had hit the press but this time not telling tales about me. A few years before, while at

West Ham for the first time a colleague said that this young journalist wanted to interview me and handed over a phone number. Later that night when I dialled the phone was answered by Carolyn Pick's young, polite female voice. That was me sucker-punched again. I just can't resist women and that includes a sexy voice on the end of a line.

We talked for a long while after I realised she was writing sod all, just flirting. End of conversation, end of relationship, as far as I was concerned. A couple of months later she phoned again and again until it became a frequent, almost annoying, occurrence. Carolyn would talk of this other professional footballer and tell me her version of their sex lives consisting of dirty talk on the phone and meetings when they consummated their fantasies. She revealed that she was religious and had decided to contact me when she saw a picture of me in a Celtic strip. That was a first. When she mentioned a yellow bikini I said, as you do, I wouldn't mind seeing her in that. Next I know it's delivered to my home in a brown paper wrapper. Telling her one of my favourite bands was Simple Minds produced a home made tape-recording of the band arriving through the mail within two days.

I moved home several times and still she found out where I lived. Then photographs of her in a yellow bikini arrived. Carolyn, an ex-model and beauty queen, was good-looking, that's for sure. But we never went further than those phone conversations. When I flitted to Gateshead it was all becoming a bit much and I changed my phone number. Within a couple of hours she had somehow sussed it and was back on the line. Again, she returned constantly to talking about this other professional footballer. It was all banter and talk as far as I was concerned. Just some woman who got a buzz out of raunchy chats on the line. Then she was arrested.

The police had lifted Carolyn Pick for stalking this other footballer. I felt heart-sorry for her and began to see that her calls to me were maybe some kind of cry for help. Her trial made for salacious reading in the press but there was something missing. Legal action had been granted to keep the footballer's name secret. At her trial the court would be closed and he would enter by special arrangement through the back of the court to give evidence against her. I always wondered what he had to hide.

You know him and I'd love to confirm it but my hands are well tied. No libel lawyer in their right mind would allow his name on to these pages. But let me help you get an idea of the type of bloke we are talking about. A top professional in England and a regular for the English national squad, though now retired from football. He regularly appears on TV.

He has a good, commercial image and is still a high earner. I guess that is what he was protecting when he applied to the court to have his identity kept secret. Seems that money talks louder than that principle of law – the one that says justice should be seen to be done.

Carolyn Pick claimed that they had had a relationship for years. He of course denied it. The list of complaints against her for stalking him sounding very close to what she related to me. At worst I found her calls annoying and intrusive. But was that stalking? Certainly not bad enough to get her into trouble in my book.

The court jailed her. That was all wrong. She needed help, counselling, not punishment. But punished she was. Her legal team were confident that she would win her appeal. On the night before she was due to go back to court, Carolyn Pick hanged herself. What a tragic waste.

But I didn't have to look into the lives of others for grief. My Dad was seriously ill. The cancer had taken over and he was wearing away, slowly slipping from life. Karen and I were up and by his bedside at every chance. Benny McAvennie was a little big man. Throughout his life he had allowed no one to harm him or his, and he wasn't about to change now. He lay and fought death with that quiet strength I recognised as my Dad's. The morphine wasn't working any more and the lines of agony creased his forehead deeper and deeper. His struggle was heroic but for those who loved him we shared his pain and were helpless to help him.

The doctors told us he would die any minute. Three days later he was still alive, his hands clenching the sheets into knots.

'Please, Dad,' I begged, 'just let go.' His glazed eyes found me and focused. 'Somebody needs to go ahead and make a deal for me so they'll let me in.' For the first time in what seemed like forever he smiled. The next day he was still alive, hanging on, his body drained and twisted with the pain.

'Oh, Dad, please just let yourself die,' I begged again. He opened his eyes and focused on me. 'No' done that deal yet, son.' I kissed his cheek and stroked his hand. A short while later he died as he had lived – quiet, peaceful, giving no trouble to anyone else.

Hard men I've known by the hundreds. None have had the strength and courage of my father, Bernard McAvennie.

I have this image of heaven. My old man is still sitting there rhyming off an endless list of the good things I've done with my life no matter how trivial. St Peter needs a bit of convincing given all the evidence he has to the contrary. But now he's considering giving me a special concession to enter through the pearly gates. After all, how bad could I be if a good man like Bernard McAvennie loved me all his life through trouble and strife, victory and loss, celebration and shame?

Keep talking, Dad.

BACK IN THE OLD ROUTINE
(2001/2002)

I had the best arrival ever at Ibrox. A charity game had been organised, the Auld Old Firm, with former Rangers and Celtic players taking each other on. When the organisers were brave enough to include me in the squad my old pal Charlie Nicholas came up with the ideal transport – a huge, long, white stretch limo. It sure as hell beat the team bus.

When the limo pulled up at the main doors of Ibrox, there was a mob of Rangers supporters hanging about trying to catch a glimpse of their heroes or blokes like Rod Stewart and Sean Connery. When they saw me they started booing and calling me a Fenian bastard. I just smiled and waved. God, how that made me feel back at home.

Almost 50,000 paying spectators turned up, which was great. Rangers won 4–1, which was terrible. No matter, the two squads went on to continue the party we had started the night before the match. We ended up at Victoria's and the rounds of champagne were in bottles, not glasses. A great night. The next day I was told there had been a ban on me at Viccies but they had lifted it for the one night only. For the life of me I couldn't remember being banned. Must have been really out of my box that night.

It was a good time. Almost as good as when I had returned to West Ham to play in George Parris's testimonial. All the old crew were there and what a welcome the supporters gave me. The deal was I'd play maybe 25 minutes. By the end of the first half they had left me on – I was dead on my feet. At half-time they talked me into going on for a few minutes of the second half. I was so knackered my very arse was aching. Finally, after a lot of protestations from me, they called for me to come off.

Instantly, a wave of supporters hit me, surrounding me, cheering and waving. When they eventually left me and ran back to the terracing I was standing there in nothing but my boxer shorts. Stripped in public for the very first time and it was by blokes. Just my bloody luck. My last game in a West Ham strip and the lot had gone home to the East End as mementoes. They are very welcome to it all. There's a bit of me that will always be in the East End with them.

After my Dad died I started playing for charity football games whenever possible. I had applied for my FIFA coaching ticket with a view to entering management. The Scottish Football Association wouldn't let me study up there so I told them to stick it up their ass and pursued a course in England. They had no trouble with bad boys as long as they knew a bit about football. On the day I was meant to be at my finals, I was asked to take part in a football match in Gateshead to raise cash for a cancer charity. There was no dilemma – the football match won.

I wouldn't say I had grown up or even changed the day my dad died. I'm as grown up as I am ever likely to be. But his loss helped me understand some priorities in life. So what the hell – a coaching exam can wait but people dying in pain need help now. No contest.

I am well over prison now and have calmed down about the obvious crude efforts to fit me up. But I tell them now, if I had gone down and been rotting in jail the day my Dad died I would have been coming after the corrupt bastards and would have got them no matter how long it took.

Then another day that would change my life. Karen and I couldn't afford a lavish wedding and it was all the more lovely for it. This was about us committing ourselves to each other but, don't get me wrong, we still had a ball – fun needs to be part of love and it is very much part of our lives.

At the part of the service where the priest asks if anyone present knows of any reason why we shouldn't get hitched, one of the guests cleared their throat as if about to speak. There was an embarrassingly long silence only broken by the nervous giggles of other guests. When it became clear nothing was going to be said, Karen looked over her shoulder at the crowd and said, 'Thank God for that.' She knows me a bit does my Karen.

Laura and Jake returned from Spain and are now well settled in Glasgow. At last we have stopped feuding and put the wee man's needs first. Karen and Laura actually get on very well and spend time together. Jake and Karen are really good pals and he comes to stay with us most weekends. He is obviously my son in every way. Journalists often ask if Jake is going to be a footballer. But how would I know? Who would have guessed what lay ahead for me when I was seven years old – thank God.

We are regular visitors to Milton to see my Mum who still lives among her friends. In writing this book, forcing myself to mull over everything that has happened to me and all that I've got up to, it's a comforting, sober reminder to have my wee Mum still there, reminding me of where I've come from and where I'll go back to.

I'm often at Upton Park on match days. Despite the ups and downs West Ham have faced and the changes that have occurred the supporters make me feel at home. Which is just as well since I'm still one of them – adopted, maybe, but I belong nevertheless.

Wherever I am on match days I always look up the results of Celtic. When you are born into the spirit of the team you die with that dedication undiluted, whatever happens. Sitting in a Glasgow pub, some guy will sidle up to me and ask me about my playing days or some current football issue. Often they leave me with no clue about which team they support – it could be Rangers, Celtic or even St Mirren.

There are those, of course, who never forget and carry their anger still fizzing. Sometimes that makes me sad but most often it makes me glad. Reminds me that I used to do something better than most – score goals.

I am waiting for the day that some beautiful woman comes on to me in a club, giving me a big smile and I'm just about to tell her that I'm flattered but I'm happily married – then she reveals how her mother was engaged to me once. It hasn't happened yet but when it does, believe me, I'll enjoy the moment. If you can't laugh at yourself you are knackered. If you have nothing to laugh at yourself about you have wasted your life.

The bankruptcy is behind me now and business ideas are always coming my way. The mistakes I have made have taught me the hard way but maybe sometimes that way is the best way. The successful guys I meet will confess to mega cock-ups in their time. The difference is that their mistakes weren't splattered all over the press and for that they are truly grateful. Me, I'm only pleased that the media took interest in me at all. Sometimes I got angry and hurt at stories that were simply wrong but these folk were just earning their crust. So I've forgiven the press because, let's face it, I'm going to go on leading my life as I always have – the only way I know how – and I think we may have a working relationship for a good few years yet.

A wee while ago an agent asked me if I would do some after-dinner speaking. To start with, I wondered what he meant. Half an hour on the highlights of my career? A new routine as a stand-up comic? Not being sure what it was all about, I decided to give it a go at least once – it's always been a principle of mine. Someone advised me that after-dinner speakers prepare a spiel, practise their jokes, and strongly recommended I do the same. It was too much like training for my tastes and I still prefer playing the game. So stuff that. I went along to the venue, had a good scoff and a score of drinks, stood up and, totally unprepared, took a deep breath. Fuck knows what I said but later the bookings rolled in.

Talking and drinking – I'm a natural. Always will be. Maybe there's a few tricks left in the old Macca yet?

Now where are those boots . . .